# WORLD HISTORY

## STUDENT ACTIVITIES

FIFTH EDITION

**World History Student Activities**
**Fifth Edition**

**Coordinating Writer**
Dennis Bollinger, PhD

**Contributing Writer**
Sarah Weaver, MEd, MA

**Editor**
Benjamin Sinnamon, MA, MLIS

**Cover**
Drew Fields

**Book Design**
Dan VanLeeuwen

**Page Layout**
Sarah Centers
Carrie Walker

**Project Coordinator**
Dan Berger

**Permissions**
Sharon Belknap
Sarah Gundlach
Ashleigh Schieber

**Photo Credits**
**front cover** © iStock.com/Byelikova_Oksana; **front matter, chs. 1–2** Dmitry Petrenko /Shutterstock.com; **chs. 3–5** © iStock.com/stock_colors; **41** arun sambhu mishra /Shutterstock.com; **chs. 6–9** feiyuezhangjie/Shutterstock.com; **chs. 10–13** Pecold /Shutterstock.com; **chs. 14–16** Keiki/Shutterstock.com; **chs. 17–19** Robert Walkley /Shutterstock.com; **173** Marzolino/Shutterstock.com; **chs. 20–22** pedrosala /Shutterstock.com; **chs. 23–24** chuyuss/Shutterstock.com; **back cover** © iStock.com /richliy

All maps from Map Resources

Text acknowledgments appear on-page with text selections.



Printed in the United States of America


ISBN: 978-1-62856-373-3

15 14 13 12 11 10 9 8 7 6

# CONTENTS


World Map . . . . . . v

## UNIT 1 THE ANCIENT WORLD: CREATION–500 BC

### Chapter 1: Foundations of World History
Activity 1: Using Historical Sources Properly . . . . . . 1
Activity 2: The Post-Flood World . . . . . . 3
Activity 3: Chapter Review . . . . . . 5

### Chapter 2: Early Civilizations
Activity 1: Ancient Near East . . . . . . 7
Activity 2: Code of Hammurabi and the Mosaic Code . . . . . . 9
Activity 3: Manu and the Flood . . . . . . 11
Activity 4: Confucius . . . . . . 13
Activity 5: Chapter Review . . . . . . 15

## UNIT 2 ADVANCE OF CIVILIZATION: 500 BC–AD 500

### Chapter 3: The Greek Civilization
Activity 1: Homer's *Odyssey* . . . . . . 17
Activity 2: Empire of Alexander the Great (323 BC) . . 19
Activity 3: Book of Daniel and Alexander's Empire . . . 20
Activity 4: Greek Philosophy and Scripture . . . . . . 21
Activity 5: Early Greek History . . . . . . 23
Activity 6: Chapter Review . . . . . . 25

### Chapter 4: The Roman Civilization
Activity 1: Roman and US Republics . . . . . . 27
Activity 2: Hannibal Crosses the Alps . . . . . . 29
Activity 3: Punic Wars . . . . . . 31
Activity 4: The Roman Empire at Its Greatest Extent (ca. AD 117) . . . . . . 32
Activity 5: Early Roman Persecution of Christians . . . . . . 33
Activity 6: Chapter Review . . . . . . 35

### Chapter 5: Civilizations in Africa and the East
Activity 1: Early Africa . . . . . . 37
Activity 2: Christianity in Ethiopia . . . . . . 39
Activity 3: Stupas in India . . . . . . 41
Activity 4: Han Dynasty China . . . . . . 42
Activity 5: Chapter Review . . . . . . 43

## UNIT 3 CULTURES OF THE WORLD: 500–1100

### Chapter 6: The Byzantine and Islamic Empires
Activity 1: The Nika Revolt . . . . . . 45
Activity 2: Byzantine Empire at Its Height (6th Century) . . . . . . 48
Activity 3: The Qur'an or the Bible? . . . . . . 49
Activity 4: Expansion of Islam . . . . . . 53
Activity 5: Chapter Review . . . . . . 55

### Chapter 7: The Civilizations of Asia
Activity 1: Asia . . . . . . 57
Activity 2: Chinese Lore . . . . . . 58
Activity 3: "A Dialogue on Poverty" . . . . . . 59
Activity 4: Korean Foundation Myths . . . . . . 60
Activity 5: Chapter Review . . . . . . 61

### Chapter 8: The Civilizations of the Americas
Activity 1: American Indian Creation/Flood Story . . . . 63
Activity 2: North America . . . . . . 65
Activity 3: Ojibwa Flood Story . . . . . . 67
Activity 4: Middle America and South America . . . . . . 69
Activity 5: Chapter Review . . . . . . 71

### Chapter 9: The Making of Medieval Europe
Activity 1: Charlemagne . . . . . . 73
Activity 2: Charlemagne's Empire . . . . . . 75
Activity 3: Treaty of Verdun (843) . . . . . . 76
Activity 4: Terminology Review . . . . . . 77
Activity 5: Chapter Review . . . . . . 79

## UNIT 4 TRANSITIONS: 1100–1650

### Chapter 10: The Reshaping of Medieval Europe
Activity 1: The Black Death . . . . . . 81
Activity 2: A Day in the Life of a University Student in 1225 . . . . . . 83
Activity 3: King John of England Swears Fealty to Pope Innocent III . . . . . . 85
Activity 4: The Battle of Crécy . . . . . . 87
Activity 5: Europe (About 1500) . . . . . . 89
Activity 6: Chapter Review . . . . . . 91

### Chapter 11: Renaissance and Reformation
Activity 1: Early History of the English Bible . . . . . . 93
Activity 2: The Spanish Armada . . . . . . 95
Activity 3: The St. Bartholomew's Day Massacre . . . . . . 97
Activity 4: Canons and Decrees of the Council of Trent . . . . . . 99
Activity 5: Chapter Review . . . . . . 101

### Chapter 12: Empires of Africa, India, and Asia
Activity 1: Early Africa . . . . . . 103
Activity 2: India . . . . . . 104
Activity 3: Sikh Scripture . . . . . . 105
Activity 4: Chapter Review . . . . . . 107

### Chapter 13: Exploration and Discovery
Activity 1: Columbus's First Voyage . . . . . . 109
Activity 2: Aztec Religion . . . . . . 111
Activity 3: Devastation of the Indies (1542) . . . . . . 113
Activity 4: Chapter Review . . . . . . 115

## UNIT 5 THE ENLIGHTENED WORLD: 1600–1800

### Chapter 14: Pursuit of Power in Europe


Activity 1: The Edict of Nantes ... 117
Activity 2: Europe (1648) ... 118
Activity 3: Revocation of the Edict of Nantes ... 119
Activity 4: Louis XIV ... 121
Activity 5: Peter the Great and Westernization ... 123
Activity 6: Chapter Review ... 125


### Chapter 15: Age of Reason


Activity 1: *The Spirit of Laws* ... 127
Activity 2: Benjamin Franklin's View of Jesus ... 129
Activity 3: Voltaire and the Bible ... 131
Activity 4: Eyewitness Account of a Whitefield Meeting ... 133
Activity 5: Chapter Review ... 135


### Chapter 16: Attempts at Liberty


Activity 1: William Pitt and the American Colonies ... 137
Activity 2: Eyewitness Account of the French Revolution ... 139
Activity 3: Execution of Louis XVI ... 141
Activity 4: Napoleon's Empire ... 143
Activity 5: Visiting the Battlefield of Waterloo ... 145
Activity 6: Chapter Review ... 147


## UNIT 6 THE EUROPEAN WORLD: 1800–1914

### Chapter 17: Reaction and Revolution


Activity 1: Metternich and European Governments .. 149
Activity 2: Europe After the Congress of Vienna (1815) ... 151
Activity 3: Young Italy ... 153
Activity 4: Chapter Review ... 155


### Chapter 18: Industrial Revolution and European Society


Activity 1: Testimonies About Child Laborers ... 157
Activity 2: *The Communist Manifesto* ... 159
Activity 3: *The Descent of Man* ... 161
Activity 4: Chapter Review ... 165


### Chapter 19: European Expansion


Activity 1: Imperialism in the Far East 1914 ... 167
Activity 2: The Middle Passage ... 169
Activity 3: Livingstone and African Slavery ... 171
Activity 4: Imperialism in Africa 1914 ... 175
Activity 5: Chapter Review ... 177


## UNIT 7 WAR AND UNREST: 1914–1945

### Chapter 20: The Great War


Activity 1: Rival Alliances (1914) ... 179
Activity 2: Armenian Genocide ... 181
Activity 3: Eyewitness Account of World War I. ... 185
Activity 4: U-boat Attack: April 1916 ... 187
Activity 5: Robert Lansing and the League of Nations ... 189
Activity 6: Chapter Review ... 191


### Chapter 21: Discontent and Experimentation


Activity 1: Fireside Chat: September 6, 1936 ... 193
Activity 2: Execution of the Czar and His Family ... 195
Activity 3: Union of Soviet Socialist Republics ... 197
Activity 4: Hitler's Impact on the Youth of Germany ... 199
Activity 5: Chapter Review ... 201


### Chapter 22: The Second World War


Activity 1: A Prisoner of War ... 203
Activity 2: War in the South Pacific ... 205
Activity 3: A Little Girl's Memories of Bombings in Berlin ... 207
Activity 4: Opposing Viewpoints on the Atomic Bomb ... 209
Activity 5: Chapter Review ... 211


## UNIT 8 THE MODERN WORLD: 1945–PRESENT

### Chapter 23: The Cold War Era


Activity 1: Cold War Europe ... 213
Activity 2: One Marine's Experience in Vietnam ... 215
Activity 3: The Berlin Wall ... 219
Activity 4: Immediate Post-Communist Eastern Europe ... 221
Activity 5: Chapter Review ... 223


### Chapter 24: To the Present


Activity 1: The Middle East ... 225
Activity 2: Israel ... 226
Activity 3: Country Comparison Chart ... 227
Activity 4: Chapter Review ... 229

# WORLD MAP

ARCTIC OCEAN
Beaufort Sea
Bering Sea
Gulf of Alaska
Hudson Bay
Baffin Bay
Labrador Sea
GREENLAND
Greenland Sea
Norwegian Sea
ICELAND
CANADA
UNITED STATES OF AMERICA
PACIFIC OCEAN
ATLANTIC OCEAN
MEXICO
Gulf of Mexico
CUBA
THE BAHAMAS
JAMAICA
BELIZE
HONDURAS
DOM. REP.
HAITI
Caribbean Sea
GUATEMALA
EL SALVADOR
NICARAGUA
COSTA RICA
PANAMA
VENEZUELA
GUYANA
SURINAME
FRENCH GUIANA
COLOMBIA
ECUADOR
PERU
BRAZIL
BOLIVIA
PARAGUAY
CHILE
ARGENTINA
URUGUAY
PACIFIC OCEAN
ATLANTIC OCEAN
FALKLAND ISLANDS
SOUTH GEORGIA ISLAND
NORWAY
SWEDEN
FINLAND
North Sea
ESTONIA
LATVIA
LITHUANIA
DENMARK
IRELAND
U.K.
NETH.
GERMANY
POLAND
BELARUS
UKRAINE
MOLDOVA
ROMANIA
BULGARIA
English Channel
Bay of Biscay
FRANCE
PORTUGAL
SPAIN
ITALY
ALBANIA
GREECE
Black Sea
TURKEY
CYPRUS
LEBANON
ISRAEL
MOROCCO
TUNISIA
Mediterranean Sea
CANARY ISLANDS
ALGERIA
LIBYA
EGYPT
WESTERN SAHARA
MAURITANIA
MALI
NIGER
CHAD
SUDAN
SENEGAL
GAMBIA
GUINEA BISSAU
GUINEA
BURKINA
NIGERIA
SIERRA LEONE
COTE D'IVOIRE
LIBERIA
GHANA
TOGO
BENIN
CAMEROON
CENTRAL AFRICAN REPUBLIC
SOUTH SUDAN
ETHIOPIA
ERITREA
DJIBOUTI
SOMALIA
SÃO TOMÉ & PRINCIPE
EQUATORIAL GUINEA
GABON
CONGO
ANGOLA
DEMOCRATIC REPUBLIC OF THE CONGO
UGANDA
KENYA
RWANDA
BURUNDI
TANZANIA
MALAWI
ZAMBIA
ZIMBABWE
NAMIBIA
BOTSWANA
MOZAMBIQUE
MADAGASCAR
SWAZILAND
SOUTH AFRICA
LESOTHO
RUSSIA
KAZAKHSTAN
GEORGIA
Caspian Sea
Aral Sea
AZERBAIJAN
ARMENIA
UZBEKISTAN
KYRGYZSTAN
TURKMENISTAN
TAJIKISTAN
SYRIA
IRAQ
IRAN
AFGHANISTAN
JORDAN
KUWAIT
QATAR
PAKISTAN
U.A.E.
Gulf of Oman
SAUDI ARABIA
Red Sea
OMAN
Arabian Sea
YEMEN
Gulf of Aden
MONGOLIA
CHINA
NORTH KOREA
SOUTH KOREA
Sea of Japan
JAPAN
Sea of Okhotsk
East China Sea
PACIFIC OCEAN
NEPAL
BHUTAN
INDIA
BANGLADESH
Bay of Bengal
MYANMAR
LAOS
TAIWAN
South China Sea
Philippine Sea
PHILIPPINES
THAILAND
CAMBODIA
VIETNAM
Andaman Sea
Gulf of Thailand
SRI LANKA
BRUNEI
MALAYSIA
INDONESIA
SINGAPORE
Java Sea
EAST TIMOR
PAPUA NEW GUINEA
Arafura Sea
Timor Sea
Gulf of Carpentaria
Coral Sea
INDIAN OCEAN
AUSTRALIA
NEW CALEDONIA
Great Australian Bight
Tasman Sea
NEW ZEALAND
ANTARCTICA

Name ______________________

# Using Historical Sources Properly

Pages 3–5 of the student text explain that a historian produces a historical account through evaluation of historical sources, synthesis of those sources into a historical narrative, and interpretation of that narrative for readers. In this activity, you will engage in a similar process by producing a historical account of one of the most famous events in ancient history: the fall of Babylon to the Medes and the Persians in 539 BC. Historians know about this event through many different sources; this activity focuses on three of the most important sources.

**Read the following excerpts from each source and then follow the directions at the end.**

## The Cyrus Cylinder

The Cyrus Cylinder is a clay cylinder located in the British Museum. An official record of the deeds of Cyrus, the first Persian emperor, it details the fall of Babylon from the conquerors' perspective. This account attributes Cyrus's victory to his claim that he was deeply committed to Marduk, the god of the Babylonians. "[Marduk] sought a righteous prince according to his heart's desire who would grasp his hands. Cyrus, the king of Anshan, whose name he uttered, [Marduk] proclaimed for lordship over everything. . . . Marduk, the great lord, the protector of his people, looked joyfully upon his pious deeds and his righteous heart. [Marduk] decreed [Cyrus's] march upon his city, Babylon. . . . Without encounter and battle [Marduk] caused [Cyrus] to enter into the midst of Babylon, his city. Nabonidus, the king who did not [honor] [Marduk], [Marduk] delivered into [Cyrus's] hands. . . . [The people of Babylon] rejoiced in his sovereignty (and) their countenances shone. . . . [Cyrus said,] 'I (am) Cyrus, . . . the king of the four quarters (of the world). . . . When I had entered into the midst of Babylon in peace, I took the seat of lordship in the palace of princes amidst jubilation and rejoicing. . . . My numerous troops advanced peacefully into the midst of Babylon. . . . The inner part of Babylon and all its cities I cared for in peace. . . . (As to) [the] dwellings, I repaired their dilapidation; I removed their ruins.'"

Raymond Philip Dougherty. *Nabonidus and Belshazzar: A Study of the Closing Events of the Neo-Babylonian Empire.* Yale Oriental Series, vol. 15 (New Haven, CT: Yale UP, 1929), 176–78.

## The Book of Daniel

**Read Daniel 5.**

(Daniel 5 refers to Darius the Mede as the conqueror of the Chaldean kingdom. This is not the same Darius as Darius I, a Persian who ruled the Medes, or Cyrus, who is mentioned in chapters one and six of Daniel.)

## *The History of Herodotus*

Having, however, thus wreaked his vengeance on the Gyndes, by dispersing it through three hundred and sixty channels, Cyrus, with the first approach of the ensuing spring, marched forward against Babylon. The Babylonians, encamped without their walls, awaited his coming. A battle was fought at a short distance from the city, in which the Babylonians were defeated by the Persian king, whereupon they withdrew within their defences. Here they shut themselves up, and made light of his siege, having laid in a store of provisions for many years in preparation against this attack; for when they saw Cyrus conquering nation after nation, they were convinced that he would never stop, and that their turn would come at last. . . .

Cyrus was now reduced to great perplexity, as time went on and he made no progress against the place. In this distress either some one made the suggestion to him, or he bethought himself

*(continued on next page)*

of a plan, which he proceeded to put in execution. He placed a portion of his army at the point where the river enters the city, and another body at the back of the place where it issues forth, with orders to march into the town by the bed of the stream, as soon as the water became shallow enough: he then himself drew off with the unwarlike portion of his host, and made for the place where Nitocris dug the basin for the river, where he did exactly what she had done formerly: he turned the Euphrates by a canal into the basin, which was then a marsh, on which the river sank to such an extent that the natural bed of the stream became fordable. Hereupon the Persians who had been left for the purpose at Babylon by the river-side, entered the stream, which had now sunk so as to reach about midway up a man's thigh, and thus got into the town. Had the Babylonians been apprised of what Cyrus was about, or had they noticed their danger, they would never have allowed the Persians to enter the city, but would have destroyed them utterly; for they would have made fast all the street-gates which gave upon the river, and mounting upon the walls along both sides of the stream, would so have caught the enemy, as it were, in a trap. But, as it was, the Persians came upon them by surprise and so took the city. Owing to the vast size of the place, the inhabitants of the central parts (as the residents at Babylon declare) long after the outer portions of the town were taken, knew nothing of what had chanced, but as they were engaged in a festival, continued dancing and revelling until they learnt the capture but too certainly. Such, then, were the circumstances of the first taking of Babylon.

Herodotus. *History of Herodotus*, bk. 1, http://en.wikisource.org/wiki/History_of_Herodotus/Book_1.

1. Write a single narrative based on the sources provided. ____________________

2. Explain why you wrote your narrative as you did (i.e., explain why you included certain facts and excluded others). ____________________

Name ______________________________

## The Post-Flood World

**Locate each term or phrase on the map and place the corresponding number in the appropriate blank.**

_______ Area settled by Ham

_______ Area settled by Japheth

_______ Area settled by Shem

_______ Black Sea

_______ Caspian Sea

_______ Euphrates River

_______ Mediterranean Sea

_______ Mount Ararat

_______ Persian Gulf

_______ Plain of Shinar

_______ Red Sea

_______ Tigris River

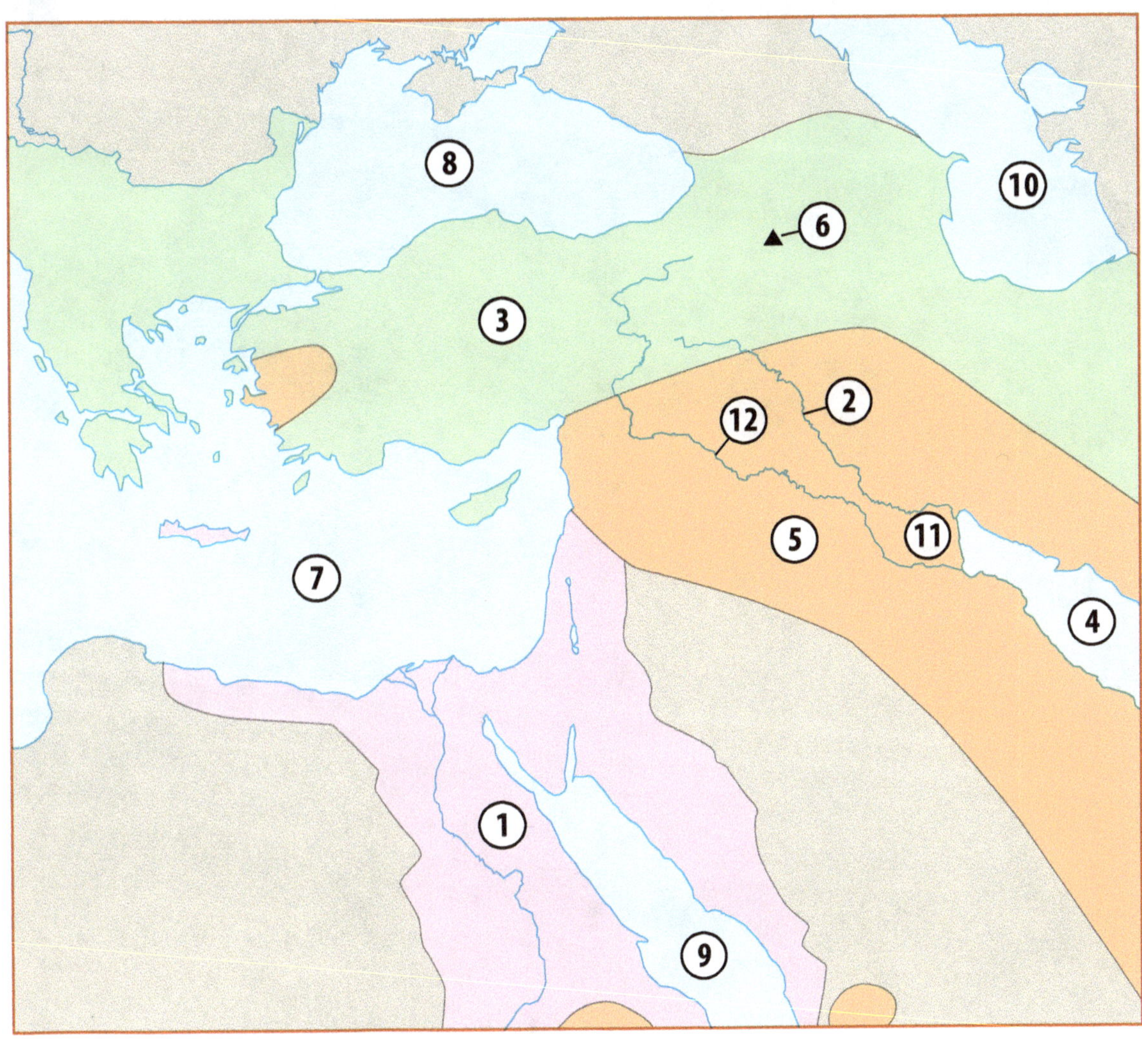

Name ______________________________

# Chapter Review

## Complete the Statement

**Underline the term that accurately completes each of the following statements.**

1. The seed of the (serpent/woman) refers primarily to Christ but also to those who are loyal to God through salvation.
2. (Primary/Secondary) sources are usually produced by people involved in the events being studied.
3. (Seth/Cain) fathered a line of people who "call[ed] upon the name of the Lord," and he was a replacement for Abel.
4. Noah placed a curse on Canaan, a son of (Ham/Japheth).
5. Historical (synthesis/interpretation) is the practice of gathering useful information and weaving it together into a narrative of the past.

## Matching

**Choose the best answer and place the letter in the blank beside the corresponding statement or description.**

| | | |
|---|---|---|
| A. civilization | C. divine providence | E. image of God |
| B. Creation Mandate | D. human sinfulness | F. specialization |

_____ 6. Man's duty to have dominion over the earth and make it useful

_____ 7. No event of history is outside God's control.

_____ 8. Human qualities that reflect part of God's personality

_____ 9. Human culture that is lived in cities or under their influence

_____ 10. All aspects of man, such as his mind, are stained by the Fall.

## Short Answer

**Write the correct answer to each question in the provided blank.**

11–13. What three central truths compose the proper Christian perspective in the Bible? ______________________

______________________________________________

14. What is the term for objects made by people in the past that give us valuable information about every-day life in past centuries? ______________________

*(continued on next page)*

15. What term describes the handing down of information by word of mouth from generation to generation?

16. What is the term for a large group of people who share the same land area and the same language?

17. Why is Genesis 10 called the Table of Nations?

18. What is the definition of the term *history*?

19. Why are written records the most important source of information to the historian?

20. What term describes a perspective from which one may examine and interpret the universe and everything in it?

Name ______________________________

## Ancient Near East

**Locate each term on the map and place the corresponding number in the appropriate blank.**

_______ Arabian Desert

_______ Assyria

_______ Babylon

_______ Canaan

_______ Egypt

_______ Euphrates River

_______ Jerusalem

_______ Jordan River

_______ Mediterranean Sea

_______ Nile River

_______ Nineveh

_______ Persia

_______ Red Sea

_______ Sinai Peninsula

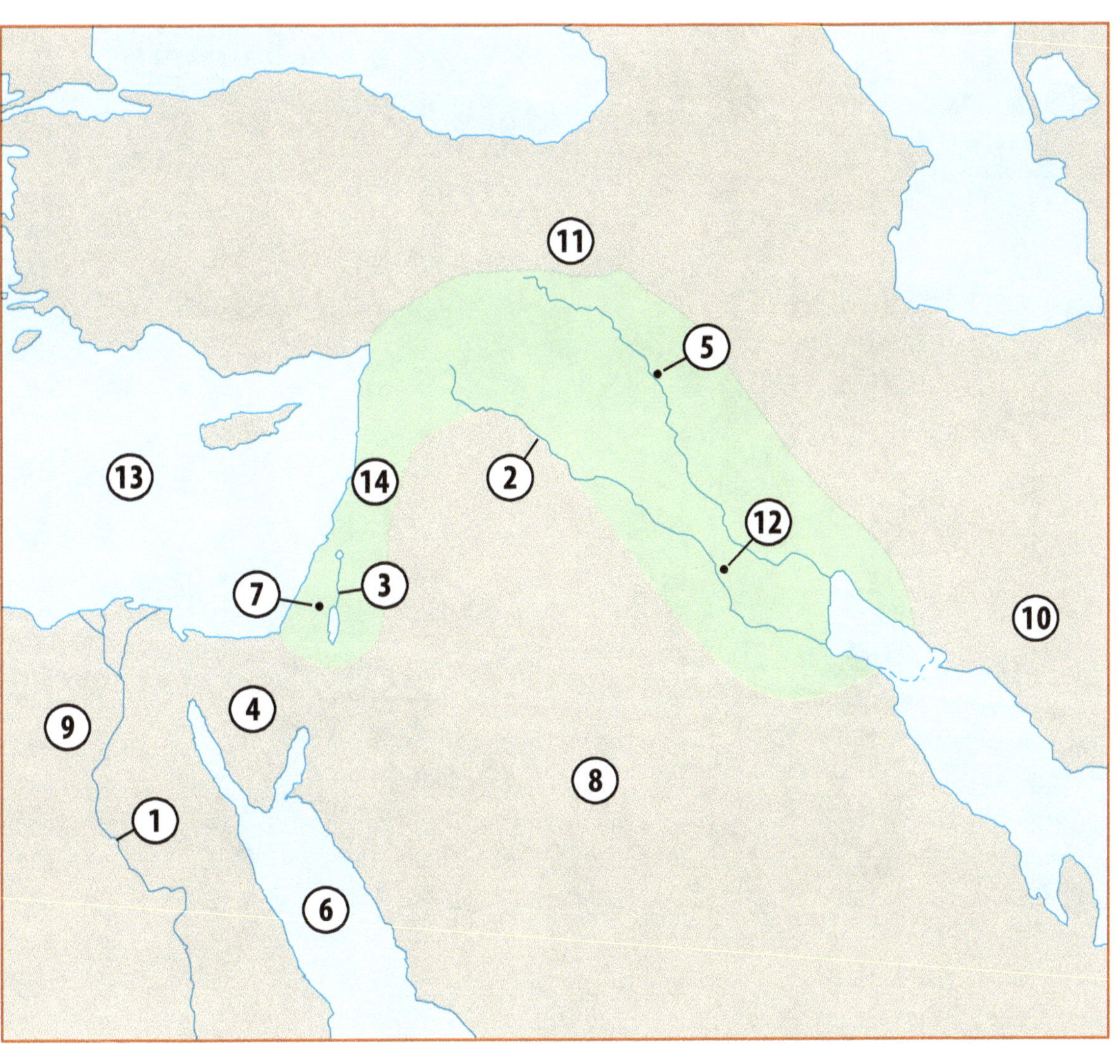

Name ______________________

# Code of Hammurabi and the Mosaic Code

Hammurabi's law code was composed of a lengthy prologue, 282 laws, and an epilogue. This activity presents a variety of topics found in Hammurabi's code to provide a sampling of his collected laws.

**Answer the questions at the end after referring to the following excerpts from the Code of Hammurabi. (The relevant Bible passages are in parentheses following each excerpt from Hammurabi.)**

1. If any one ensnare another, putting a ban upon him, but he can not prove it, then he that ensnared him shall be put to death. . . . (Exod. 20:16)

14. If any one steal the minor son of another, he shall be put to death. . . . (Exod. 21:16; Deut. 24:7)

21. If any one break a hole into a house (break in to steal), he shall be put to death before that hole and be buried. (Exod. 22:1–3)

22. If any one is committing a robbery and is caught, then he shall be put to death. . . .

60. If any one give over a field to a gardener, for him to plant it as a garden, if he work at it, and care for it for four years, in the fifth year the owner and the gardener shall divide it, the owner taking his part in charge. . . . (Lev. 19:23–25)

129. If a man's wife be surprised (in lying) with another man, both shall be tied and thrown into the water, but the husband may pardon his wife and the king his slaves. . . . (Deut. 22:22)

157. If any one be guilty of incest with his mother after his father, both shall be burned. . . . (Lev. 18:7; 20:11)

195. If a son strike his father, his hands shall be hewn off. . . . (Exod. 21:15)

198. If [anyone] put out the eye of a freed man, or break the bone of a freed man, he shall pay one gold mina. (Exod. 21:18–19)

199. If he put out the eye of a man's slave, or break the bone of a man's slave, he shall pay one-half of its value. . . . (Exod. 21:20–21, 26–27)

211. If a woman of the free class lose her child by a blow, [the attacker] shall pay five shekels in money. (Exod. 21:22–25)

212. If this woman die, [the attacker] shall pay half a mina.

213. If he strike the maid-servant of a man, and she lose her child, [the attacker] shall pay two shekels in money.

214. If this maid-servant die, [the attacker] shall pay one-third of a mina. . . .

250. If while an ox is passing on the street (market) some one push it, and kill it, the owner can set up no claim in the suit (against the hirer). (Exod. 21:28–36)

251. If an ox be a goring ox, and it shown that he is a gorer, and he do not bind his horns, or fasten the ox up, and the ox gore a free-born man and kill him, the owner shall pay one-half a mina in money.

252. If he kill a man's slave, he shall pay one-third of a mina.

Hammurabi. *Code of Hammurabi.* http://en.wikisource.org/wiki/Codex_Hammurabi_%28King_translation%29.

*(continued on next page)*

1. What actions forbidden by the Amorites are also forbidden in the Bible?

2. How does Hammurabi's code show preference for certain people?

3. Contrast punishments assigned by Hammurabi's law and the Mosaic code regarding theft.

4. Contrast Hammurabi's punishment for a person striking his parents with the punishment found in the Mosaic code. Why do you think one is more severe than the other?

5. Who or what was the source of Hammurabi's code? Who or what was the source of the Mosaic code?

6. In what ways are laws 250–52 of Hammurabi's code very similar to Exodus 21:28–36? In what ways are they different? Which one places a higher value on human life?

7. What might account for the similarities between Hammurabi's code and parts of the Mosaic law according to Romans 2:14–15? What might account for the differences?

Name ________________________

# Manu and the Flood

**Answer the questions at the end after reading the following Hindu account of the Flood. (The fish was an avatar [manifestation] of the Hindu god Vishnu.)**

## EIGHTH ADHYÂYA. FIRST BRÂHMANA.

THE IDÂ.

1. In the morning they brought to Manu water for washing, just as now also they (are wont to) bring (water) for washing the hands. When he was washing himself, a fish came into his hands.

2. It spake to him the word, 'Rear me, I will save thee!' 'Wherefrom wilt thou save me?' 'A flood will carry away all these creatures: from that I will save thee!' 'How am I to rear thee?'

3. It said, 'As long as we are small, there is great destruction for us: fish devours fish. Thou wilt first keep me in a jar. When I outgrow that, thou wilt dig a pit and keep me in it. When I outgrow that, thou wilt take me down to the sea, for then I shall be beyond destruction.'

4. It soon became a ghasha (a large fish); for that grows largest (of all fish). Thereupon it said, 'In such and such a year that flood will come. Thou shalt then attend to me (i.e. to my advice) by preparing a ship; and when the flood has risen thou shalt enter into the ship, and I will save thee from it.'

5. After he had reared it in this way, he took it down to the sea. And in the same year which the fish had indicated to him, he attended to (the advice of the fish) by preparing a ship; and when the flood had risen, he entered into the ship. The fish then swam up to him, and to its horn he tied the rope of the ship, and by that means he passed swiftly up to yonder northern mountain.

6. It then said, 'I have saved thee. Fasten the ship to a tree; but let not the water cut thee off, whilst thou art on the mountain. As the water subsides, thou mayest gradually descend!' Accordingly he gradually descended, and hence that (slope) of the northern mountain is called 'Alarm's descent.' The flood then swept away all these creatures, and Manu alone remained here.

7. Being desirous of offspring, he engaged in worshipping and austerities. During this time he also performed a . . . sacrifice: he offered up in the waters clarified butter, sour milk, whey, and curds. Thence a woman was produced in a year: becoming quite solid she rose; clarified butter gathered in her footprint. Mitra and Varuna met her.

8. They said to her, 'Who art thou?' 'Manu's daughter,' she replied. 'Say (thou art) ours,' they said. 'No,' she said, 'I am (the daughter) of him who begat me.' They desired to have a share in her. She either agreed or did not agree, but passed by them. She came to Manu.

9. Manu said to her, 'Who art thou?' 'Thy daughter,' she replied. 'How, illustrious one, (art thou) my daughter?' he asked. She replied, 'Those offerings (of) clarified butter, sour milk, whey, and curds, which thou madest in the waters, with them thou hast begotten me. I am the blessing (benediction): make use of me at the sacrifice! If thou wilt make use of me at the sacrifice, thou wilt become rich in offspring and cattle. Whatever blessing thou shalt invoke through me, all that shall be granted to thee!' He accordingly made use of her (as the benediction) in the middle of the sacrifice; for what is intermediate between the fore-offerings and the after-offerings, is the middle of the sacrifice.

10. With her he went on worshipping and performing austerities, wishing for offspring. Through her he generated this race, which is this race of Manu; and whatever blessing he invoked through her, all that was granted to him.

*http://sacred-texts.com/hin/sbr/sbe12/sbe1234.htm*

*(continued on next page)*

1. How does Manu learn of an impending flood? ______________________________

2. How did Manu preserve the fish? ______________________________

______________________________

3. How did Manu escape the flood? ______________________________

______________________________

4. What emerged from Manu's offering of clarified butter, sour milk, whey, and curds?

______________________________

5. What did the answer to number four call itself? ______________________________

6. Where did mankind come from? ______________________________

7. Contrast this account with the biblical account.

______________________________

______________________________

______________________________

______________________________

Name ______________________

## Confucius

**Answer the questions at the end after reading the following excerpts of Confucius.**

Book 12

1. Yan Yuan asked about humaneness. The Master said, To master the self and return to ritual is to be humane. For one day master the self and return to ritual, and the whole world will become humane. Being humane proceeds from you yourself. How could it proceed from others?

Yan Yuan said, May I ask how to go about this?

The Master said, If it is contrary to ritual, don't look at it. If it is contrary to ritual, don't listen to it. If it is contrary to ritual, don't utter it. If it is contrary to ritual, don't do it.

Yan Yuan said, Lacking in cleverness though I am, I would like if I may, to honor these words.

2. Zhonggong asked about humaneness. The Master said, When you go out the door, behave as though you were going to meet an important guest. When you employ the common people, do so as though you were conducting an important sacrifice. What you do not want others to do to you, do not do to others. In the domain, let there be no grievances against you; in the family, let there be no grievances against you.

Zhonggong said, Lacking in cleverness though I am, I would like, if I may, to honor these words.

. . . .

15. The Master said, Acquire broad learning in cultural matters, focus it through ritual, and you are hardly likely to go far astray—isn't that so?

16. The Master said, The gentleman brings out what is most admirable in people; he does not bring out what is bad in them. The petty man does the opposite.

. . . .

19. Ji Kangzi asked Confucius about government, saying, If I kill those who don't follow the Way, and thereby encourage those who do follow the Way, how would that be?

Confucius replied, Your task is to govern. What need is there for killing? If you desire goodness, the common people will be good. The virtue of the gentleman is like the wind; the virtue of the petty people like the grass. When the wind blows over the grass, surely it will bend.

Burton, Watson, trans. *The Analects of Confucius.* (New York: Columbia University Press, 2007), 80–83.

1. According to Confucius, how is humaneness attained? ______________________

______________________

2. According to Confucius, what kind of a man brings out the good in people?

______________________

3. According to Confucius, what is the responsibility of government? What did he believe would be the effect of a good government? ______________________

4. Evaluate the statements above. Which are contrary to Scripture and which are not? Explain.

______________________

______________________

Name ______________________________

# Chapter Review

## Complete the Statement

**Underline the term(s) that accurately complete(s) each of the following statements.**

1. (Sargon/Hammurabi) united the land of Mesopotamia and is remembered for his code of laws.
2. (Sargon/Hammurabi) established the first known empire.
3. Khufu built the Great Pyramid at Giza in the (Old/Middle) Kingdom.
4. Moses probably led the Israelites out of Egypt during the reign of (Amenhotep II/Thutmose III).
5. The Israelites wandered in the wilderness for (forty/seventy) years before entering the land of Canaan.
6. Jerusalem was destroyed, and many Jews were taken as captives to Babylon in (722/586) BC.
7. The (Phoenicians/Hittites) excelled in the production of iron.

8–9. Abraham traveled from (Sumer/Ur) and became the founder of the nation of (Israel/Syria).

10–11. (Sennacherib/Nebuchadnezzar) destroyed Jerusalem and carried the Jews into exile for (forty/seventy) years.

12. The leading religion in China was (Taoism/ancestor worship).
13. The (Middle Kingdom/Fertile Crescent) encompasses Mesopotamia and the land of Canaan.
14. (Sanskrit/Aryan) was a new language in India brought by the Aryans.
15. The study of celestial bodies is called (astrology/astronomy).
16. The earliest known form of writing was known as (cuneiform/hieroglyphics).
17. (Brahman/Zoroaster) rejected polytheism and instituted the worship of one god, Ahura Mazda.
18. (Sumer/Mesopotamia) is the term used to describe the fertile region between the Tigris and Euphrates Rivers.
19. (Khufu/Diaspora) refers to the time when the Jews were scattered after the destruction of Jerusalem.
20. The belief in many gods is known as (polytheism/monotheism).

*(continued on next page)*

## Matching

**Choose the best answer and place the letter in the blank beside the corresponding description. Not all answers will be used.**

| | | |
|---|---|---|
| A. Belshazzar | F. Hatshepsut | K. Sennacherib |
| B. Confucius | G. Laozi | L. Siddhartha Gautama |
| C. Cyrus | H. Menes | M. Solomon |
| D. Darius the Great | I. Ramses II | |
| E. David | J. Sargon II | |

_____ 21. Used by God to free His people from captivity in Babylon

_____ 22. Profaned golden vessels from God's temple in Jerusalem

_____ 23. Assyrian leader who defeated Samaria and northern Israel

_____ 24. Founded the religion of Buddhism

_____ 25. Under his reign the Persian Empire reached its height

_____ 26. Under his reign the kingdom of Israel reached its peak

_____ 27. After his death, Egypt gradually declined

_____ 28. Known as "the Master" to the Chinese

_____ 29. Founded the religion of Taoism

_____ 30. Assyrian king defeated by the Israelites

Name ______________________

## Homer's *Odyssey*

In the *Odyssey*, Ulysses, who participated in the ten-year-long Trojan War, undergoes a series of events that delay his return home for an additional ten years as the Greek gods struggle over his fate. Most people in Ithaca, Ulysses's homeland, assume that he is dead. In Ulysses's absence, over one hundred men court Penelope, Ulysses's wife, demanding that she marry one of them. When Ulysses returns, he appears in disguise to confront his enemies.

**Answer the questions below after reading the following excerpts from Homer's *Odyssey*.**

### From Book I

Tell me, O muse, of that ingenious hero who traveled far and wide after he had sacked the famous town of Troy. Many cities did he visit, and many were the nations with whose manners and customs he was acquainted; moreover he suffered much by sea while trying to save his own life and bring his men safely home; but do what he might he could not save his men, for they perished through their own sheer folly in eating the cattle of the Sun-god Hyperion; so the god prevented them from ever reaching home. Tell me, too, about all these things, O daughter of Jove, from whatsoever source you may know them.

1. How is Ulysses described? ______________________

______________________

2. Why is Ulysses unable to save his men? ______________________

______________________

### From Book II

[Antinous (one of Penelope's suitors) speaks to Telemachus (Ulysses's son) about Penelope.]

"And then there was that other trick she played us. She set up a great tambour frame in her room, and began to work on an enormous piece of fine needlework. 'Sweet hearts,' said she, 'Ulysses is indeed dead, still do not press me to marry again immediately, wait—for I would not have skill in needlework perish unrecorded—till I have completed a pall for the hero Laertes, to be in readiness against the time when death shall take him. He is very rich, and the women of the place will talk if he is laid out without a pall.'

"This was what she said, and we assented; whereon we could see her working on her great web all day long, but at night she would unpick the stitches again by torchlight. She fooled us in this way for three years and we never found her out, but as time wore on and she was now in her fourth year, one of her maids who knew what she was doing told us, and we caught her in the act of undoing her work, so she had to finish it whether she would or no."

3. What trick does Penelope play on her suitors? ______________________

______________________

4. How do the suitors discover Penelope's trick? ______________________

5. How much time passes before Penelope's trick is revealed? ______________________

*(continued on next page)*

## From Book XXI

[Penelope tells the suitors what they must do to win and marry her.]

Minerva now put it in Penelope's mind to make the suitors try their skill with the bow and with the iron axes, in contest among themselves, as a means of bringing about their destruction. . . . [A]nd Penelope stepped upon the raised platform, where the chests stood in which the fair linen and clothes were laid by along with fragrant herbs: reaching thence, she took down the bow with its bow case from the peg on which it hung. . . . [S]he went to the cloister where the suitors were, carrying the bow and the quiver, with the many deadly arrows that were inside it. . . . When she reached the suitors, she stood by one of the bearing-posts supporting the roof of the cloister, holding a veil before her face, and with a maid on either side of her. Then she said:

"Listen to me you suitors, who persist in abusing the hospitality of this house because its owner has been long absent, and without other pretext than that you want to marry me; this, then, being the prize that you are contending for, I will bring out the mighty bow of Ulysses, and whomsoever of you shall string it most easily and send his arrow through each one of twelve axes, him will I follow."

6. What does Penelope say that the suitors must do to win her? ______________________

______________________________________________

7. Who gives Penelope this idea? ______________________

[After all the suitors try in vain to string Ulysses's bow, Ulysses—disguised as a beggar—strings the bow and shoots an arrow through twelve ax handles.]

Ulysses, when he had taken [the bow] up and examined it all over, strung it as easily as a skilled bard strings a new peg of his lyre and makes the twisted gut fast at both ends. Then he took it in his right hand to prove the string, and it sang sweetly under his touch like the twittering of a swallow. The suitors were dismayed, and turned colour as they heard it; at that moment, moreover, Jove thundered loudly as a sign, and the heart of Ulysses rejoiced as he heard the omen that the son of scheming Saturn had sent him.

He took an arrow that was lying upon the table—for those which the Achaeans [Penelope's suitors] were so shortly about to taste were all inside the quiver—he laid it on the centre-piece of the bow, and drew the notch of the arrow and the string toward him, still seated on his seat. When he had taken aim he let fly, and his arrow pierced every one of the handle-holes of the axes from the first onwards till it had gone right through them, and into the outer courtyard.

Homer. *The Odyssey.* (New York, 1898), bk. 1, bk. 2, bk. 21, http://en.wikisource.org/wiki/The_Odyssey_%28Butler%29.

8. What occurs after Ulysses strings his bow? ______________________

______________________________________________

9. Who will soon feel all the arrows in Ulysses's quiver? ______________________

Name ______________________________

## Empire of Alexander the Great (323 BC)

**Locate each term on the map and place the corresponding number in the appropriate blank.**

_______ Alexandria

_______ Babylon

_______ Black Sea

_______ Caspian Sea

_______ Euphrates River

_______ Indus River

_______ Mediterranean Sea

_______ Nile River

_______ Persepolis

_______ Persian Gulf

_______ Red Sea

_______ Tigris River

_______ Tyre

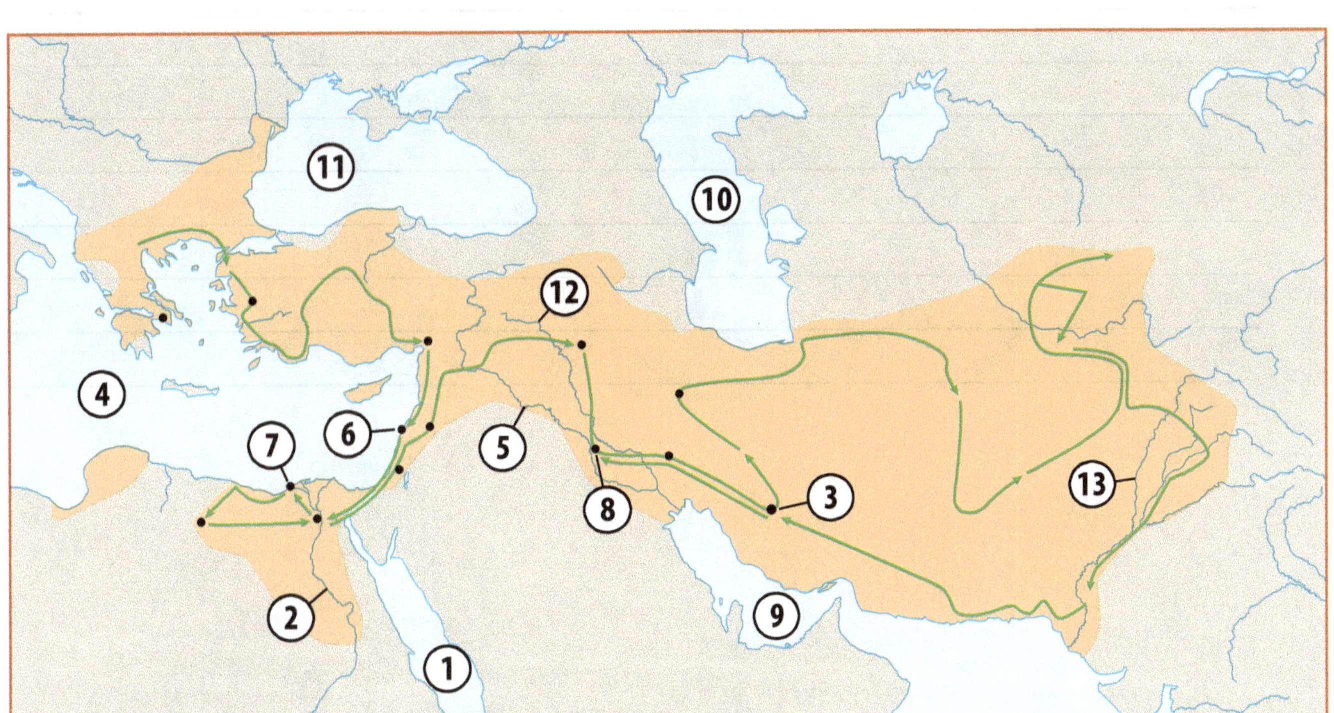

Name ______________________________

## Book of Daniel and Alexander's Empire

**Using the information in the student text and chapter eight of the book of Daniel, synthesize the two accounts of Alexander's conquests and the division of Alexander's empire.**

Name ____________________

## Greek Philosophy and Scripture

**This is an enrichment activity for those who are interested in this subject.**

**Write a brief response to each of the Greek philosophies cited using the Bible passages provided. (Note that the word translated "happy" from the philosophers does not mean *feeling* happy. It means to be in a happy or flourishing condition.)**

| Summary of Philosophy | Bible Reference | Student Summary |
|---|---|---|
| ***Plato***<br>"In many dialogues Plato grapples with the question of how we are to live a good life. He begins from an assumption which he shares with the rest of his society, namely that we all seek happiness (eudaimonia). . . . Where do most people go wrong? They think their life will go well, and that they will be happy, if they have the things that most people think are good—health, wealth, good looks, and so on. . . . [T]hey do not do you any good until you put them to use, that is, do something with them. Moreover, you have to do the right thing with them, put them to use which is expert and intelligent, or they will not benefit you—indeed may do you harm. Someone who wins the lottery, for example, may well not be made any happier by just having the money. Unless she puts it to intelligent use, the money may do nothing for her, or even ruin her life. Happiness cannot just be the stuff you have; you have to put it to good use."<br>Julia Annas. *Plato: A Very Short Introduction*. (New York: Oxford, 2003), 53–54. | Psalm 1:1–4; Prov. 3:5–8, 13–18 | |
| ***Aristotle***<br>"To know how to live well, we need to know the goal of human life, since knowing how well any activity has gone is a matter of knowing how far it has achieved its goal. Human life, says Aristotle, goes well when we achieve happiness, but only happiness of a certain sort, namely, happiness approved by reason. Only then are we exercising the capacities that nature intends us to exercise, and 'living well.' . . . Nature intends us to enjoy the happiness of a good person. . . . To make progress, we must examine the particular virtues—reason, temperance, fidelity, courage, justice, and so on—and discover how they contribute to the good life. This is what Aristotle does."<br>Alan Ryan. *On Politics: A History of Political Thought: From Herodotus to the Present*. (New York: Norton, 2012), 1:79. | Isaiah 5:20–21; 2 Peter 1:3–8 | |



*(continued on next page)*

| Summary of Philosophy | Bible Reference | Student Summary |
|---|---|---|
| ***Epicureanism***<br>"Above all, his philosophy of life was explicitly focused on 'pleasure', and that does not sound very virtuous. . . . he saw pleasure in a largely negative way: in its purest form it was just the absence of pain. . . . [P]ain lurks around every corner, especially if one tries too hard to pursue a life of intensely agreeable sensations. . . . [T]he pain of unsatisfiable desire is never far away when one gives free rein to one's greediest appetites. The life of unalloyed pleasures, then, will have to be a rather quiet affair. It will be a life in which all potential sources of distress have been eliminated."<br>Anthony Gottlieb. *The Dream of Reason: A History of Philosophy from the Greeks to the Renaissance.* (New York: Norton, 2000), 292–93. | Matthew 5:3–4, 10–12 | |
| ***Stoicism***<br>"For the Stoics, as for Heraclitus, a key ingredient in the recipe for happiness was learning to live with the inevitable. As a later, Roman Stoic put it: 'Do not seek to have everything that happens happen as you wish, but wish for everything to happen as it does happen, and your life will be serene.' . . . [T]he Stoics said that everything unfolds according to fate in an inexorable chain of cause and effect, and, moreover, that it will unfold in exactly the same way again and again in a cycle of cosmic creation and destruction." . . . One Stoic "drew a distinction between the things which are under our control, namely our thoughts and desires, and those which are not, namely what happens to our bodies, our families, our property, our reputation and fortune in life. He argued that if you suppress or redirect your emotions in order to focus on what is in your power, and ignore everything else, then 'no one will ever be able to exert compulsion upon you, no one will hinder you—neither is there any harm that can touch you.'"<br>Anthony Gottlieb. *The Dream of Reason: A History of Philosophy from the Greeks to the Renaissance.* (New York: Norton, 2000), 309–10, 313–14. | Philippians 4:11–13 | |

Name ____________________

# Early Greek History

**Answer the questions at the end after reading the following excerpt from Thucydides's *History of the Peloponnesian War.***

Thucydides, an Athenian, wrote the history of the war in which the Peloponnesians and the Athenians fought against one another. He began to write when they first took up arms, believing that it would be great and memorable above any previous war. For he argued that both states were then at the full height of their military power, and he saw the rest of the Hellenes [Greeks] either siding or intending to side with one or other of them. No movement ever stirred Hellas [Greece] more deeply than this; it was shared by many of the Barbarians, and might be said even to affect the world at large. The character of the events which preceded, whether immediately or in more remote antiquity, owing to the lapse of time cannot be made out with certainty. But, judging from the evidence which I am able to trust after most careful enquiry, I should imagine that former ages were not great either in their wars or in anything else.

The country which is now called Hellas [Greece] was not regularly settled in ancient times. The people were migratory, and readily left their homes whenever they were overpowered by numbers. There was no commerce, and they could not safely hold intercourse with one another either by land or sea. The several tribes cultivated their own soil just enough to obtain a maintenance from it. But they had no accumulations of wealth, and did not plant the ground; for, being without walls, they were never sure that an invader might not come and despoil them. Living in this manner and knowing that they could anywhere obtain a bare subsistence, they were already ready to migrate; so that they neither had great cities nor any considerable resources. The richest districts were most constantly changing their inhabitants; for example, the countries which are now called Thessaly and Boeotia, the greater part of Peloponnesus with the exception of Arcadia, and all the best parts of Hellas. For the productiveness of the land increased the power of individuals; this in turn was a source of quarrels by which communities were ruined, while at the same time they were more exposed to attacks from without. Certainly Attica, of which soil was poor and thin, enjoyed a long freedom from civil strife, and therefore retained its original inhabitants. And striking confirmation of my argument is afforded by the fact that Attica through immigration increased in population more than any other region. For the leading men of Hellas, when driven out of their own country by war or revolution, sought an asylum at Athens; and from the very earliest times, being admitted to rights of citizenship, so greatly increased the number of inhabitants that Attica became incapable of containing them, and was at last obliged to send out colonies to Ionia.

The feebleness of antiquity is further proved to me by the circumstance that there appears to have been no common action in Hellas before the Trojan War. And I am inclined to think that the very name was not as yet given to the whole country, and in fact did not exist at all before the time of Hellen, the son of Deucalion; the different tribes, of which the Pelasgian was the most widely spread, gave their own names to different districts. But when Hellen and his sons became powerful in Phthiotis, their aid was invoked by other cities, and those who associated with them gradually began to be called Hellenes, though a long time elapsed before the name prevailed over the whole country. Of this Homer affords the best evidence; for he, although he lived long after the Trojan War, nowhere uses this name collectively, but confines it to the followers of Achilles from Phthiotis, who were the original Hellenes; when speaking of the entire host he calls them Danaäns, or Argives, or Achaeans. Neither is there any mention of Barbarians in his poems, clearly because there were as yet no Hellenes opposed to them by a common distinctive name. Thus the several Hellenic tribes (and I mean by the term Hellenes

*(continued on next page)*

those who, while forming separate communities, had a common language, and were afterwards called by a common name), owing to their weakness and isolation, were never united in any great enterprise before the Trojan War.

Thucydides, trans. Benjamin Jowett. *History of the Peloponnesian War* 1.1-3

1. What war does Thucydides discuss in the first paragraph? ______________________________

______________________________________________________________________

2. Why did he think it would be a major historical event? ______________________________

______________________________________________________________________

3. What information in this passage shows that most of Greece was decentralized and lacked unity before the Trojan War? ______________________________

______________________________________________________________________

______________________________________________________________________

4. Which regions did tribes invade repeatedly because of their fertile soil? ______________________________

______________________________________________________________________

5. What region prospered because its poor soil discouraged invasion? ______________________________

6. What city in this region became overcrowded as it attracted refugees? ______________________________

7. Who united the regions of ancient Greece by alliance? What name was eventually given to inhabitants of ancient Greece? ______________________________

______________________________________________________________________

Name ______________________

# Chapter Review

## Complete the Statement

**Underline the term that accurately completes each of the following statements.**

1. (Dorians/Egyptians) invaded Mycenae around 1200 BC.
2. The (*Avesta*/*Iliad*) is a long epic poem about the Greek Dark Ages.
3. The earliest center of civilization in the Aegean region was populated by the (Mycenaean/Minoan) people.
4. (Solon/Zeno) led Athens toward democracy when he became archon around 594 BC.
5. The (polis/archon), or "city-state," was the basic political unit of Greece.
6. (Sparta/Athens) emerged victorious in 404 BC at the end of the Peloponnesian War.
7. In 460 BC, Pericles became the influential leader of (Athens/Corinth).
8. Darius I led a (Greek/Persian) force that landed twenty-five miles north of Athens in 490 BC.
9. The Greeks defeated the Persian fleet at the Battle of (Salamis Bay/Marathon).
10. Alexander the Great was originally from (Persia/Macedonia), a region located north of Greece.

## Short Answer

**Write the correct answer to each question in the provided blank.**

11. Which Greek philosopher believed that reality was in the physical world? ______________________
12. Who took the motto "Know thyself" and drank a cup of hemlock after being convicted of undermining institutions in Athens? ______________________
13. Who was the Father of Geometry and founded a school of mathematics in Alexandria, Egypt? ______________________
14. What was the function of the Parthenon? ______________________
15. What god did the Greeks regard as the "king of gods" who ruled Mount Olympus? ______________________
16. What term describes the Greeks' belief that gods have human form or attributes? ______________________
17. What is the breakdown of government and order? ______________________

*(continued on next page)*

18. What name is given to those that seek to find answers to basic life questions through man's reason?

_______________

19. What term means "like the Greek"? _______________

20. What is the name for a three-step logical process of thinking? _______________

21. In Greek society, what involved qualified adult male citizens sharing in the responsibility of ruling?

_______________

22. What is the formal study of human thought and culture? _______________

23. Name the organization of city-states that was led by Sparta. _______________

24. Name the leader of the Persian army that was confronted by Alexander the Great.

_______________

25. Name the organization of city-states that was led by Athens. _______________

## Matching

**Choose the best answer and place the letter in the blank beside the corresponding description. Not all answers will be used.**

| | | |
|---|---|---|
| A. Aristophanes | F. Homer | K. Thucydides |
| B. Epicurus | G. Plato | L. Xerxes |
| C. Eratosthenes | H. Pythagoras | M. Zeno |
| D. Herodotus | I. Sophocles | |
| E. Hippocrates | J. Thales | |

_____ 26. formulated lines of latitude and longitude

_____ 27. believed that avoidance of pain and fear brings happiness

_____ 28. a writer of tragedy

_____ 29. believed that every sickness has a natural cause

_____ 30. Darius's son who continued the conquest of Greece

_____ 31. regarded water as the original substance of all things

_____ 32. a writer of epic poems

_____ 33. studied under Socrates; wrote the *Republic*

_____ 34. the Father of History

_____ 35. concluded that the universe could be explained in mathematical terms

Name ______________________

## Roman and US Republics

**Complete the chart below, comparing the Roman Republic with the modern US republic.**

| | | Roman Republic | United States Republic |
|---|---|---|---|
| Written Law | Date the monarchy was replaced | ____________ BC | ____________ or 1783 |
| | Name of the written law of the land and date of its adoption | ______________________; ____________ BC | ______________________; 1787 or 1789 |
| | Purpose of the written law | | To settle the form of government and to limit the powers of government |
| Separation of Powers | Elected body with power to pass laws and control finances | | |
| | Term of office for senators | | |
| | Plebeian elected body with power to pass laws | | |
| | Term of office for consuls/ representatives | | |
| | Executive(s) empowered to carry out laws | | |
| | Term of office for the executive(s) | | |
| | Commander(s) of the army | | |
| | Supreme judge(s), or supreme interpreter(s) of the law | | |

*(continued on next page)*

| | | Roman Republic | United States Republic |
|---|---|---|---|
| Checks and Balances | Checks on executive power | | Congress can impeach the president.<br>Congress can override presidential vetoes.<br>The Senate can reject the president's appointees.<br>The House can impeach federal officials. |
| | Checks on the Senate's power | | |
| | Checks on the represen-tative assembly's power | | |

Name ____________________

# Hannibal Crosses the Alps

**Answer the questions at the end after reading the following excerpt from Livy's *History of Rome*.**

Though the elephants were driven through steep and narrow roads with great loss of time, yet wherever they went they rendered the army safe from the enemy, because men unacquainted with such animals were afraid of approaching too nearly. On the ninth day they came to a summit of the Alps, chiefly through places trackless; and after many mistakes of their way, which were caused either by the treachery of the guides, or, when they were not trusted, by entering valleys at random, on their own conjectures of the route. For two days they remained encamped on the summit; and rest was given to the soldiers, exhausted with toil and fighting: and several beasts of burden, which had fallen down among the rocks, by following the track of the army arrived at the camp. A fall of snow, it being now the season of the setting of the constellation of the Pleiades, caused great fear to the soldiers, already worn out with weariness of so many hardships. On the standards being moved forward at daybreak, when the army proceeded slowly over all places entirely blocked up with snow, and languor and despair strongly appeared in the countenances of all, Hannibal, having advanced before the standards, and ordered the soldiers to halt on a certain eminence, whence there was a prospect far and wide, points out to them Italy and the plains of the Po, extending themselves beneath the Alpine mountains; and said "that they were now surmounting not only the ramparts of Italy, but also of the city of Rome; that the rest of the journey would be smooth and down-hill; that after one, or, at most, a second battle, they would have the citadel and capital of Italy in their power and possession." The army then began to advance, the enemy now making no attempts beyond petty thefts, as opportunity offered. But the journey proved much more difficult than it had been in the ascent, as the declivity [slope] of the Alps being generally shorter on the side of Italy is consequently steeper; for nearly all the road was precipitous, narrow, and slippery, so that neither those who made the least stumble could prevent themselves from falling, nor, when fallen, remain in the same place, but rolled, both men and beasts of burden, one upon another.

They then came to a rock much more narrow, and formed of such perpendicular ledges, that a light-armed soldier, carefully making the attempt, and clinging with his hands to the bushes and roots around, could with difficulty lower himself down. The ground, even before very steep by nature, had been broken by a recent falling away of the earth into a precipice of nearly a thousand feet in depth. Here when the cavalry had halted, as if at the end of their journey, it is announced to Hannibal, wondering what obstructed the march that the rock was impassable. Having then gone himself to view the place, it seemed clear to him that he must lead his army round it, by however great a circuit, through the pathless and untrodden regions around. But this route also proved impracticable; for while the new snow of a moderate depth remained on the old, which had not been removed, their footsteps were planted with ease as they walked upon the new snow, which was soft and not too deep; but when it was dissolved by the trampling of so many men and beasts of burden, they then walked on the bare ice below, and through the dirty fluid formed by the melting snow. Here there was a wretched struggle, both on account of the slippery ice not affording any hold to the step, and giving way beneath the foot more readily by reason of the slope; and whether they assisted themselves in rising by their hands or their knees, their supports themselves giving way, they would stumble again; nor were there any stumps or roots near; by pressing against which, one might with hand or foot support himself; so that they only floundered on the smooth ice and amid the melted snow. The beasts of burden sometimes also went into this lower ice by merely treading upon it, at others they broke it completely through, by the violence with which they struck in their hoofs in their struggling, so that most of them, as if taken in a trap, stuck in the hardened and deeply frozen ice.

*(continued on next page)*

At length, after the men and beasts of burden had been fatigued to no purpose, the camp was pitched on the summit, the ground being cleared for that purpose with great difficulty, so much snow was there to be dug out and carried away. The soldiers being then set to make a way down the cliff by which alone a passage could be effected, and it being necessary that they should cut through the rocks, having felled and lopped a number of large trees which grew around, they make a huge pile of timber; and as soon as a strong wind fit for exciting the flames arose, they set fire to it, and, pouring vinegar on the heated stones, they render them soft and crumbling. They then open a way with iron instruments through the rock thus heated by the fire, and soften its declivities by gentle windings, so that not only the beasts of burden, but also the elephants could be led down it. Four days were spent about this rock, the beasts nearly perishing through hunger: for the summits of the mountains are for the most part bare, and if there is any pasture the snows bury it. The lower parts contain valleys, and some sunny hills, and rivulets flowing beside woods, and scenes more worthy of the abode of man. There the beasts of burden were sent out to pasture, and rest given for three days to the men, fatigued with forming the passage: they then descended into the plains, the country and the dispositions of the inhabitants being now less rugged.

Livy. *The History of Rome.* Public domain.

1. How did the presence of elephants protect Hannibal's army as it crossed the Alps? ____________________

____________________________________________________________

2. What did Hannibal show his troops to encourage them? ____________________

____________________________________________________________

3. What obstacles did Hannibal's army encounter as it tried to march into Italy by descending the Alps?

____________________________________________________________

____________________________________________________________

4. Why did the animals almost starve? ____________________

____________________________________________________________

Name ______________________________

## Punic Wars

**Locate each term or phrase on the map and place the corresponding number in the appropriate blank.**

| | |
|---|---|
| _______ Adriatic Sea | _______ Mediterranean Sea |
| _______ Alps | _______ North Africa |
| _______ Cannae | _______ Rome |
| _______ Carthage | _______ Sardinia |
| _______ Corsica | _______ Spain |
| _______ Hannibal's route | _______ Zama |

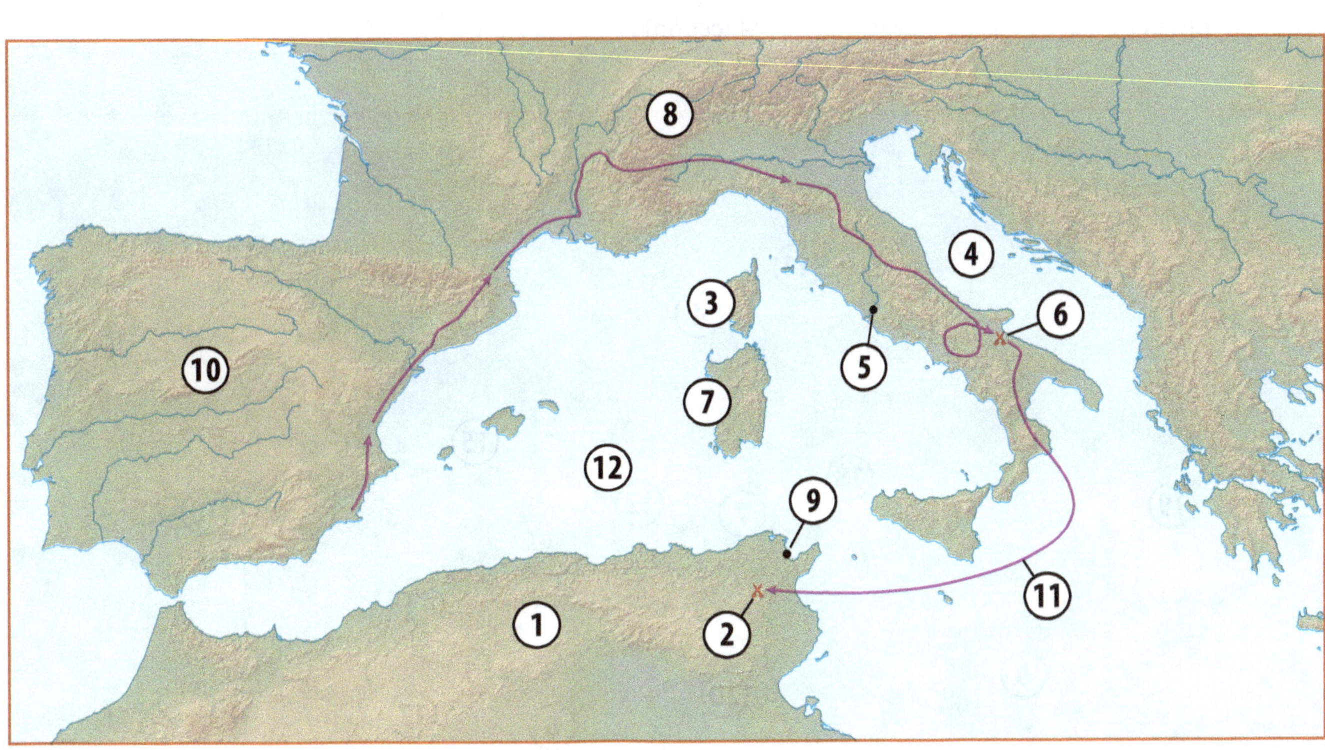

Name ______________________

## The Roman Empire at Its Greatest Extent (ca. AD 117)

**Locate each term on the map and place the corresponding number in the appropriate blank.**

______ Adriatic Sea

______ Black Sea

______ Britain

______ Crete

______ Cyprus

______ Danube River

______ Egypt

______ Euphrates River

______ Gaul

______ Germania

______ Italy

______ Jerusalem

______ Judea

______ Macedonia

______ Mediterranean Sea

______ Nile River

______ North Africa

______ Red Sea

______ Spain

______ Tigris River

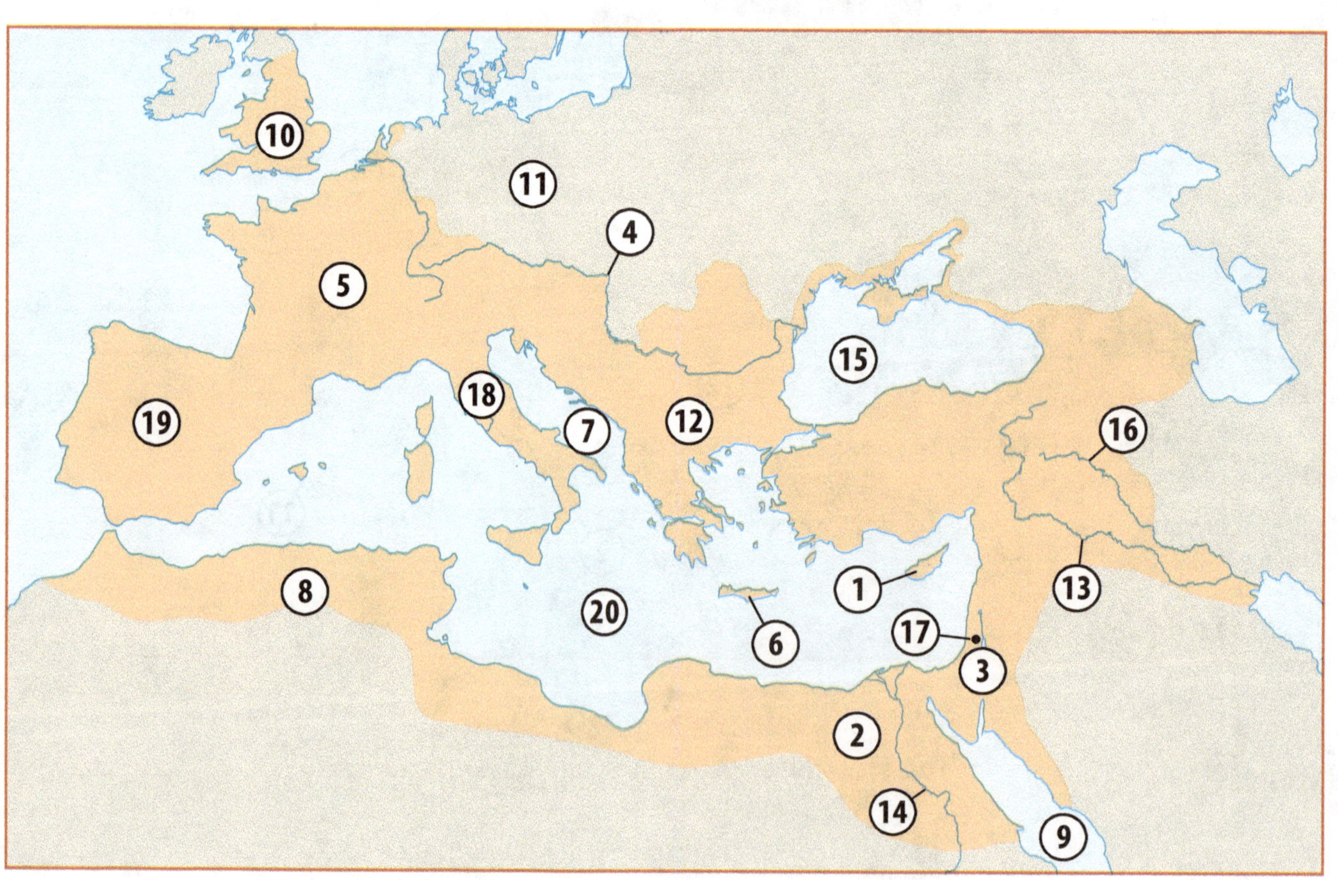

Name ____________________

# Early Roman Persecution of Christians

**Answer the questions below after reading the following excerpts from the correspondence of Pliny the Younger.**

Letter XCVII. *To* the Emperor Trajan.

It is my invariable rule, Sir, to refer to you in all matters where I feel doubtful; for who is more capable of removing my scruples, or informing my ignorance? Having never been present at any trials concerning those who profess Christianity, I am [unacquainted] not only with the nature of their crimes, or the measure of their punishment, but how far it is proper to enter into an examination concerning them. Whether, therefore, any difference is usually made with respect to ages, or no distinction is to be observed between the young and the adult; whether repentance entitles them to a pardon; or if a man has been once a Christian, it avails nothing to desist from his error; whether the very profession of Christianity, unattended with any criminal act, or only the crimes themselves inherent in the profession are punishable; on all these points I am in great doubt. In the meanwhile, the method I have observed towards those who have been brought before me as Christians is this: I asked them whether they were Christians; if they admitted it, I repeated the question twice, and threatened them with punishment; if they persisted, I ordered them to be at once punished: for I was persuaded, whatever the nature of their opinions might be, a contumacious and inflexible obstinacy certainly deserved correction. There were others also brought before me possessed with the same infatuation, but being Roman citizens, I directed them to be sent to Rome. But this crime spreading (as is usually the case) while it was actually under prosecution, several instances of the same nature occurred. An anonymous information was laid before me, containing a charge against several persons, who upon examination denied they were Christians, or had ever been so. They repeated after me an invocation to the gods, and offered religious rites with wine and incense before your statue (which for that purpose I had ordered to be brought, together with those of the gods), and even reviled the name of Christ: whereas there is no forcing, it is said, those who are really Christians into any of these compliances: I thought it proper, therefore, to discharge them.

1. How did Pliny determine whether certain people were truly Christians? ____________________

____________________

2. Where did he send Christians who were also Roman citizens? ____________________

3. What did Pliny discover about the result of persecuting Christians? ____________________

____________________

4. What did Pliny do when he received an anonymous accusation that several people were Christians?

____________________

____________________

5. What did Pliny discover about forcing real Christians to invoke the gods and revile the name of Christ?

____________________

____________________

*(continued on next page)*

Letter XCVIII. Trajan *to* Pliny.

You have adopted the right course, my dearest Secundus in investigating the charges against the Christians who were brought before you. It is not possible to lay down any general rule for all such cases. Do not go out of your way to look for them. If indeed they should be brought before you, and the crime is proved, they must be punished; with the restriction, however, that where the party denies he is a Christian, and shall make it evident that he is not, by invoking our gods, let him (notwithstanding any former suspicion) be pardoned upon his repentance. Anonymous informations ought not to be received in any sort of prosecution. It is introducing a very dangerous precedent, and is quite foreign to the spirit of our age.

Pliny the Younger. *The Letters of Caius Plinius Caecilius Secundus*. trans. Melmoth (New York: Macmillan, 1909), 393–94, 396–97.

6. Is Trajan pleased or displeased with Pliny's current course of action? ______

7. What does Trajan caution Pliny not to "go out of [his] way" for? ______

8. What counsel does Trajan give Pliny about those who were accused of being Christians but denied the charge? ______

9. What does Trajan warn Pliny not to receive or act on? ______

10. Why does Trajan warn Pliny against this practice? How does this warning parallel modern law in the United States? ______

Name ______________________

## Chapter Review

### Complete the Statement

**Underline the term that accurately completes each of the following statements.**

1. The Roman Republic was formed in 509 BC to replace the Etruscan (oligarchy/monarchy).
2. (Julius Caesar/Octavian) was murdered in the Senate on the Ides of March in 44 BC.
3. The (plebeians/patricians) were privileged citizens who held the highest positions in society.
4. In the first century BC, Rome was transformed into a government ruled by (an imperator/ consuls).
5. (Constantine/Arius) was the Roman emperor who made Christianity legal.
6. (Assembly of Centuries/Roman forum) passed laws that could be vetoed by the Senate.
7. (Stoics/Epicureans) pursued happiness and rejected the afterlife and divine judgment.

### Short Answer

**Write the correct answer to each question in the provided blank.**

8. According to tradition, what city did Romulus and Remus found in 753 BC? ______________
9. What group established one of Italy's earliest civilizations around 800 BC? ______________
10. What foundation of Roman law was displayed in the Roman Forum? ______________
11. In 287 BC, what plebeian assembly gained power to pass laws binding upon all the people of Rome?
    ______________________________
12. In Roman society, what group was responsible for collecting taxes in Roman provinces? ______________
    ______________________________
13. Who was reigning at the beginning of the *Pax Romana*? ______________
14. Who was the Roman emperor at the time of Christ's death and resurrection? ______________
15. Which Roman emperor was the first to persecute Christians? ______________
16. Give the name for the wars between Carthage and Rome. ______________
17. What became the most powerful and important body of the republic of Rome?
    ______________________________
18. What edict made Christianity legal in 313? ______________
19. What church council affirmed Christ's deity and the doctrine of the Trinity in 325? ______________
    ______________________________

*(continued on next page)*

20. Which emperor initiated the final and most widespread persecution of Christians in the Roman Empire?

______________________________

21. What Germanic tribe defeated the Roman army and killed the emperor? ______________________________

______________________________

22. Who was the fierce leader of the Huns? ______________________________

23. When did Octavian defeat Antony and Cleopatra? ______________________________

24. Give the name for the villages that were the beginning of the city of Rome.

______________________________

25. Name the group of people that protected the rights and interests of the common people of Rome.

______________________________

26. Give the name for the message of the good news of the kingdom of God. ______________________________

27. Name the Germanic tribe that established a kingdom in North Africa. ______________________________

28. What year did Octavian become the sole ruler of Rome? ______________________________

29. These were built to supply water to Roman cities. ______________________________

30. View that the earth was the center of the universe. ______________________________

## Matching

**Choose the best answer and place the letter in the blank beside the corresponding statement or description.**

| | | |
|---|---|---|
| A. Arius | D. Livy | F. Scipio |
| B. Cicero | E. Ptolemy | G. Seneca |
| C. Hannibal | | |

_____ 31. invaded Italy by marching through the Alps in the winter

_____ 32. tutor to Nero; a leading Stoic

_____ 33. wrote a history of Rome

_____ 34. revered as the greatest orator of his day; born in 106 BC

_____ 35. believed the earth was the center of the universe

Name ______________________________

## Early Africa

**Locate each term on the map and place the corresponding number in the appropriate blank.**

_______ Aksum

_______ Gulf of Aden

_______ Mecca

_______ Mediterranean Sea

_______ Nile River

_______ Persian Gulf

_______ Red Sea

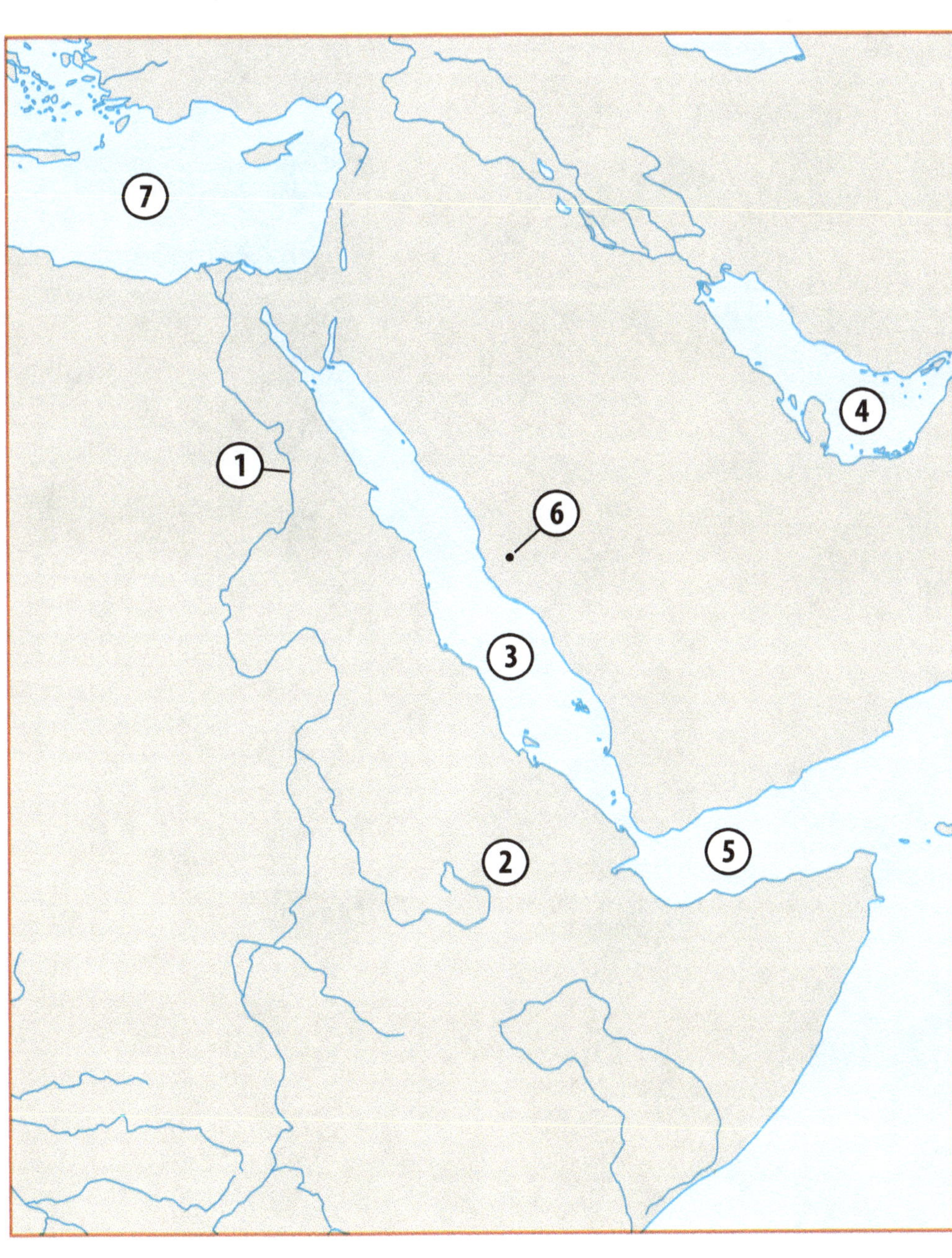

Name ______________________

# Christianity in Ethiopia

**Answer the questions at the end after reading the following selection on the spread of Christianity in Ethiopia.**

*The Nine Saints.* For the century after the death of Ezana (c. 400) Christianity was confined to "a narrow corridor between Adulis and Axum along the main caravan routes." The successors of Ezana, such as Kaleb and Gabre Maskal, were sincere Christians who puzzled over how to bring the Good News of the kingdom to the masses.

An answer came in the form of a new missionary force entering the country. Beginning in the fifth century Syrian monks of mildly Monophysite persuasion filtered into Ethiopia, possibly to escape persecution from the pro-Chalcedonian Byzantine emperor. Ethiopian church tradition identifies a select group of these missionary refugees as the *tesseatou Kidoussan* (the Nine Saints). These nine monks (Abba Aregawi, Abba Guerima, Abba Aftse, Penteleon, Likanos, Alef, Tsihma, Ym'ata, and Gouba) learned the local languages, translated Scriptures in Ge'ez, preached, planted monasteries and churches, and traveled extensively throughout the Axumite lands. Abba Aregawi was the most revered. His legacy was the founding of monasticism in Ethiopia, which emanated from his center, Dabra Damo.

Although other missionaries like the *Sadqan* and Abba Libanos were significant in the spread of the faith in Ethiopia, the Nine Saints are given the primary credit for rooting Christianity among the people. For centuries after, the stories and church murals of the Nine Saints would be a significant part of Ethiopian tradition.

The coming of the Syrian monks and their introduction of the rule of St. Pachomius changed the character of Ethiopian Christianity. Monasteries more than churches became the bases from which Christianity was established and extended in the kingdom. It was to the monasteries, says Roland Oliver, that "the faithful repaired at great festivals and in times of personal need." When King Gabre Maskal granted land to Abba Aregawi, a tradition was established that would eventually make "the Church the largest landowner in the country."

Yet the work of the monks and their successors was not without flaws. To their credit they did present apolitical Christianity that clearly distinguished the acceptance of Christ as King from submission to the king sitting in Axum.

However, the conversion process used by the monks had unintended side effects. The new missionaries of the fifth century and their successors established a ritual for conversion that involved a profession of faith, the experience of baptism, and the assigning of a new name. Little teaching or training was given. This meant that "many new Christians had only a minimal commitment to their faith." Combined with the lack of trained clergy, such converts frequently slipped into syncretism or eventual apostasy. Belief in sacred groves and trees persisted within the community of the church into modern times. Beneath the numeric successes of the monastic missionaries lay a deeper failure to bring converts beyond the "threshold of Christianity" to the point of "an irreversible commitment."

Linked with Egyptian Coptic Christianity (the *abun* or chief bishop of the church continued to be an Egyptian) and armed with vernacular Scriptures, Christian kings, and great numbers of local churches, the church of Ethiopia entered the Middle Ages where, in Gibbon's exaggerated phrase, they "slept near a thousand years, forgetful of the world, by whom they were forgotten."

Shaw, Mark R. *The Kingdom of God in Africa.* (Grand Rapids: Baker Books, 1996), 64–65.

*(continued on next page)*

1. Where was Christianity found in Ethiopia after the death of Ezana?

2. What was the response to the lack of Christianity in Ethiopia?

3. What is the name that the Ethiopian church traditionally identifies as the select group of missionaries?

4. What became the bases of Christianity in Ethiopia?

5–6. Describe the conversion process used by the monks. Evaluate the problems with this method.

7. What was Ethiopian Christianity linked with?

Name ______________________________

## Stupas in India

**Answer the questions at the end after reading the following selection on stupas in India.**

*The Great Stupa at Sanchi, Madhya Pradesh, India*

Buddhist stupas and cave temples were built in India as early as the second century B.C.E. Stupas were round structures that held relics of the Buddha and were perambulated by devotees. They were built through donations of kings and laypeople from at least the time of Ashoka. The earliest freestanding Hindu temples in the subcontinent, however, date only to the Gupta period (fourth–mid-sixth centuries C.E.) These structures were small in comparison to the temples of later centuries; most had flat roofs and were built of thick masonry without mortar. The temple design of sixth century C.E. has remained the standard even to the modern period. At the center of the temple is a small, dark shrine room containing the image of the chief deity, and outside this is a larger hall and a porch through which worshippers enter. A large tower rises over the core shrine room, and the whole building complex is set within a rectangular courtyard, sometimes (in later buildings) enclosing a temple tank. The great Hindu temples were built under the patronage of the South Indian dynasties of the fifth to 12th centuries: the Pallavas, Chalukyas, and Cholas. In the north many older temples were destroyed by Muslim invaders, and most large temples, even in Varanasi, are recent. Two large famous temple complexes dating to the 12th and 13th centuries can be found in Orissa: the Jagannatha temple in the city of Puri and the temple to Surya (the sun god) at nearby Konarak.

Walsh, Judith E. *A Brief History of India*. (New York: Facts on File, 2011), 57.

1. Give the name for the round structures that held relics of the Buddha.

______________________________

2. During what Indian empire discussed in this chapter were the earliest freestanding Hindu temples built?

______________________________

3. Who often funded the building of the temples?

______________________________

4. What happened to many older temples?

______________________________

5. Evaluate the stupas from a biblical worldview.

______________________________

______________________________

______________________________

Name ______________________________

# Han Dynasty China

**Locate each term on the map and place the corresponding number in the appropriate blank.**

| | |
|---|---|
| ______ Great Wall | ______ Sea of Japan (East Sea) |
| ______ Grand Canal | ______ South China Sea |
| ______ Huang He River | ______ Xi River |
| ______ Korea | ______ Yangtze River |
| ______ Pacific Ocean | ______ Yellow Sea |

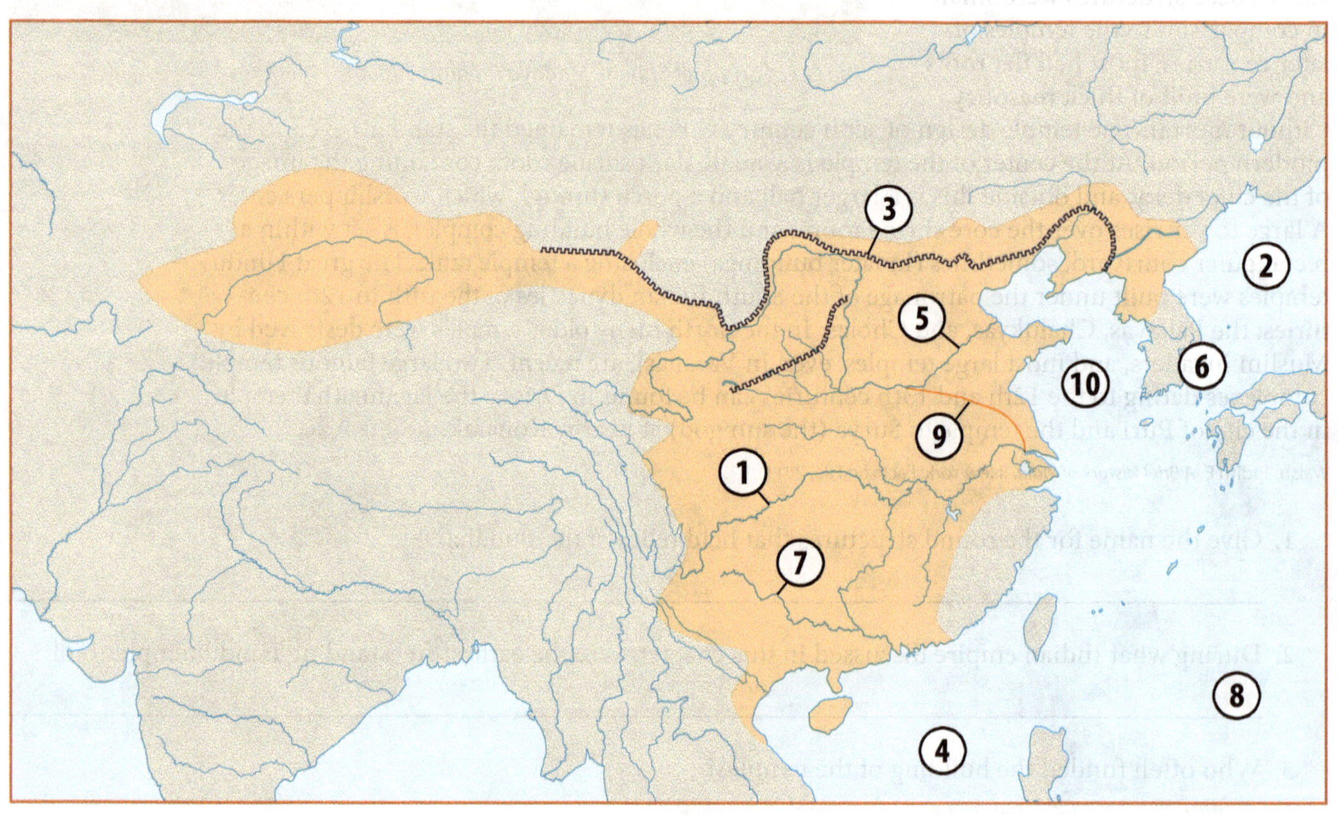

Name ______________________

# Chapter Review

## Matching

**Choose the best answer and place the letter in the blank beside the corresponding description.**

| | | |
|---|---|---|
| A. Aksum | C. Han dynasty | E. Mauryan empire |
| B. Gupta empire | D. Kush | F. Qin dynasty |

_____ 1. Began connecting structures to form the Great Wall of China

_____ 2. First period in which India was unified; arose after the end of Greek invasions

_____ 3. Traded with Greece and Rome

_____ 4. Period in which Kalidasa wrote his plays

_____ 5. Won its independence from Egypt and began to seize territory

_____ 6. Kingdom ruled by King Ezana

## Short Answer

**Write the correct answer to each question in the provided blank.**

7. Name the teacher known for his wise sayings. ______________________
8. What Greek military commander threatened India with his armies in 326 BC? ______________________
9. Who promoted Christianity in Aksum? ______________________
10. What term means the practice of having more than one spouse? ______________________
11. Who founded the first strong empire of India in the fourth century AD? ______________________
12. Who was the most famous ruler of the Han dynasty? ______________________
13. Whose plays earned him the title "the Indian Shakespeare"? ______________________
14. Give the name for the "Chinese Peace" during the Han dynasty. ______________________
15. What may have been the first trace of people in Africa? ______________________
16. What African city is believed to be the oldest in Africa? ______________________
17. What is the name for the southern area of Africa? ______________________
18. Who was the most famous of the Mauryan rulers? ______________________

*(continued on next page)*

19. What West African culture was known for its iron working and weaponry? ______________________

20. Who was the first to unite the provinces of China under one strong centralized government?

______________________

21. What tall structures were built with carefully designed stones in Aksum? ______________________

22. What religion became more popular in India during the Gupta Empire? ______________________

23–25. List three of the contributions of the Gupta Empire. ______________________

______________________

______________________

Name ____________________

## The Nika Revolt

Known as the Nika Revolt or the Nika Riots, this violent event in 532 lasted only one week, but it nearly destroyed the capital of the Byzantine Empire. By the time forces loyal to the government successfully crushed the revolt, nearly half the city was destroyed and thousands of people were dead.

**Answer the questions below after reading the following excerpts from the writings of Procopius.**

At this same time an insurrection broke out unexpectedly in Byzantium among the populace, and, contrary to expectation, it proved to be a very serious affair, and ended in great harm to the people and to the senate, as the following account will shew. In every city the population has been divided for a long time past into the Blue and the Green factions; but within comparatively recent times it has come about that, for the sake of these names and the seats which the rival factions occupy in watching the games, they spend their money and abandon their bodies to the most cruel tortures, and even do not think it unworthy to die a most shameful death. And they fight against their opponents knowing not for what end they imperil themselves, but knowing well that, even if they overcome their enemy in the fight, the conclusion of the matter for them will be to be carried off straightway to the prison, and finally, after suffering extreme torture, to be destroyed. So there grows up in them against their fellow men a hostility which has no cause, and at no time does it cease or disappear, for it gives place neither to the ties of marriage nor of relationship nor of friendship, and the case is the same even though those who differ with respect to these colours be brothers or any other kin. They care neither for things divine nor human in comparison with conquering in these struggles; and it matters not whether a sacrilege is committed by anyone at all against God, or whether the laws and the constitution are violated by friend or by foe; nay even when they are perhaps ill supplied with the necessities of life, and when their fatherland is in the most pressing need and suffering unjustly, they pay no heed if only it is likely to go well with their "faction"; for so they name the bands of partisans. And even women join with them in this unholy strife, and they not only follow the men, but even resist them if opportunity offers, although they neither go to the public exhibitions at all, nor are they impelled by any other cause; so that I, for my part, am unable to call this anything except a disease of the soul. This, then, is pretty well how matters stand among the people of each and every city.

But at this time the officers of the city administration in Byzantium were leading away to death some of the rioters. But the members of the two factions, conspiring together and declaring a truce with each other, seized the prisoners and then straightway entered the prison and released all those who were in confinement there, whether they had been condemned on a charge of stirring up sedition, or for any other unlawful act. And all the attendants in the service of the city government were killed indiscriminately; meanwhile, all of the citizens who were sane-minded were fleeing to the opposite mainland, and fire was applied to the city as if it had fallen under the hand of an enemy. The sanctuary of Sophia and the baths of Zeuxippus, and the portion of the imperial residence from the propylaea as far as the so-called House of Ares were destroyed by fire, and besides these both the great colonnades which extended as far as the market place which bears the name of Constantine, in addition to many houses of wealthy men and a vast amount of treasure. During this time the emperor and his consort with a few members of the senate shut themselves up in the palace and remained quietly there. Now the watchword which the populace passed around to one another was Nika ["Conquer"], and the insurrection has been called by this name up to the present time.

1. In what city did the Nika Revolt occur? ____________________

2. What two groups competed with each other at games? ____________________

(continued on next page)

3. Why did these two groups that usually hated each other make a pact and an alliance? ______________

______________________________________________

______________________________________________

4. What actions started the Nika Revolt? ______________________________________________

______________________________________________

5. What was the "watchword" during the revolt? What does this term mean? ______________

______________________________________________

Now the emperor and his court were deliberating as to whether it would be better for them if they remained or if they took to flight in the ships. And many opinions were expressed favouring either course. And the Empress Theodora also spoke to the following effect: "As to the belief that a woman ought not to be daring among men or to assert herself boldly among those who are holding back from fear, I consider that the present crisis most certainly does not permit us to discuss whether the matter should be regarded in this or in some other way. For in the case of those whose interests have come into the greatest danger nothing else seems best except to settle the issue immediately before them in the best possible way. My opinion then is that the present time, above all others, is inopportune for flight, even though it bring safety. For while it is impossible for a man who has seen the light not also to die, for one who has been an emperor it is unendurable to be a fugitive. May I never be separated from this purple [a costly fabric that denoted royalty], and may I not live that day on which those who meet me shall not address me as mistress. If, now, it is your wish to save yourself, O Emperor, there is no difficulty. For we have much money, and there is the sea, here the boats. However consider whether it will not come about after you have been saved that you would gladly exchange that safety for death. For as for myself, I approve a certain ancient saying that royalty is a good burial-shroud." When the queen had spoken thus, all were filled with boldness, and, turning their thoughts towards resistance, they began to consider how they might be able to defend themselves if any hostile force should come against them. Now the soldiers as a body, including those who were stationed about the emperor's court, were neither well disposed to the emperor nor willing openly to take an active part in fighting, but were waiting for what the future would bring forth. All the hopes of the emperor were centred upon Belisarius and Mundus [Byzantine military commanders], of whom the former, Belisarius, had recently returned from the Persian war bringing with him a following which was both powerful and imposing, and in particular he had a great number of spearmen and guards who had received their training in battles and the perils of warfare. Mundus had been appointed general of the Illyrians, and by mere chance had happened to come under summons to Byzantium on some necessary errand, bringing with him Erulian barbarians.

When Hypatius [a relative of a previous emperor and one whom the mob appointed emperor in place of Justinian] reached the hippodrome, he went up immediately to where the emperor is accustomed to take his place and seated himself on the royal throne from which the emperor was always accustomed to view the equestrian and athletic contests. And from the palace Mundus went out through the gate which, from the circling descent, has been given the name of the Snail. Belisarius meanwhile began at first to go straight up toward Hypatius himself and the royal throne, and when he came to the adjoining structure where there has been a guard of soldiers from of old, he cried out to the soldiers commanding them to open the door for him as quickly as possible, in order that he might go against the tyrant. But since the soldiers had decided to support neither side, until one of them should be manifestly victorious, they pretended not to hear at all and thus put him off. So Belisarius returned to the emperor and declared that the day was lost for them, for the soldiers who guarded the palace were rebelling against him. The emperor therefore commanded him to go to the so-called Bronze Gate and the propylaea there. So Belisarius, with difficulty and not without danger and great exertion, made his way over ground covered by ruins and half-burned buildings, and ascended to the stadium. And when he had reached the Blue Colonnade which is on the right of

*(continued on next page)*

the emperor's throne, he purposed to go against Hypatius himself first; but since there was a small door there which had been closed and was guarded by the soldiers of Hypatius who were inside, he feared lest while he was struggling in the narrow space the populace should fall upon him, and after destroying both himself and all his followers, should proceed with less trouble and difficulty against the emperor. Concluding, therefore, that he must go against the populace who had taken their stand in the hippodrome—a vast multitude crowding each other in great disorder—he drew his sword from its sheath and, commanding the others to do likewise, with a shout he advanced upon them at a run. But the populace, who were standing in a mass and not in order, at the sight of armoured soldiers who had a great reputation for bravery and experience in war, and seeing that they struck out with their swords unsparingly, beat a hasty retreat. Then a great outcry arose, as was natural, and Mundus, who was standing not far away, was eager to join in the fight,—for he was a daring and energetic fellow—but he was at a loss as to what he should do under the circumstances; when, however, he observed that Belisarius was in the struggle, he straightway made a sally into the hippodrome through the entrance which they call the Gate of Death. Then indeed from both sides the partisans of Hypatius were assailed with might and main and destroyed. When the rout had become complete and there had already been great slaughter of the populace, Boraedes and Justus, nephews of the Emperor Justinian, without anyone daring to lift a hand against them, dragged Hypatius down from the throne, and, leading him in, handed him over together with Pompeius [a military officer] to the emperor. And there perished among the populace on that day more than thirty thousand. But the emperor commanded the two prisoners to be kept in severe confinement. Then, while Pompeius was weeping and uttering pitiable words (for the man was wholly inexperienced in such misfortunes), Hypatius reproached him at length and said that those who were about to die unjustly should not lament. For in the beginning they had been forced by the people against their will, and afterwards they had come to the hippodrome with no thought of harming the emperor. And the soldiers killed both of them on the following day and threw their bodies into the sea. The emperor confiscated all their property for the public treasury, and also that of all the other members of the senate who had sided with them. Later, however, he restored to the children of Hypatius and Pompeius and to all others the titles which they had formerly held, and as much of their property as he had not happened to bestow upon his friends. This was the end of the insurrection in Byzantium.

Procopius, *Procopius*. trans. H. B. Dewing, vol.1, *History of the Wars: Books 1 and 2* (Cambridge, MA: Harvard Univ. Press, 1971), 219, 221, 223, 231, 233, 235, 237, 239.

6. When the emperor Justinian contemplated fleeing, who convinced him to stay and fight? ______________

7. What did this person say that encouraged Justinian and his court to subdue the mob? ______________

8. How did Belisarius and Mundus end the revolt? ______________

9. How many rioters were killed to end the revolt? ______________

10. How did the emperor punish treasonous members of the senate? ______________

11. What act of mercy did the emperor perform after calm had been restored? ______________

Name ______________________

## Byzantine Empire at Its Height (6th Century)

**Locate each term on the map and place the corresponding number in the appropriate blank.**

_______ Alexandria

_______ Arabia

_______ Asia Minor

_______ Black Sea

_______ Constantinople

_______ Danube River

_______ Egypt

_______ Greece

_______ Jerusalem

_______ Mediterranean Sea

_______ Nile River

_______ North Africa

_______ Red Sea

_______ Rome

_______ Venice

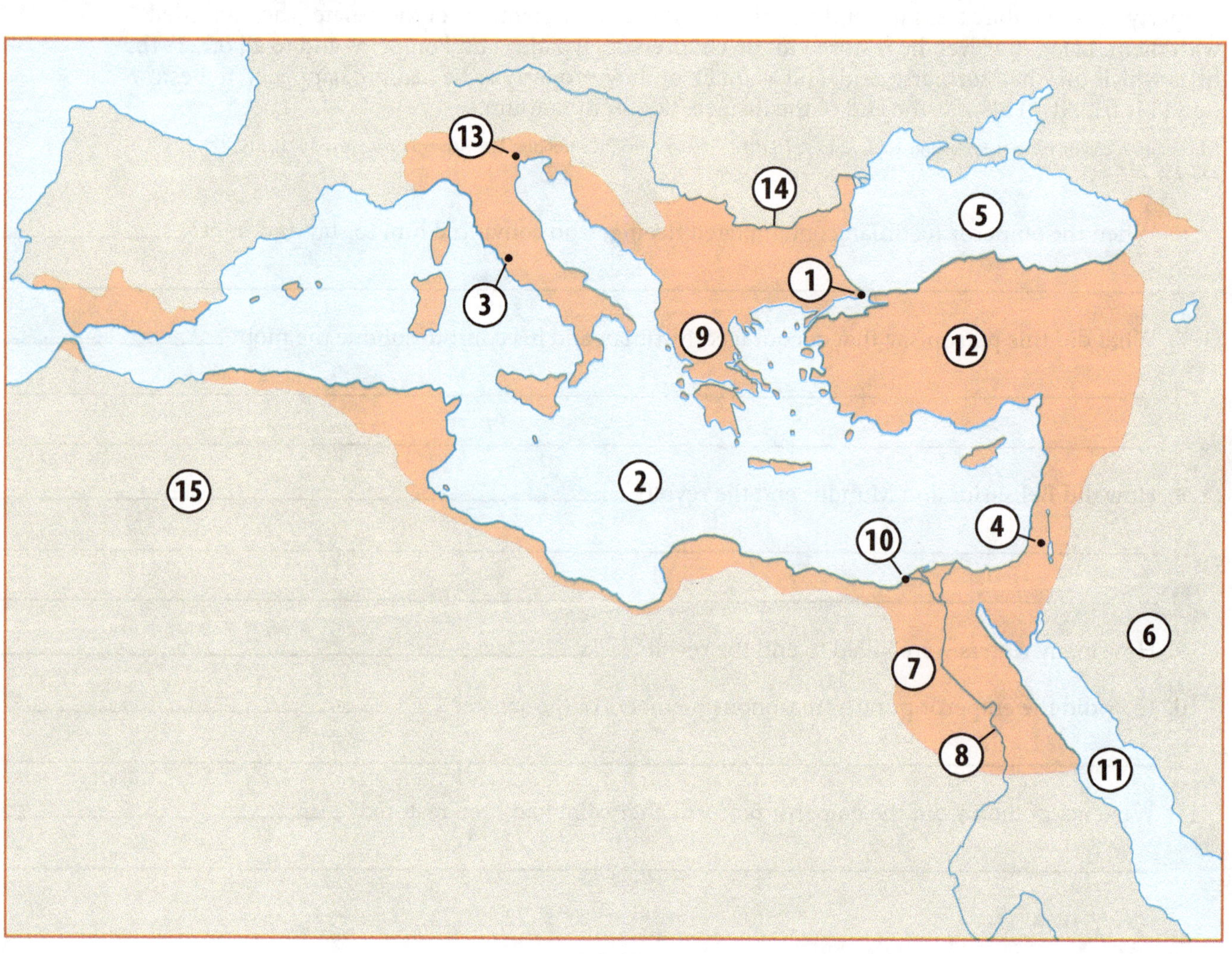

Name ______________________

# The Qur'an or the Bible?

To defend your faith against the false claims of Islam, you must understand some basics about the Qur'an. Muslims revere the Qur'an as Allah's final revelation to mankind and honor Muhammad as the greatest prophet. Below are some passages from the Qur'an that cover important topics, including sin, salvation, and the nature of Allah. As you read each selection, remember that Allah, not Muhammad, is the speaker.

**Answer the questions below after reading the following excerpts from the Qur'an.**

## Sura II: "The Cow"

Call to Believe (2:23–25)

And if ye are in doubt concerning that which We reveal unto Our slave (Muhammad), then produce a surah of the like thereof, and call your witnesses beside Allah if ye are truthful.

And if ye do it not—and ye can never do it—then guard yourselves against the fire prepared for disbelievers, whose fuel is of men and stones.

And give glad tidings (O Muhammad) unto those who believe and do good works; that theirs are Gardens underneath which rivers flow; as often as they are regaled with food of the fruit thereof, they say: This is what was given us aforetime; and it is given to them in resemblance. There for them are pure companions; there for ever they abide.

Importance of Fighting (2:190–93)

Fight in the way of Allah against those who fight against you, but begin not hostilities. Lo! Allah loveth not aggressors.

And slay them wherever ye find them, and drive them out of the places whence they drove you out, for persecution is worse than slaughter. And fight not with them at the Inviolable Place of Worship until they first attack you there, but if they attack you (there) then slay them. Such is the reward of disbelievers.

But if they desist, then lo! Allah is Forgiving, Merciful.

And fight them until persecution is no more, and religion is for Allah. But if they desist, then let there be no hostility except against wrongdoers.

1. Who is the "slave" through whom Allah provided the Qur'an? ______________________

2. What is Allah's challenge to those who doubt the Qur'an? ______________________

______________________

3. What is promised to those who do good works as described in the Qur'an? ______________________

______________________

______________________

4. How are Muslims commanded to spread and protect Islam? ______________________

______________________

*(continued on next page)*

## Sura III: "The 'Imrans"

Story of Jesus' Birth and Ministry (3:42–47, 54–59)

And then the angels said: O Mary! Lo! Allah hath chosen thee and made thee pure, and hath preferred thee above (all) the women of creation.

O Mary! Be obedient to thy Lord, prostrate thyself and bow with those who bow (in worship).

This is of the tidings of things hidden. We reveal it unto thee (Muhammad). Thou wast not present with them when they threw their pens (to know) which of them should be the guardian of Mary, nor wast thou present with them when they quarreled (thereupon).

(And remember) when the angels said: O Mary! Lo! Allah giveth thee glad tidings of a word from Him, whose name is the Messiah, Jesus, son of Mary, illustrious in the world and the Hereafter, and one of those brought near (unto Allah).

He will speak unto mankind in his cradle and in his manhood, and he is of the righteous.

She said: My Lord! How can I have a child when no mortal hath touched me? He said: So (it will be). Allah createth what He will. If He decree such a thing, He saith unto it only: Be! And it is. . . .

And they (the disbelievers) schemed, and Allah schemed (against them): and Allah is the best of schemers.

(And remember) when Allah said: O Jesus! Lo! I am gathering thee and cause thee to ascend unto Me, and am cleansing thee of those who disbelieve and am setting those who follow thee above those who disbelieve until the Day of Resurrection. Then unto Me ye will (all) return, and I shall judge between you as to that wherein ye used to differ.

As for those who disbelieve I shall chastise them with a heavy chastisement in the world and the Hereafter; and they will have no helpers.

And as for those who believe and do good works, He will pay them their wages in full. Allah loveth not wrongdoers.

This (which) We recite unto thee is a revelation and a wise reminder.

Lo! The likeness of Jesus with Allah is as the likeness of Adam. He created him of dust, then He said unto him: Be! And he is.

5. What do the angels tell Mary that Jesus will do from the cradle? ______

6. When Allah's enemies seek to deceive, how does Allah respond? How is Allah described in this context?
______

7. How does Allah feel about "wrongdoers" (sinners)? ______

8. How is Jesus compared with Adam? ______

## Sura V: "The Table"

Jesus and the Apostles Before Allah (5:109–16)

In the day when Allah gathereth together the messengers, and saith: What was your response (from mankind)? They say: We have no knowledge. Lo! Thou, only Thou art the Knower of Things Hidden,

When Allah saith: O Jesus, son of Mary! Remember My favour unto thee and unto thy mother; how I strengthened thee with the holy Spirit, so that thou spakest unto mankind in the cradle as in maturity . . . and how thou didst shape of clay as it were the likeness of a bird [and made it alive] by My permission, and thou didst heal him who was born blind and the leper by My permission; and how I restrained the Children of Israel from (harming) thee when thou camest unto them with clear proofs, and those of them who disbelieved exclaimed: This is naught else than mere magic;

And when I inspired the disciples, (saying): Believe in Me and in My messenger, they said: We believe. Bear witness that we have surrendered (unto Thee). . . .

*(continued on next page)*

Jesus, son of Mary, said: O Allah, Lord of us! Send down for us a table spread with food from heaven, that it may be a feast for us, for the first of us and for the last of us, and a sign from Thee. Give us sustenance, for Thou art the Best of Sustainers.

Allah said: Lo! I send it down for you. And whoso disbelieveth of you afterward, him surely will I punish with a punishment wherewith I have not punished any of (My) creatures.

And when Allah saith: O Jesus, son of Mary! Didst thou say unto mankind: Take me and my mother for two gods beside Allah? He saith: Be glorified! It was not mine to utter that to which I had no right. If I used to say it, then Thou knewest it. Thou knowest what is in my mind, and I know not what is in Thy Mind. Lo! Thou, only Thou art the Knower of Things Hidden?

I spake unto them only that which Thou commandest me, (saying): Worship Allah, my Lord and your Lord.

9. According to the Qur'an, Allah strengthened Jesus to do miracles through the Holy Spirit. List two of these miracles. ______________________________

______________________________

10. According to the Qur'an, is Jesus omniscient (all-knowing)? Why or why not? ______________________________

______________________________

11. When Allah refers to Jesus as the "son of Mary," whom is he omitting? ______________________________

______________________________

12. According to the Qur'an, what did Jesus tell people to do? ______________________________

13. Does the Qur'an teach that Jesus is a Muslim? ______________________________

## Sura XXIII: "The Believers"

Future Judgment (23:95–111)

Until, when death cometh unto one of them, he saith: My Lord! Send me back,

That I may do right in that which I have left behind! But nay! It is but a word that he speaketh; and behind them is a barrier until the day when they are raised.

And when the trumpet is blown there will be no kinship among them that day, nor will they ask of one another.

Then those whose scales are heavy, they are the successful.

And those whose scales are light are those who lose their souls, in hell abiding.

The fire burneth their faces, and they are glum therein.

(It will be said): Were not My revelations recited unto you, and then ye used to deny them?

They will say: Our Lord! Our evil fortune conquered us, and we were erring folk.

Our Lord! Oh, bring us forth from hence! If we return (to evil) then indeed we shall be wrong-doers.

He saith: Begone therein, and speak not unto Me.

Lo! There was a party of My slaves who said: Our Lord! We believe, therefor[e] forgive us and have mercy on us for Thou are best of all who show mercy;

But he chose them for a laughing-stock until they caused you to forget remembrance of Me, while ye laughed at them.

Lo! I have rewarded them this day forasmuch as they were stedfast; and they verily are the triumphant.

*The Meaning of the Glorious Koran: An Explanatory Translation* by Marmaduke Pickthall (Alfred A. Knopf, 1930) public domain

*(continued on next page)*

14. According to the Qur'an, when sinners die, what do they request of Allah? ______________________________

______________________________________________________________________________

15. Will Allah grant sinners' requests? ______________________________________________

16. Whom will Allah reward? ______________________________________________________

17. According to the Qur'an, when will Allah mete out his judgment? ______________________

18. What will Allah weigh on the day of judgment? ______________________________________

19. Whom will Allah send to hell? _________________________________________________

______________________________________________________________________________

______________________________________________________________________________

Name ___________________________

## Expansion of Islam

**Locate each term or phrase on the map and place the corresponding number in the appropriate blank.**

| | |
|---|---|
| _______ Arabia | _______ Medina |
| _______ Baghdad | _______ Mediterranean Sea |
| _______ Cairo | _______ Nile River |
| _______ Constantinople | _______ Persia |
| _______ Damascus | _______ Persian Gulf |
| _______ Egypt | _______ Rome |
| _______ Euphrates River | _______ Sahara |
| _______ Jerusalem | _______ Spain |
| _______ Kingdom of the Franks | _______ Tigris River |
| _______ Mecca | _______ Tours |

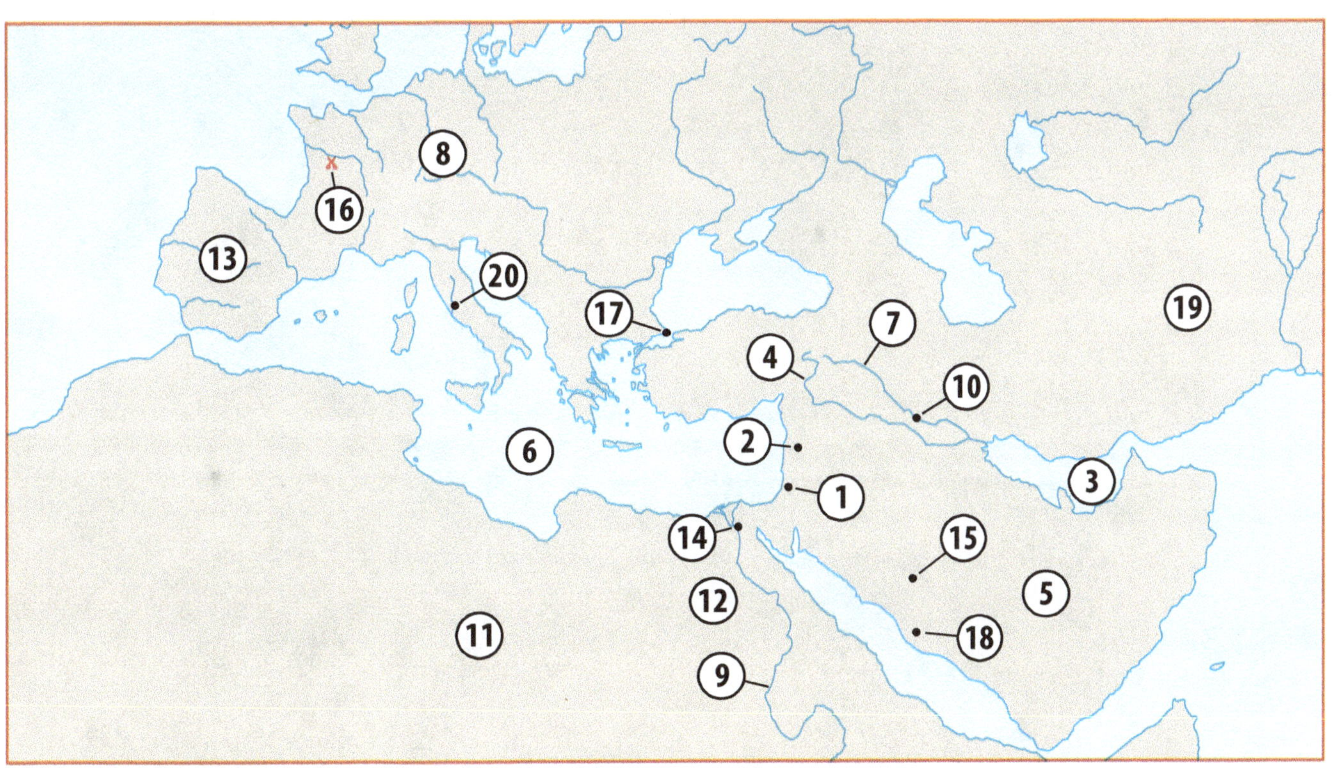

Name ______________________

# Chapter Review

## Complete the Statement

**Underline the term that accurately completes each of the following statements.**

1. Seljuk Turks annihilated the Byzantine army at the Battle of (Adrianople/Manzikert).
2. Cyril and Methodius were missionaries to the (Russians/Arabs).
3. Damascus was the capital of the (Umayyad/Abbasid) caliphate.
4. The (Spanish/Franks) stopped Muslim advancement into Europe at the Battle of Tours.
5. Arabs are descendants of (Jacob/Ishmael).

## Short Answer

**Write the correct answer to each question in the provided blank.**

6. What revolt that broke out in Constantinople in 532 threatened to topple Justinian's reign? ______________________
7. What city dedicated by Constantine in 330 was called "New Rome"? ______________________
8. Whose reign, beginning in 527, resulted in a golden age of Byzantine culture? ______________________
9. What powerful Byzantine ruler was known as the "Bulgar Slayer"? ______________________
10. What is calligraphy? ______________________
11. What Slavic designation meaning "rowers" or "seafarers" was possibly used to create the name of a country? ______________________
12. Name the largest people group whose ancestors played a major role in establishing the early Russian state. ______________________
13. What were painted images of Christ and the saints called? ______________________
14. What were military expeditions to free the East from Muslim invaders? ______________________
15. Give the name for the basic religious practices the Muslims observe. ______________________
16. What bands of Swedish Norsemen plundered Slavic villages? ______________________
17. What procedure involved depriving an individual of the sacraments and excluding him from the fellowship of the church? ______________________

*(continued on next page)*

18. What people group sacked Constantinople? ____________________

19. What type of decorative art graced the walls and ceilings of Byzantine churches? ____________________

20. During this caliphate many non-Arabs became increasingly influential and Islamic culture flourished.

____________________

## Matching: Section 1

**Choose the best answer and place the letter in the blank beside the corresponding description.**

| | | |
|---|---|---|
| A. Abu Bakr | D. Muhammad | G. Vladimir I |
| B. al-Rāzi | E. Omar Khayyam | H. Yaroslav |
| C. Ibn Sina | F. Rurik | |

_____ 21. Made Eastern Orthodox Christianity the religion of Russia

_____ 22. Second leader of Islam

_____ 23. Gained control of Novgorod and began Russian history

_____ 24. First leader and founder of Islam

_____ 25. Led Kiev to reach the height of its power

## Matching: Section 2

| | | |
|---|---|---|
| A. caliph | D. Ka'bah | G. Qur'an |
| B. Hegira | E. mosque | |
| C. jihad | F. muezzin | |

_____ 26. The spread of Islam through war on non-Muslims

_____ 27. Muhammad's flight to escape persecution

_____ 28. Any successor who led Islam after Muhammad's death

_____ 29. Calls Muslims to the place of prayer

_____ 30. Muslim place of worship

Name ______________________

## Asia

**Locate each term on the map and place the corresponding number in the appropriate blank.**

_______ Angkor

_______ Champa

_______ Dai Viet

_______ Great Wall

_______ Hokkaido

_______ Honshu

_______ Huang He River

_______ Korea

_______ Kyushu

_______ Mekong River

_______ Pacific Ocean

_______ Sea of Japan (East Sea)

_______ Xi River

_______ Yangtze River

_______ Yellow Sea

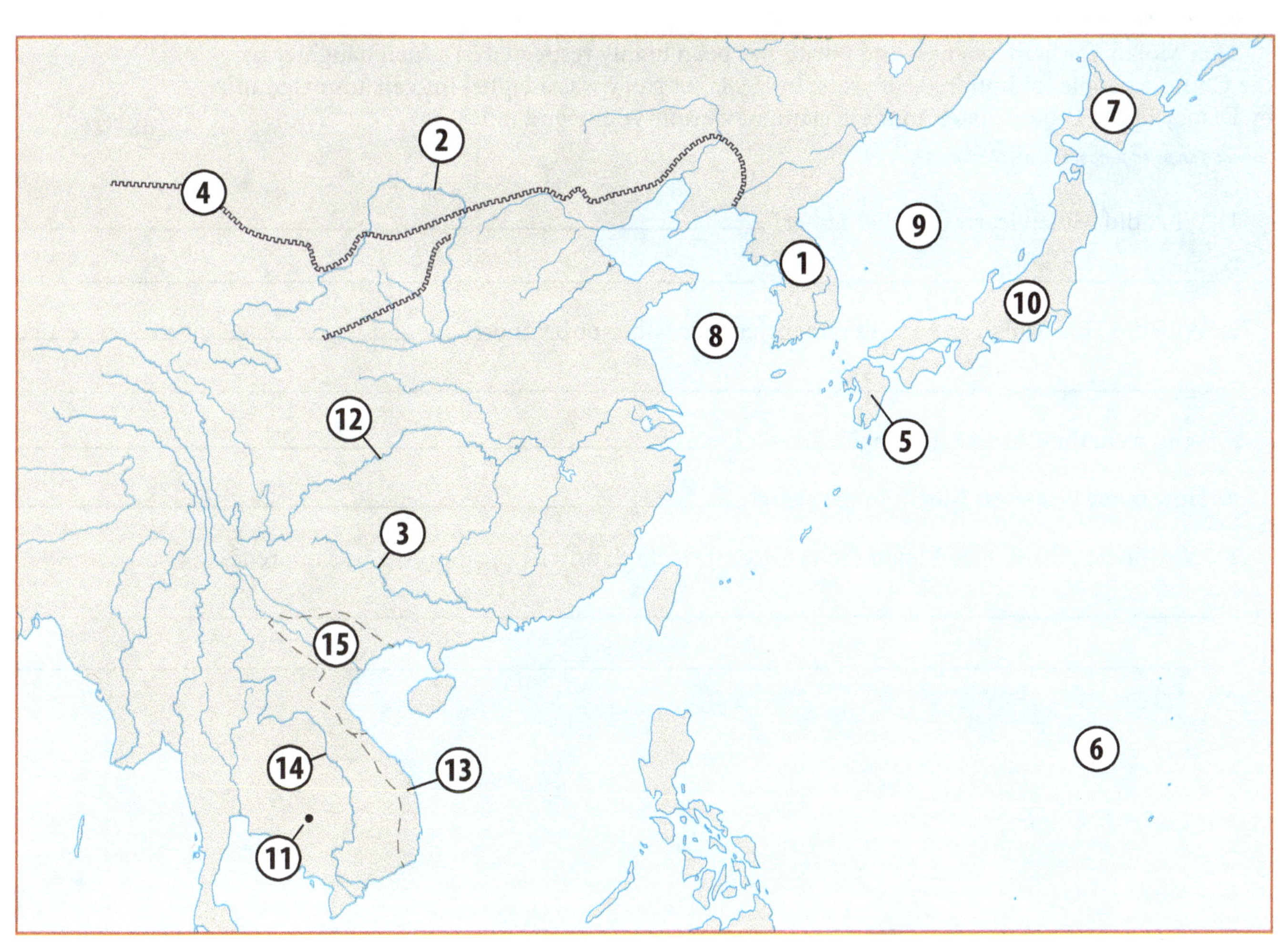

Name ______________________

# Chinese Lore

**Answer the questions at the end after reading the following account of Hua Mulan.**

"Click, click, click. Mulan wove cloth in the house. Yet we could not hear the sound of the shuttle, but the sound of Mulan's sighs..." This is the opening of the *The Ballad of Mulan*, a well-known folk song in north China. The heroine of this ballad was a heroic woman in the north named Hua Mulan. The song tells how Hua Mulan disguised herself as a man, and joined the army in place of her father.

It is said that Mulan lived in the Northern Wei Dynasty, and that people in the north were fond of practicing martial arts. When Mulan was about ten years old, her father, an ex-soldier, taught her military skills, including martial arts, horse riding, archery and swordsmanship. Hua Mulan also read her father's books on military science in her spare time.

After Emperor Xiaowen's reform, the Northern Wei Dynasty saw a picture of socio-economic development and more stable lives. To ward off incursions by Rouran nomads, the ruler of the Northern Wei ordered that every household provide a man to join an expedition against them. Mulan's father was old then, and her younger brother was too young to go and fight. So Mulan decided to join the army instead of her father. Mulan spent 12 years in the army. Fighting at the border is even hard for many men, let alone a girl such as Mulan because she had to conceal her identity while fighting against the enemy with her partner. But Hua Mulan finally completed her mission, and returned home with victory 12 years later. In view of her exploits on the battlefield, the ruler of the Northern Wei offered Mulan a high official position, but she refused it.

Hua Mulan, for her braveness and purity, has been highly respected as a filial daughter by the Chinese people for hundreds of years. In 1998, her story was adapted into an animated film by Disney in the United States, to the acclaim of viewers young and old.

*Common Knowledge about Chinese History*, 87.

1. What did Mulan learn from her father? ______________________

______________________

2. Why did Hua Mulan go to fight rather than her father or brother? ______________________

______________________

3. Who were the Chinese fighting? ______________________
4. How many years was Mulan in the army? ______________________
5. Why do you think Hua Mulan did not accept the high official position she was offered?

______________________

______________________

Name ____________________

## "A Dialogue on Poverty"

**Answer the questions at the end after reading the following poem by Japanese poet Yamanoue Okura.**

On the night when the rain beats,
Driven by the wind,
On the night when the snowflakes mingle
With the sleety rain,
I feel so helplessly cold.
I nibble at a lump of salt,
Sip the hot, oft-diluted dregs of saké;
And coughing, snuffling,
And stroking my scanty beard,
I say in my pride,
"There's none worthy, save I!"
But I shiver still with cold.
I pull up my hempen bedclothes,
Wear what few sleeveless clothes I have,
But cold and bitter is the night!
As for those poorer than myself,
Their parents must be cold and hungry,
Their wives and children beg and cry.
Then, how do you struggle through life?
Wide as they call the heaven and earth,
For me they have shrunk quite small;
Bright though they call the sun and moon,
They never shine for me.
Is it the same with all men,
Or for me alone?
By rare chance I was born a man
And no meaner than my fellows,
But, wearing unwadded sleeveless clothes
In tatters, like weeds waving in the sea,
Hanging from my shoulders,
And under the sunken roof,
Within the leaning walls,
Here I lie on straw
Spread on bare earth,
With my parents at my pillow,
My wife and children at my feet,
All huddled in grief and tears.
No fire sends up smoke
At the cooking-place,
And in the cauldron
A spider spins its web.
With not a grain to cook,
We moan like the night thrush.
Then, 'to cut,' as the saying is,
'The ends of what is already too short,'
The village headman comes,
With rod in hand, to our sleeping place,
Growling for his dues.
Must it be so hopeless—
The way of this world?



1. What emotions are mentioned in this poem? ____________________
2. What possessions are mentioned in the poem? ____________________

   ____________________
3. What metaphor is used to describe the poor's clothing? ____________________
4. What animals are mentioned in the poem? ____________________
5. What do the last seven lines of the poem refer to? ____________________
6. What does the Bible have to say about poverty? ____________________

   ____________________

   ____________________

   ____________________

   ____________________

Name ______________________________

## Korean Foundation Myths

**Answer the questions at the end after reading the following account of the Tan'gun Myth.**

The *Book of Wei* relates: Two thousand years ago Tan'gun Wanggŏm established his capital in Asadal and founded a state which he called Chosŏn. He was a contemporary of Yao [mythical Chinese emperor, third millennium B.C.]. The Ancient Records relate that in remote times, the son of Huan In by a concubine, Huan Ung, often thought of the world and desired to help man. He was called Lord of Heaven. The father was aware of his son's thoughts. Below he saw the three peaks of Mount T'aebaek by which he could generously benefit mankind. Then he gave Huan Ung the three Heavenly Seals and sent him to go and manage the world. Ung descended beneath the divine Tan tree on Mount T'aebaek leading 3,000 followers. He is the one called Huan Ung, King of Heaven. He commanded the Gods of Wind, Rain, and Clouds and ruled over the grains, life, sickness, punishments, good and evil. In all, he ruled over the 360 some affairs concerning man, and in the world he regulated change. At this time there were a bear and a tiger who lived in the same cave. They constantly prayed to the God Ung desiring to be changed into humans. Then, the God Ung gave them one stick of wonder-working mugwort and twenty stalks of garlic telling them: If you eat this and do not look at the sun's rays for 100 days, you will attain human form. The bear and the tiger took it and ate it, and avoided the sun for 21 days. The bear attained the body of woman but the tiger was unable to avoid the sun and did not attain the body of man. The bear-woman was without anyone to marry, therefore, she repeatedly went beneath the Tan tree and prayed of her desire to be pregnant. Ung then temporarily transformed himself and married her. She became pregnant and bore a son. He was called Tan'gun Wanggŏm. The capital was the walled city of P'yŏngyang. In the beginning they called it Chosŏon; they also moved the capital to Mount Paegak in Asadal. He governed the nation for 1,500 years. King Wu of Chou (dynasty of ancient China) ascended the throne and enfeoffed the Viscount of Ch'i (Kija) with Chosŏn. Tan'gun then moved to Changdang-gyŏong. Later he returned and hid himself in Asadal as a mountain god. His age was 1,908 years.

Henthorn, William E. *A History of Korea.* (New York: The Free Press, 1971), 228–29.

1. What did one of the gods in this myth desire to do? ______________________________
2. What did Huan Ung have power over? ______________________________
______________________________
3. What two animals prayed to be turned into humans? ______________________________
4. Who married the woman that was changed from an animal? ______________________________
5. What happened to the son of Huan Ung? ______________________________
6. What are your thoughts about this myth? ______________________________
______________________________
______________________________
______________________________
______________________________

Name ____________________

# Chapter Review

## Matching

**Choose the best answer and place the letter in the blank beside the corresponding description.**

| | | |
|---|---|---|
| A. Fujiwara | C. Song | E. Tang |
| B. Han | D. Sui | F. Yamato |

_____ 1. forged a united Japanese state

_____ 2. witnessed the height of Chinese painting, printing, and porcelain making

_____ 3. conquered Korea in 108 BC and northern Vietnam around 100 BC

_____ 4. period in which Li Po wrote his poems

_____ 5. ruled Japan as regents of the infant emperor

## Short Answer

**Write the correct answer to each question in the provided blank.**

6. What was the title of the powerful individuals who held the real power over Japan, beginning in 1192?
____________________

7. What ruler of Japan made Buddhism the country's favored national religion? ____________________

8. What was the name of the empire in Cambodia? ____________________

9. Who was the leader of the Minamoto clan who was granted the title shogun? ____________________

10. What dynasty was overthrown by General Li Yuan? ____________________

11. What was the name for the kingdom in central and southern Vietnam? ____________________

12. What name was given to the turnabout in Japanese political and economic structure? ____________________

13. Give the name for a Japanese warrior. ____________________

14. What painful Chinese custom was ended during the nineteenth century? ____________________

15. What project connected the Yellow and Yangtze Rivers? ____________________

16. What popular Chinese poet wrote thousands of poems expressing emotional and sentimental themes?
____________________

*(continued on next page)*

17. Give the name for the early Vietnamese kingdom that broke free of Chinese domination.

______________________________________________

18. What religion supports the belief in the divine origin of the emperor? ______________

19. What is the unwritten Japanese military code for warriors? ______________

20. Give the name for the first emperor of Japan. ______________

Name ____________________

## American Indian Creation/Flood Story

**Answer the questions at the end after reading the following Indian account of a flood and creation.**

The people before the present people were wild and did not know how to do anything. The Creator did not like the way they lived. He thought, "I will make a new world." He had the chief pipe. He went outdoors, hung the pipe on three sticks, and picked up four buffalo chips. He put one under each of the three sticks that supported the pipe, and took the fourth chip for his own seat.

The Creator said, "I will sing three times and shout three times. After I have done these things, I will kick the earth, and water will come out of the cracks. There will be heavy rain. There will be water over all the earth."

Then he began to sing. After he sang three times, he shouted three times. Then he kicked the ground and it cracked. The water came out, and it rained for days, and over all the earth was water. Because of the buffalo chips, he and the pipe floated. Then it stopped raining. There was water everywhere. For days he drifted, floating where the wind took him. Above him the Crow flew about. All the animals and birds were drowned.

The Crow became tired. It flew about crying, "My father, I am tired, and I want to rest."

Three times Crow said this. After the third time, the Creator replied, "Alight yourself on the pipe and rest." Repeatedly the Crow cried to him, and each time was allowed to alight on the pipe.

Finally the Creator became tired from sitting in one position and he cried. He did not know what to do. After he had cried a long time, he began to unwrap the chief pipe which contained all the animals. He selected those that have a long breath to dive through water. First he selected the Large Loon. The Loon was not alive, but the Creator had its body wrapped up in the pipe. The Creator sang to it and then commanded it to dive and try to bring up some mud. Not half way down, Large Loon lost its breath and immediately turned back. Almost drowned, it reached the Creator.

Then the Creator took Small Loon's body and sang. Then the Small Loon dived and nearly reached the bottom before it lost its breath and turned back. It was almost dead when it came back to the surface. Then the Creator took Turtle from the pipe, sang until it became alive, and sent it down for some mud.

Meanwhile, Crow flew about, crying for rest. The Creator did not listen. After a long time, Turtle came up from the water, nearly dead. It had filled its feet and the cracks along its sides with mud. When it reached the Creator, all the mud had been washed away.

"Did you reach the mud?" asked the Creator.

"Yes," answered Turtle. "I had much of it in my feet and around my sides, but it was washed away before I came to you."

"Come to me." The Creator looked inside its feet and in the cracks of its sides. On the inside of its feet he found a little earth. He scraped this into his hand. . . . Then he began to sing. Three times he sang, and three times he shouted.

"I will throw this little dust in my hand into the water," he said. "Little by little, let there be enough to make a strip of land large enough for me."

He began to drop it, little by little, into the water, opening and closing his hand carefully. When he had finished, there was a small strip of land, large enough for him to sit on. Then he said to Crow, "Come down and rest. I have made a piece of land for myself and for you."

Then Crow came down and rested, and then flew up again. The Creator took from his pipe two long wing feathers, held one in each hand, and began to sing. Three times he sang, and

*(continued on next page)*

three times he shouted, "Youh, hou, hou!" Then he spread out his arms, closed his eyes. When he had done this, he said "Let there be land as far as my eyes can see around me."

When he opened his eyes, then indeed there was land. After he had made the land, there was no water anywhere. He went about with his pipe and with the Crow. When he became thirsty, he did not know what to do to get water. Then he thought, "I will cry." He cried. While he cried, he closed his eyes. He tried to think how he could get water. He shed tears, and they dropped to the ground. They made a large spring in front of him. Soon, a stream ran from out of the spring. When the Creator stopped crying, a large river was flowing. Thus he made rivers and streams.

When he became tired of being alone with Crow and his pipe, he decided to make persons and animals. First, he took earth, and made it into the shape of a man. He made also the shape of a woman. Then he made more figures of earth, until he had many men and women.

When the Creator thought he had enough people, he made animals of all kinds in pairs. When he had finished making these shapes, he named the tribes of people and the kinds of animals. He sang three times, shouted three times. After he had shouted, he kicked the ground, and there were living pairs of being standing before him, animals and men. . . . He called the world Turtle because Turtle was the animal that had helped him to make the world. Then he made bows and arrows for men, and told them how to use them. The pipe, he gave to a tribe called Haa-ninin (Gros Ventres).

He said to the people, "If you are good, there will be no more water and no more fire." Long before the flood came, the world had been burned. Now this is the third life.

Then he showed them the rainbow and said, "This rainbow is the sign that the earth will not be covered with water again. Whenever you have rain, you will see the rainbow; and when you see it, it will mean that the rain has gone by. There will be another world after this one." He told the people to separate in pairs and to select habitations for themselves. That is why human beings are scattered.

Kroeber, A. L. *Anthropological Papers of the American Museum of Natural History.* Vol. I, Part III. (New York: Order of the Trustees, 1907), 59–61

1. Why did the Creator destroy the world? ______________________

2. What does the Creator do when he does not know what to do? ______________________

3. What animal survived the flood? ______________________

4. What animal helped the Creator make land? ______________________

5. What did the Creator do when he became lonely? ______________________

6. What sign did the Creator give the people when he promised there would not be another flood?

______________________

7. Compare and contrast the biblical Creation and Flood accounts with this account.

______________________

______________________

______________________

Name ______________________________

## North America

**Locate each term or phrase on the map and place the corresponding number in the appropriate blank.**

_______ Apache

_______ Atlantic Ocean

_______ Cherokee

_______ Cheyenne

_______ Comanche

_______ Great Plains

_______ Iroquois

_______ Mississippi River

_______ Nez Perce

_______ Northeast Woodlands

_______ Pacific Ocean

_______ Pueblo

_______ Seminole

_______ Sioux

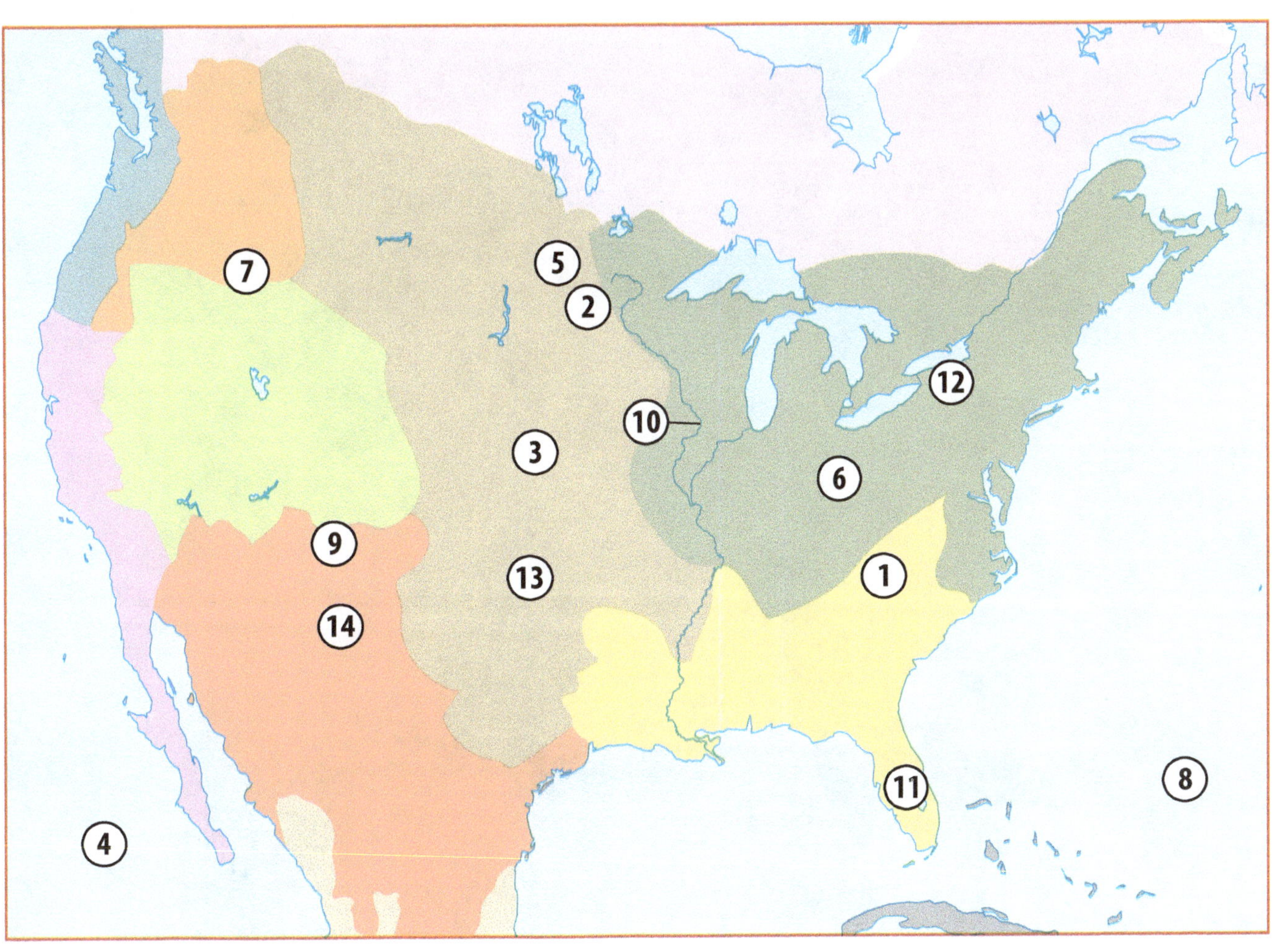

Name ______________________

# Ojibwa Flood Story

**Answer the questions at the end after reading the following Indian account of the Flood.**

**(There are many versions of this story. American Indians believed that Menaboshu, a great primeval hero, either created the world or gave it its present form.)**

Menaboshu lived on very friendly terms with the animals, whom he regarded as his kinsfolk and with whom he could converse in their own language. [In a time of distress he joined a tribe of wolves and hunted with them.]

This they did for ten days, but on the tenth day they came to a cross-road. The wolves wished to go one way, and Menaboshu wished to go another, and as neither would give way, it was resolved to part company. But Menaboshu said . . . the youngest wolf must go with him, for he loved the animal dearly and called him his little brother. . . Menaboshu and the little wolf camped in the middle of the wood and hunted together, but sometimes the little wolf hunted alone. Now Menaboshu was anxious for the safety of the little wolf, and he said to him, 'My dear little brother, have you seen that lake which lies near our camp to the west? Go not thither, never tread the ice on it! Do you hear?' This he said because he knew that his worst enemy, the serpent-king, dwelt in the lake and would do anything to vex him. The little wolf promised to do as Menaboshu told him, but he thought within himself, 'Why does Menaboshu forbid me to go on the lake? Perhaps he thinks I might meet my brothers the wolves there! After all I love my brothers!' Thus he thought for two days, but on the third day he went on the lake and roamed about on the ice to see whether he could find his brothers. But just as he came to the middle of the lake, the ice broke, and he fell in and was drowned. [Menaboshu waited for his little brother for many days and then realized that the serpent-king had killed him.] . . . When spring came at last, [Menaboshu] went one bright warm day to the lake in which his little brother had perished. . . . He saw the footprints of his lost brother, and when he saw them he broke into lamentations so loud that they were heard far and near.

The serpent-king heard them also, and curious to know what was the matter, he popped his head out of the water. 'Ah, there you are,' said Menaboshu to himself, wiping away the tears with the sleeve of his coat, 'you shall pay for your misdeed.' He turned himself at once into a tree-stump and stood in that likeness stiff and stark on the water's edge. The serpent-king and all the other serpents, who popped out after him, looked about very curiously to discover who had been raising this loud lament, but they could discover nothing but the tree-stump, which they had never seen there before. As they were sniffing about it, 'Take care,' said one of them, 'there's more there than meets the eye. Maybe it is our foe, the sly Menaboshu, in disguise.' So the serpent-king commanded one of his attendants to go and search the matter out. The gigantic serpent at once coiled itself round the tree-stump and squeezed it so hard, that the bones in Menaboshu's body cracked, but he bore the agony [in silence], not betraying his anguish by a single sound. So the serpents were easy in their minds and said, 'No, it is not he. We can sleep safe. It is only wood!' And the day being warm, they all lay down on the sandy beach of the lake and fell fast asleep.

Scarcely had the last snake closed his eyes, when Menaboshu slipped from his ambush, seized his bow and arrows, and shot the serpent-king dead. . . . At that the other serpents awoke, and glided back into the water, crying 'Woe! Woe! Menaboshu is among us! Menaboshu is killing us!' . . . Those of them who had the most powerful magic brought forth their medicine-bags, opened them, and scattered the contents all around on the banks and the wood and in the air. Then the water began to run in whirlpools and to swell. They sky was overcast with clouds, and torrents of rain fell. First the neighbourhood, then half the earth, then the whole world was flooded. Frightened to death, Menaboshu fled away, hopping from mountain to mountain

*(continued on next page)*

like a squirrel, but finding no rest for the soles of his feet, for the swelling waves followed him everywhere. At last he escaped to a very high mountain, but soon the water rose even over its summit. On the top of the mountain grew a tall fir-tree, and Menaboshu climbed up it to its topmost bough. Even there the flood pursued him and had risen to his mouth, when it suddenly stood still. . . .

Menaboshu remained five days and five nights [in this painful position], wondering how he could escape. At last he saw a solitary bird, a loon, swimming on the face of the water. He called the bird and said, 'Brother loon, thou skillful diver, be so good as to dive into the depths and see whether thou canst find any earth, without which I cannot live.' Again and again the loon dived, but no earth could he find. Menaboshu was almost in despair. But next day he saw the dead body of a drowned musk-rat drifting towards him. He caught it, took it in his hand, breathed on it, and brought it to life again. Then he said to the rat, 'Little brother rat, neither you nor I can live without earth. Dive into the water and bring me up a little earth. If it be only three grains of sand, yet will I make something out of it for you and me.' The rat dived and after a long time reappeared on the surface. It was dead, but Menaboshu caught it and examined its paws. On one of the fore-paws he found two grains of sand or dust. So he took them, dried them on his hand in the sun, and blew them away over the water. Where they fell they grew into little islands, and these united into larger ones, till at last Menaboshu was able to jump down from the tree-top on one of them. On it he floated about as on a raft, and helped the other islands to grow together, until at last they formed lands and continents. Then Menaboshu walked from place to place, restoring nature to its former beauty and variety. He found little roots and tiny plants which he planted, and they grew into meadows, shrubs, and forests. Many of the dead bodies of animals had drifted ashore. Menaboshu gathered them and blew on them, and they came to life. . . . Moreover, Menaboshu walked to and fro with a measuring-line, determining the length of the rivers, the depth of the lakes, the height of the mountains, and the form of the lands.

Frazer, James George. *Folk-Lore in the Old Testament: Studies in Comparative Religion Legend and Law*, Vol. 1. (London, Macmillan and Co., Limited, 1919), 301–04.

1. Whom did the serpent-king kill? ______________________________

2. Where did the serpent-king live? ______________________________

3. What caused the serpent-king to surface? ______________________________

4. How did Menaboshu disguise himself when seeking revenge? ______________________________

5. What did the surviving serpents do in response to the serpent-king's death? ______________________________

______________________________

6. Contrast this flood account with the biblical flood account. ______________________________

______________________________

______________________________

______________________________

Name ______________________________

## Middle America and South America

**Locate each term or phrase on the map and place the corresponding number in the appropriate blank.**

_______ Andes Mountains

_______ Chichén Itzá

_______ Chile

_______ Cuzco

_______ Gulf of Mexico

_______ Lake Titicaca

_______ Pacific Ocean

_______ Tenochtitlán

_______ Valley of Mexico

_______ Yucatán Peninsula

Name ______________________

# Chapter Review

## Matching

**Choose the best answer and place the letter in the blank beside the corresponding description.**

| | | |
|---|---|---|
| A. Eastern Woodlands Indians | C. Hopi | E. Mound Builders |
| B. Hopewell | D. Mississippian | F. Pueblo Indians |

_____ 1. Southwestern tribe known for its peaceful culture

_____ 2. a wide and dispersed group of Indians believed to be united by trade

_____ 3. Southwestern Indians known as "cliff dwellers"

_____ 4. established agricultural communities in the Southeast

_____ 5. Cahokia Indians were a large part of this group

## Short Answer

**Write the correct answer to each question in the provided blank.**

6. Give the name of a city that sought to become influential in the Mayan Classic Period.

______________________________

7. What was the system that Incans used to record data?

______________________________

8. What was a group of several families that shared common customs?

______________________________

9. What god did some Aztecs worship but was rejected by the Toltecs?

______________________________

10. What was the name of the precise Mayan calendar?

______________________________

11. What did the Mayans believe supported the sky?

______________________________

12. What is the name given to the possible land bridge over the Bering Sea from Asia?

______________________________

*(continued on next page)*

13. What Aztec city was built on an island in the middle of a lake in central Mexico?

______________________________

14. What group of Indians in South America had a system of runners for communication?

______________________________

15. What effigy mound in southern Ohio is over 1,300 feet long?

______________________________

16. What warlike Mesoamerican civilization required every able-bodied man to serve in the army?

______________________________

17. What Mayan artifact is carved with inscriptions?

______________________________

18. What groups of Indian languages are believed to have had a single ancestral language?

______________________________

19. What Mesoamerican civilization believed that the sun fell into the underworld each evening?

______________________________

20. Did all Indian civilizations remain stationary in location?

______________________________

21. What name was given to the union of the Aztecs and the city-states of Texcoco and Tlacopan?

______________________________

22. What term defines Indians that shared similar customs, means of livelihood, and levels of civilization?

______________________________

Name ______________________

# Charlemagne

**Answer the questions at the end after reading the following excerpts from the writings of Einhard.**

VII. . . . [T]he Saxon war, that seems to have been only laid aside for the time, was taken up again. No war ever undertaken by the Frank nation was carried on with such persistence and bitterness, or cost so much labor, because the Saxons, like almost all the tribes of Germany, were a fierce people, given to the worship of devils, and hostile to our religion, and did not consider it dishonorable to transgress and violate all law, human and divine. Then there were peculiar circumstances that tended to cause a breach of peace every day. Except in a few places, where large forests or mountain ridges intervened and made the bounds certain, the line between ourselves and the Saxons passed almost in its whole extent through an open country, so that there was no end to the murders, thefts, and arsons on both sides. In this way the Franks became so embittered that they at last resolved to make reprisals no longer, but to come to open war with the Saxons. Accordingly war was begun against them, and was waged for thirty-three successive years with great fury; more, however, to the disadvantage of the Saxons than of the Franks. It could doubtless have been brought to an end sooner, had it not been for the faithlessness of the Saxons. It is hard to say how often they were conquered, and, humbly submitting to the King, promised to do what was enjoined upon them, gave without hesitation the required hostages, and received the officers sent them from the King. They were sometimes so much weakened and reduced that they promised to renounce the worship of devils, and to adopt Christianity, but they were no less ready to violate these terms than prompt to accept them, so that it is impossible to tell which came easier to them to do; scarcely a year passed from the beginning of the war without such changes on their part. But the King did not suffer his high purpose and steadfastness—firm alike in good and evil fortune—to be wearied by any fickleness on their part, or to be turned from the task that he had undertaken; on the contrary, he never allowed their faithless behavior to go unpunished, but either took the field against them in person, or sent his counts with an army to wreak vengeance and exact righteous satisfaction. At last, after conquering and subduing all who had offered resistance, he took ten thousand of those that lived on the banks of the Elbe [a river that flows through Germany], and settled them, with their wives and children, in many different bodies here and there in Gaul [France] and Germany. The war that had lasted so many years was at length ended by their acceding to the terms offered by the King; which were renunciation of their national religious customs and the worship of devils, acceptance of the sacraments of the Christian faith and religion, and union with the Franks to form one people. . . .

XXII. Charles [Charlemagne] was large and strong, and of lofty stature, though not disproportionately tall (his height is well known to have been seven times the length of his foot); the upper part of his head was round, his eyes very large and animated, nose a little long, hair fair, and face laughing and merry. Thus his appearance was always stately and dignified, whether he was standing or sitting; although his neck was thick and somewhat short, and his belly rather prominent; but the symmetry of the rest of his body concealed these defects. His gait was firm, his whole carriage manly, and his voice clear, but not so strong as his size led one to expect. His health was excellent, except during the four years preceding his death, when he was subject to frequent fevers; at the last he even limped a little with one foot. Even in those years he consulted rather his own inclinations than the advice of physicians, who were almost hateful to him, because they wanted him to give up roasts, to which he was accustomed, and to eat boiled meat instead. In accordance with the national custom, he took frequent exercise on horseback and in the chase, accomplishments in which scarcely any people in the world can equal the Franks. He enjoyed the exhalations from natural warm springs, and often practiced swimming, in which

*(continued on next page)*

he was such an adept that none could surpass him; and hence it was that he built his palace at Aix-la-Chapelle [Aachen, Germany], and lived there constantly during his latter years until his death. . . .

XXIV. Charles was temperate in eating, and particularly so in drinking, for he abominated drunkenness in anybody, much more in himself and those of his household; but he could not easily abstain from food, and often complained that fasts injured his health. He very rarely gave entertainments, only on great feastdays, and then to large numbers of people. His meals ordinarily consisted of four courses, not counting the roast, which his huntsmen used to bring in on the spit; he was more fond of this than of any other dish. While at table, he listened to reading or music. The subjects of the readings were the stories and deeds of olden time: he was fond, too, of St. Augustine's books, and especially of the one entitled "The City of God." He was so moderate in the use of wine and all sorts of drink that he rarely allowed himself more than three cups in the course of a meal. . . .

XXV. Charles had the gift of ready and fluent speech, and could express whatever he had to say with the utmost clearness. He was not satisfied with command of his native language merely, but gave attention to the study of foreign ones, and in particular was such a master of Latin that he could speak it as well as his native tongue; but he could understand Greek better than he could speak it. He was so eloquent, indeed, that he might have passed for a teacher of eloquence. . . .

XXVI. He cherished with the greatest fervor and devotion the principles of the Christian religion, which had been instilled into him from infancy. Hence it was that he built the beautiful basilica [the Cathedral of Aachen] at Aix-la-Chapelle, which he adorned with gold and silver and lamps, and with rails and doors of solid brass. He had the columns and marbles for this structure brought from Rome and Ravenna, for he could not find such as were suitable elsewhere. He was a constant worshipper at this church as long as his health permitted, going morning and evening, even after nightfall, besides attending mass; and he took care that all the services there conducted should be administered with the utmost possible propriety, very often warning the sextons not to let any improper or unclean thing be brought into the building or remain in it. He provided it with a great number of sacred vessels of gold and silver and with such a quantity of clerical robes that not even the doorkeepers who fill the humblest office in the church were obliged to wear their everyday clothes when in the exercise of their duties.

Eginhard. *Life of Charlemagne*, trans. Samuel Epes Turner (NY: American Book, 1880), 25–28, 56–57, 59–64.

1. Which fierce German tribe resisted the Franks' repeated efforts to conquer it? ____________

2. How did geography contribute to the ongoing struggle between this tribe and the Franks? ____________

____________

____________

3. How did Charlemagne set an example in academic pursuit? ____________

____________

4. What structure did Charlemagne build? What expensive items did he add to beautify it? ____________

____________

____________

____________

Name ______________________________

## Charlemagne's Empire

**Locate each term or phrase on the map and place the corresponding number in the appropriate blank.**

_______ Aix-la-Chapelle

_______ Alps

_______ Carolingian Empire

_______ Danube River

_______ Lombards' territory

_______ Mediterranean Sea

_______ North Sea

_______ Paris

_______ Rhine River

_______ Rome

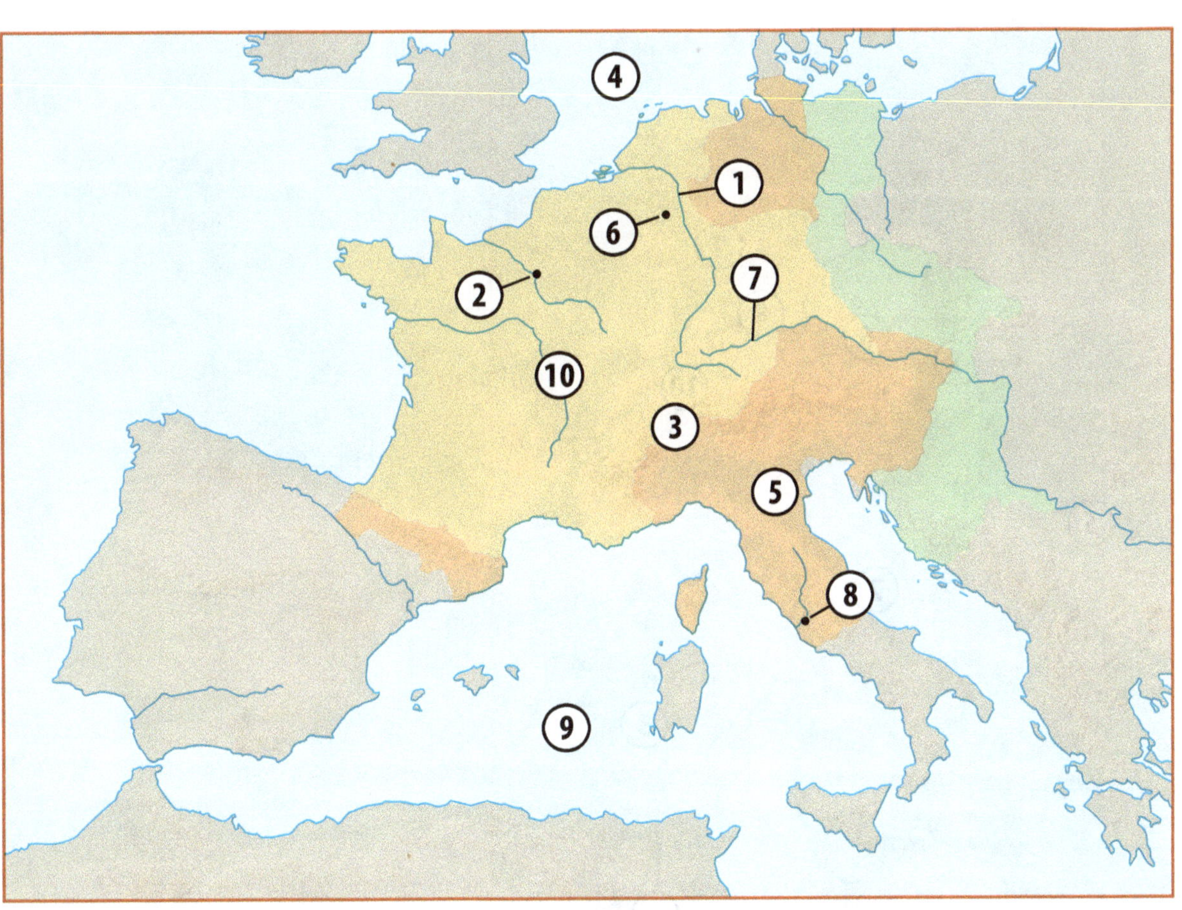

Name ______________________

## Treaty of Verdun (843)

**Locate each term or phrase on the map and place the corresponding number in the appropriate blank.**

| | |
|---|---|
| ______ Charles the Bald's territory | ______ Papal States |
| ______ Cordova | ______ Paris |
| ______ Danube River | ______ Rhine River |
| ______ Lothair's territory | ______ Rome |
| ______ Louis the German's territory | ______ Verdun |

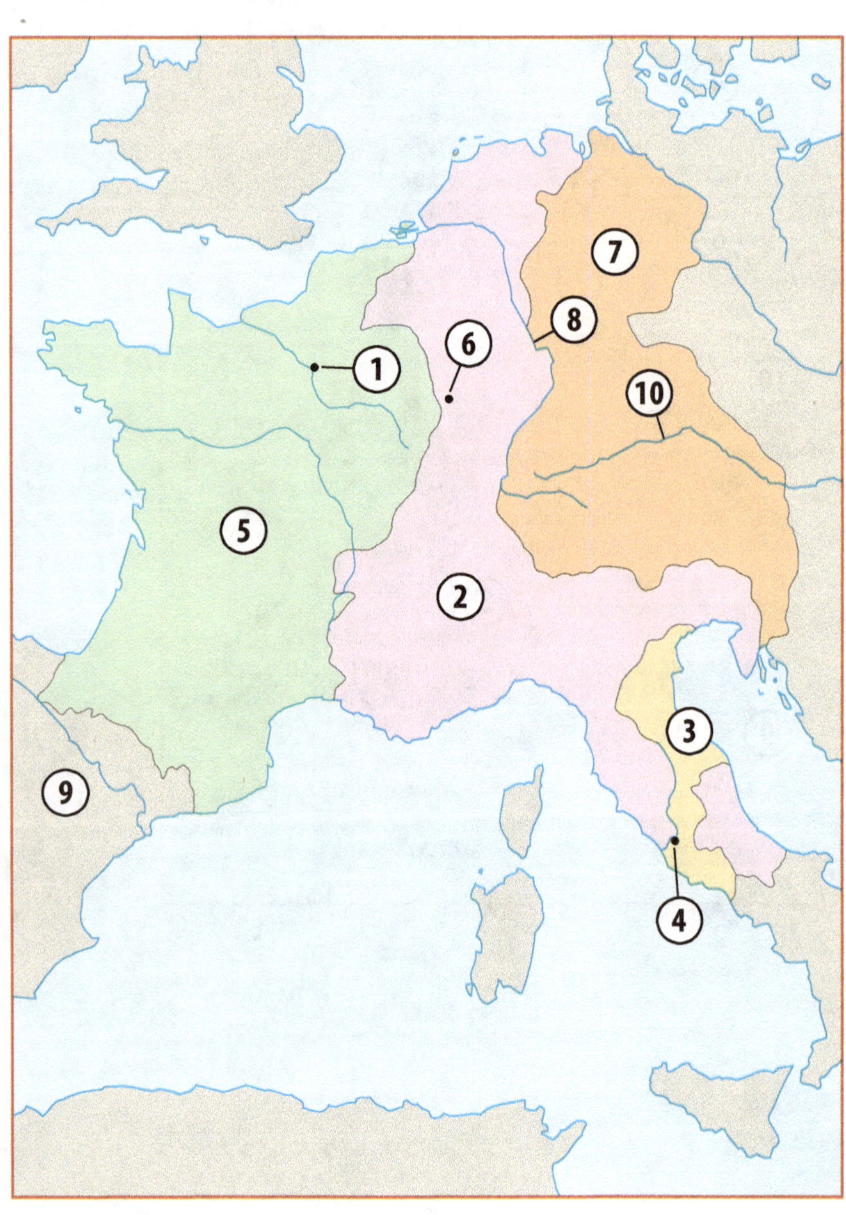

Name ____________________

# Terminology Review

## Matching

**Choose the best answer and place the letter in the blank beside the corresponding description.**

| | | |
|---|---|---|
| A. baptism | D. Extreme Unction | G. matrimony |
| B. Boniface | E. Gregory I | H. Patrick |
| C. Charles Martel | F. Lothair | |

_____ 1. Administered to a very sick or dying person

_____ 2. Apostle of the Germans

_____ 3. Greatly expanded the authority of the bishop of Rome

_____ 4. Missionary to Ireland

_____ 5. Initiates one into the Catholic Church

_____ 6. Unites a man and woman as husband and wife

_____ 7. Defeated Muslims at the Battle of Tours

## Complete the Statement

**Underline the term that accurately completes each of the following statements.**

8. Early Christians used the term (*sacramental*/*catholic*) to describe the church's universal nature.
9. (Leo I/Gregory I) persuaded Attila the Hun to spare the city of Rome in 452.
10. The term *pope* was initially used to praise the actions of (Leo I/Constantine).
11. The Petrine theory was used to enhance the position of the bishops of (Rome/Constantinople).
12. The (Orthodox/Roman Catholic) Church defines a sacrament as an act that grants grace by its very performance, based on the recipient's intentions.
13. According to the Roman Catholic Church, (Holy Orders/Holy Eucharist) is both a sacrament and a sacrifice.
14. (Holy Orders/Holy Eucharist) sets an individual apart for the service of the Roman Catholic Church.
15. The service during which Holy Communion is celebrated is known as the (mass/penance).

*(continued on next page)*

16. According to the Roman Catholic Church, one earns forgiveness through (mass/penance) for sin committed after baptism.

17. The leaders of the Roman Catholic Church are called the (laity/clergy).

18. In the Roman Catholic Church, the priests who conduct religious services and administer the mass are known as (secular/regular) clergy.

19. The clergy who live secluded lives in monasteries are known as (secular/regular) clergy.

20. The Benedictine Rule regulated the lives of (secular/regular) clergy.

Name ______________________

# Chapter Review

## Complete the Statement

**Underline the term that accurately completes each of the following statements.**

1. (Demesne/Homage) was the ceremony by which a man became a vassal and thus eligible for a fief.
2. Clovis founded a line of rulers called the (Carolingian/Merovingian) House.

## Matching: Section 1

**Choose the best answer and place the letter in the blank beside the corresponding description.**

| | | |
|---|---|---|
| A. Benedict | F. Frederick II | K. Louis the German |
| B. Boniface | G. Gregory I | L. Charles Martel |
| C. Hugh Capet | H. Gregory VII | N. Philip II |
| D. Charles the Bald | I. Henry the Fowler | M. Otto I |
| E. Frederick I | J. Leo I | |

_____ 3. Regarded by many as the Roman Church's first pope (late 500s)

_____ 4. Father of Western Monasticism

_____ 5. Persuaded a barbarian tribe to leave Rome rather than pillage it

_____ 6. Missionary to the Germans

_____ 7. Defeated Muslim invaders at the Battle of Tours in 732

_____ 8. Powerful German ruler who proclaimed himself king of Italy

_____ 9. Formally prohibited laymen from appointing church officials

_____ 10. Count of Paris; founded a dynasty after the Carolingians' decline

_____ 11. His death marked the decline of the Holy Roman Empire.

_____ 12. Tripled the size of his royal French domain and was called "Augustus"

_____ 13. First of the Saxon line of German kings

*(continued on next page)*

## Matching: Section 2

| | | |
|---|---|---|
| A. Franks | C. Magyars | E. Vikings |
| B. Lombards | D. Saxons | |

_____ 14. One of the northern German tribes who transformed "Roman" Britain into England

_____ 15. People in northern Gaul; united by Clovis

_____ 16. Germanic invaders from Norway, Sweden, and Denmark

_____ 17. Germanic invaders in northern Italy; defeated by Pepin the Short

_____ 18. Savage horsemen who terrorized southeastern Europe

## Short Answer

**Write the correct answer to each question in the provided blank.**

19. What is the Petrine theory? ______________________________

______________________________

______________________________

20. What writing style developed in the monasteries during Charlemagne's rule? ______________________________

______________________________

21. For which three major modern European nations did Charlemagne lay the foundation? ______________________________

______________________________

22. What is the designation for the ineffective Merovingian rulers who lost the throne in the eighth century?

______________________________

23. What form of government became prevalent in Europe after the collapse of the Carolingian Empire?

______________________________

24. What royal line ruled the Holy Roman Empire from 1024 to 1125, succeeding the Saxon kings? ______________________________

______________________________

25. What organization was created in 1059 to ensure that churchmen rather than Roman nobles or German kings would choose the popes? ______________________________

Name ______________________________

# The Black Death

**Answer the questions at the end after reading the following excerpt from the writings of Henry Knighton, who witnessed the Black Death.**

Then the grievous plague penetrated the seacoasts from Southampton, and came to Bristol, and there almost the whole strength of the town died, struck, as it were, by sudden death; for there were few who kept their beds more than three days, or two days, or half a day; and after this the fell [sudden] death broke forth on every side with the course of the sun. There died at Leicester in the small parish of St. Leonard more than 380; in the parish of Holy Cross, more than 400; in the parish of St. Margaret of Leicester, more than 700; and so in each parish a great number. Then the bishop of Lincoln sent through the whole bishopric, and gave general power to all and every priest, both regular and secular, to hear confessions, and absolve with full and entire episcopal authority except in matters of debt, in which case the dying man, if he could, should pay the debt while he lived, or others should certainly fulfill that duty from his property after his death. Likewise, the pope granted full remission of all sins to whoever was absolved in peril of death, and granted that this power should last till next Easter, and every one could choose a confessor at his will. In the same year there was a great plague of sheep everywhere in the realm, so that in one place there died in one pasturage more than 5000 sheep, and so rotted that neither beast nor bird would touch them. And there were small prices for everything on account of the fear of death. For there were very few who cared about riches or anything else; for a man could have a horse, which before was worth 40 *s.* [shillings], for 6 *s.* 8 *d.* [pence], a fat ox for 4 *s.*, a cow for 12 *d.*, a heifer for 6 *d.*, a fat wether [ram] for 4 *d.*, a sheep for 3 *d.*, a lamb for 2 *d.*, a big pig for 5 *d.*, a stone of wool for 9 *d.* Sheep and cattle went wandering over fields and through crops, and there was no one to go and drive or gather them, so that the number cannot be reckoned which perished in the ditches and hedges in every district, for lack of herdsmen; for there was such a lack of servants that no one knew what he ought to do. In the following autumn no one could get a reaper for less than 8 *d.* with his food, a mower for less than 12 *d.* with his food. Wherefore many crops perished in the fields for want [lack] of some one to gather them; but in the pestilence year, as is above said of other things, there was such abundance of grain that no one troubled about it. . . .

Meanwhile the king sent proclamation into all the counties that reapers and other laborers should not take more than they had been accustomed to take under a penalty appointed by statute. But the laborers were so lifted up and obstinate that they would not listen to the king's command: if any one wished to have them he had to give them what they wanted, and either lose his fruit and crops, or satisfy the lofty and covetous wishes of the workmen. And when it was known to the king that men had not observed his command, and had given greater wages to the laborers, he levied heavy fines upon abbots, priors, knights, greater and lesser, and other great folk and small folk of the realm, of some 100 s., of some 40 s., of some 20 s., from each according to what he could give. He took from each plowland of the realm 20 s., and, notwithstanding this, a fifteenth. And afterwards the king had many laborers arrested and sent them to prison; many withdrew themselves and went into the forests and woods; and those who were taken were heavily fined. Their ringleaders were made to swear that they would not take daily wages beyond the ancient custom, and then were freed from prison. And in like manner it was done with the other craftsmen in the boroughs and villages. . . . After the aforesaid pestilence many buildings, great and small, fell into ruins in every city, borough, and village for lack of inhabitants, likewise many villages and hamlets became desolate, not a house being left in them, all having died who dwelt there; and it was probable that many such villages would never be inhabited. In the winter following there was such a want of servants in work of all kinds, that one would scarcely believe that in times past there had ever been such a lack. . . . And so all

*(continued on next page)*

necessaries became so much dearer [more expensive] that what in times past had been worth a penny was then worth 4 d. or 5 d.

Magnates and lesser lords of the realm who had tenants made abatements of the rent in order that the tenants should not go away on account of the want of servants and the general dearness [expensiveness], some half the rent, some more, some less, some for two years, some for three, some for one year, according as they could agree with them. Likewise, those who received of their tenants day work throughout the year, as is the practice with villains [peasants], had to give them more leisure and remit such works, and either entirely to free them or give them an easier tenure at a small rent, so that homes should not be everywhere irrecoverably ruined, and the land everywhere remain entirely uncultivated.

Edward P. Cheyney. *Readings in English History Drawn from the Original Sources: Intended to Illustrate "A Short History of England."* (Boston: Ginn, 1908), 255–57.

1. How widespread and serious was the plague in England? ____________________

2. How did the Roman Church respond to the plague? ____________________

3. How did the plague affect livestock? ____________________

4. How did the plague change the value of items, the harvest of crops, and the maintenance of buildings in England? ____________________

5. How did common laborers use the plague to their advantage? ____________________

Name ______________________

# A Day in the Life of a University Student in 1225

**Answer the questions at the end after reading the following fictional account.**

Greetings, Mother and Father,

I ask your forgiveness for not writing sooner to thank you for your generous financial gift that arrived several weeks ago. Please believe me when I tell you that the funds were desperately needed and will be spent with the utmost care. The cost of food and housing here is very high, as the local citizens take every advantage of the students. In fact, several months ago we had to organize a university strike to force several merchants to stop charging students more for necessities than they charged others.

My intention was to write you as soon as the courier delivered your letter of credit. However, it has been very busy here at Bologna, and some exciting events forced me to postpone this note. Lest you think I am exaggerating, let me remind you of my daily schedule:

We must rise at four ante meridiem [a.m.].

Attendance at an arts lecture at five is required.

Before we can eat breakfast, we are required to attend mass at six.

Then we attend class from eight to ten.

This is followed by formal debates before we eat lunch at noon.

Lunch is followed by repetitions in small groups to help us memorize our lessons. (Hardly anyone here can afford wax tablets on which to write notes.)

Our repetitions are followed by another class from three to five post meridiem [p.m.].

Then we take turns practicing our skill in disputations until dinner at six.

We end our day with two to three hours of repetitions in order to memorize the lecture from our afternoon class.

We are expected to be in bed by nine post meridiem. (I am usually so tired that no one has to urge me to my bed!)

Students who are having difficulty are also required to attend an "extraordinary lecture" where a graduate student reviews the material discussed in class. I am happy to report that I have not needed to attend any of these special sessions this year. In fact, I may be able to earn some money next year by tutoring first-year students who struggle with one or more of their subjects. That should lessen my future need for support. I am also glad to report that my Latin has improved; I am now able to understand the class lectures without missing any of the teachers' finer details.

Despite the long days and short nights, I am thrilled to spend two hours each morning (sitting on a floor covered with straw) under the instruction of Professor Cornerius. His lectures on rhetoric and Roman civil law are rich in detail. In the afternoon, I walk to another rented building and sit on a wooden bench near the front of the room to learn from Master Strauts. Of the two professors' lectures, I consider Master Strauts's lectures on Peter Lombard's great work *Sentences* to be more challenging and yet more rewarding.

Then, as if the daily schedule were not exhausting enough, we have had quite a stir with the recent threat posed by Emperor Frederick II of the Holy Roman Empire. He sent an emissary to announce his plans to close our school and compel us to attend his new university in Naples. Many of us were in a panic since we already paid rent for the buildings we use for classes; the citizens who own those buildings were not going to refund our payments. Then, at the last moment, our benefactor, Pope Honorius III, used his great influence to force the emperor to withdraw his demands. Needless to say, we were greatly relieved, and every student signed a note of

*(continued on next page)*

thanks to our patron—written on the finest parchment that money could buy. What a year it has been thus far!

Please do not think that I am complaining about how hard it is at the university. When I hear stories about other schools, I am glad that you made it possible for me to get an education at Bologna. For example, I heard that the university at Paris is controlled by the faculty rather than by the students! And someone else told me that the leaders of the university at Padua passed a resolution requiring the professors to teach for exactly two hours and not one minute less. The students were even forbidden to beat on their benches to force the professor to finish his lecture early. Although I have never seen anyone behave in such a manner here, we do get to leave our lectures early on the rare occasion when the teacher finishes before the assigned two hours are ended. Some students complain about not getting their money's worth, but I treasure those few moments of free time.

I doubt that this note will be delivered any quicker than the letter of credit you sent recently. Based on the note you included with it, I calculated that your letter took more than six weeks to arrive! So you will probably not get this until I am well into the second half of my school year. But rest assured that I pray for you daily, and I look forward to returning home in a few years. Give my regards to the rest of the family and share this note with them.

Your devoted son,

Michael

1. What resource did the students at Bologna use to protect themselves from local merchants' abuse?

______________________________

2. How many classes did the students attend each day? How long was each class? ______________

3. What type of lecture did struggling students have to attend? What was the purpose of this lecture?

______________________________

4. In what language were lectures conducted? What was the advantage of using this language? What was a disadvantage of using it? ______________________________

______________________________

5. What seating accommodations did the students have in class? ______________________________

______________________________

6. What role did kings and popes play in medieval universities? ______________________________

______________________________

Name ____________________

## King John of England Swears Fealty to Pope Innocent III

**Answer the questions at the end after reading the following document signed by King John of England.**

John, by the grace of God king of England, lord of Ireland, duke of Normandy and Aquitaine, earl of Anjou, to all the faithful in Christ who shall inspect this present charter, greeting. We will it to be known by all of you by this our charter, confirmed by our seal, that we, having offended God and our mother the holy Church in many things, and being on that account known to need the Divine mercy, and unable to make any worthy offering for the performance of due satisfaction to God and the Church, unless we humble ourselves and our realms—we, willing to humble ourselves for Him who humbled Himself for us even to death, by the inspiration of the Holy Spirit's grace, under no compulsion of force or of fear, but of our good and free will, and by the common consent of our barons, offer and freely grant to God and His holy apostles Peter and Paul, and the holy Roman Church, our mother, and to our lord the Pope Innocent [III] and his catholic successors, the whole realm of England and the whole realm of Ireland with all their rights and appurtenances, for the remission of our sins and those of all our race, as well quick [living] as dead; and from now receiving back and holding these, as a feudal dependant, from God and the Roman Church, in the presence of the prudent man Pandulf, subdeacon and familiar of the lord the pope, do and swear fealty for them to the aforesaid our lord the Pope Innocent and his catholic successors and the Roman Church, according to the form written below, and will do liege homage to the same lord the Pope in his presence if we shall be able to be present before him; binding our successors and heirs by our wife, for ever, that in like manner to the supreme pontiff for the time being, and to the Roman Church, they should pay fealty and acknowledge homage without contradiction. Moreover, in proof of this our perpetual obligation and grant, we will and establish that from the proper and special revenues of our realms aforesaid, for all service and custom that we should render for ourselves, saving in all respects the penny of blessed Peter, the Roman Church receive 1000 marks sterling each year, to wit at the feast of St. Michael 500 marks, and at Easter 500 marks; 700 to wit for the realm of England, and 300 for the realm of Ireland; saving to us and our heirs, our rights, liberties, and royalties. All which, as aforesaid, we willing them to be perpetually ratified and confirmed, bind ourselves and our successors not to contravene. And if we or any of our successors shall presume to attempt this, whoever he be, unless he come to amendment after due admonition, let him forfeit right to the kingdom, and let this charter of obligation and grant on our part remain in force for ever.

*The Oath of Fealty.*

I, John, by the grace of God king of England and lord of Ireland, from this hour forward will be faithful to God and the blessed Peter and the Roman Church, and my lord the Pope Innocent and his successors following in catholic manner: I will not be party in deed, word, consent, or counsel, to their losing life or limb or being unjustly imprisoned. Their damage, if I am aware of it, I will prevent, and will have removed if I can; or else, as soon as I can, I will signify it, or will tell such persons as I shall believe will tell them certainly. Any counsel they entrust to me, immediately or by their messengers or their letter, I will keep secret, and will consciously disclose to no one to their damage. The patrimony of blessed Peter, and specially the realm of England and the realm of Ireland, I will aid to hold and defend against all men to my ability. So help me God and these holy gospels. Witness myself at the house of the Knights of the Temple near Dover, in the presence of the lord H. Archbishop of Dublin; the lord J. Bishop of Norwich; G. Fitz-Peter, Earl of Essex, our justiciar; W. Earl of Salisbury, our brother; W. Marshall, Earl of Pembroke; R. Count of Boulogne; W. Earl of Warenne; S. Earl of Winchester; W. Earl of Arundel; W. Earl of Ferrers; W. Brewer; Peter, son of Herbert; Warren, son of Gerald. The 15th day of May in the 14th year of our reign [1213].

Henry Gee and William John Hardy, comps. *Documents Illustrative of English Church History.* (London: Macmillan, 1914), 75–77.

*(continued on next page)*

1. Which of John's statements indicate that the Roman Church had much political power during his reign?

2. What was John's stated reason for swearing fealty to the pope?

3. What lands did John perpetually subject to the Roman Church?

4. What did John expect to receive in exchange for his subjection?

5. What does he say he will do to prove that he is submitting his kingdom to the pope?

Name ______________________

# The Battle of Crécy

**Answer the questions at the end after reading the following excerpt from the writings of Froissart, a French historian.**

The Englishmen, who were in three battles [at Crécy], lying on the ground to rest them, as soon as they saw the Frenchmen approach, rose upon their feet fair and easily without any haste and arranged their battles. In the first, which was the prince's battle, the archers stood in the manner of a herse [wedge], and the men of arms in the bottom of the battle. The earl of Northampton and the earl of Arundel, with the second battle, were on a wing in good order, ready to comfort the prince's battle, if need were.

The lords and knights of France came not to the assembly in good order, for some came before and some came after in such evil order that one of them did trouble another. When the French king saw the Englishmen his blood changed, and he said to his marshals, "Make the Genoways [Genoese] go on before and begin the battle in the name of God and St. Denis [patron saint of France]." There were of the Genoways crossbows about fifteen thousand, but they were so weary of going afoot that day a six leagues armed with their crossbows, that they said to their constables: "We be not well ordered to fight this day, for we be not in the case to do any great feats of arms: we have more need of rest." These words came to the earl of Alençon, who said, "A man is well at ease to be charged with such a set of rascals, to be faint and fail now at most need." Also the same season there fell a great rain and lightning with terrible thunder, and before the rain there came flying over both battles a great number of crows for fear of the tempest coming. Then anon the air began to wax clear, and the sun to shine fair and bright, the which was right in the Frenchmen's eye[s] and on the Englishmen's backs. When the Genoways were assembled together and began to approach, they uttered very great cries to abash the Englishmen, but [the Englishmen] stood still and stirred not for all that; then the Genoways again the second time made a great and a fell [fierce] cry, and stept forward a little, and the Englishmen removed not one foot; thirdly again they cried out and then they shot fiercely with their crossbows. Then the English archers stept forth one pace and let fly their arrows [from longbows], so wholly and so thick that it seemed snow. When the Genoways felt the arrows piercing through heads, arms, and breasts, many of them did cast down their crossbows and did cut their strings and returned discomfited [defeated]. When the French king saw them fly away, he said, "Slay these rascals, for they shall let and trouble us without reason." Then ye should have seen the men of arms dash in among them and kill a great number of them; and ever still the Englishmen shot whereas they saw thickest press; the sharp arrows ran into the men of arms and into their horses, and many fell, horse and men, among the Genoways, and when they were down they could not rise again; the press was so thick that one overthrew another. And also among the Englishmen there were certain rascals that went afoot with great knives, and they went in among the men of arms and slew and murdered many as they lay on the ground, both earls, barons, knights, and squires, whereof the king of England was after displeased, for he had rather they had been taken prisoners. . . .

In the morning, the day of the battle, certain Frenchmen and Almains [Germans] perforce opened [broke through] the archers of the Prince's battle and came and fought with the men of arms, hand to hand. Then the second battle of the Englishmen came to succor [help] the Prince's battle, the which was time, for they had as then much ado; and they with the Prince sent a messenger to the king who was on a little windmill hill. Then the knight said to the king: "Sir, the earl of Warwick, and the earl of Oxford, Sir Raynold Cobham, and other, such as be about the Prince, your son, are fiercely fought withal and are sorely handled; wherefore they desire you that you and your battle will come and aid them; for if the Frenchmen increase, as they doubt [fear] they will, your son and they shall have much ado." Then the king said, "Is my son

*(continued on next page)*

dead or hurt on the earth felled?" "No, sir," quoth the knight, "but he is hardly matched [outnumbered]; wherefore he hath need of your aid." "Well," said the king, "return to him and to them that sent you hither, and say to them that they send no more to me for any adventure that falleth, as long as my son is alive; and also say to them that they suffer him this day to win his spurs; for if God be pleased, I will this journey be his and the honor thereof, and to them that be about him." Then the knight returned again to them and shewed the king's words, the which greatly encouraged them. . . .

In the evening the French king, who had left about him no more than a threescore persons, one and other, whereof Sir John of Hainault was one, who had remounted once the king, for his horse was slain with an arrow, then he said to the king, "Sir, depart hence, for it is time; lose not yourself wilfully; if ye have loss at this time, ye shall recover it again another season." And so he took the king's horse by the bridle and led him away in a manner perforce [by necessity]. Then the king rode until he came to the castle of Broye. The gate was closed, because it was by that time dark; then the king called the captain, who came to the walls and said, "Who is it that calleth there this time of night?" Then the king said, "Open your gate quickly, for this is the fortune of France." The captain knew then it was the king, and opened the gate and let down the bridge. Then the king entered, and he had with him but five barons, Sir John of Hainault, Sir Charles of Montgomery, the lord of Beaujeu, the lord d'Aubigny, and the lord of Montsault. The king would not tarry there, but drank and departed thence about midnight, and so rode by such guides as knew the country till he came in the morning to Amiens, and there he rested.

This Saturday the Englishmen never departed from their battles for chasing of any man, but kept still their field, and ever defended themselves against all such as came to assail them. This battle ended about evensong time.

Edward P. Cheyney. *Readings in English History Drawn from the Original Sources: Intended to Illustrate "A Short History of England."* (Boston: Ginn, 1908), 242–45.

1. What factors made fighting difficult for the French before the battle began? ______________________

______________________________________________________________

______________________________________________________________

2. With what new weapon did the English fight the French? How effective was this weapon? ______________

______________________________________________________________

______________________________________________________________

3. How did the English "rascals" displease the king? ______________________________________

______________________________________________________________

4. Why did the English king refuse to send reinforcements to assist his son (the Prince of Wales)? __________

______________________________________________________________

5. What was the outcome of the battle? ______________________________________________

______________________________________________________________

Name ______________________________

## Europe (About 1500)

**Locate each term on the map and place the corresponding number in the appropriate blank.**

_______ Austria

_______ Baltic Sea

_______ Denmark

_______ England

_______ France

_______ Holy Roman Empire

_______ Hungary

_______ Ireland

_______ Kingdom of Naples

_______ Mediterranean Sea

_______ Netherlands

_______ North Sea

_______ Norway

_______ Ottoman Empire

_______ Papal States

_______ Poland

_______ Portugal

_______ Russia

_______ Spain

_______ Sweden

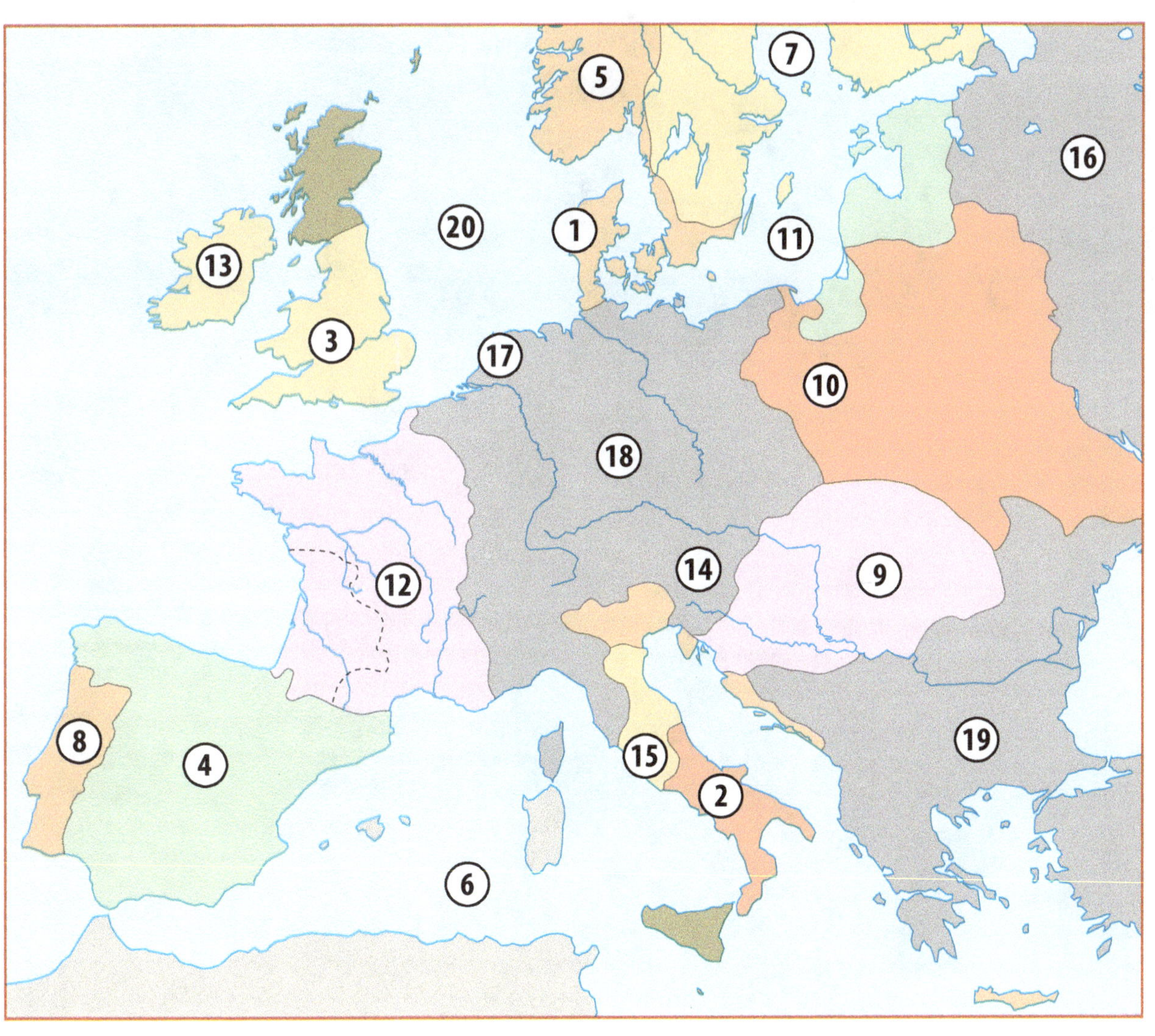

Name ______________________________

# Chapter Review

## Matching

**Choose the best answer and place the letter in the blank beside the corresponding description.**

A. Peter Abelard
B. Dante Alighieri
C. Anselm
D. Thomas Aquinas
E. Roger Bacon
F. Boniface VIII
G. Geoffrey Chaucer
H. Edward III
I. Ferdinand
J. Henry VII
K. Louis IX
L. Maximilian I
M. Philip IV

_____ 1. Wrote *The Canterbury Tales*

_____ 2. Wrote the *Divine Comedy*

_____ 3. Sought to prove God's existence with reason

_____ 4. Claimed France's throne, beginning a war with Philip VI

_____ 5. Founded the Tudor dynasty in England

_____ 6. King of Spain; promoted the Inquisition

_____ 7. Promoted critical reasoning

_____ 8. Strengthened the Habsburg line through marriage

_____ 9. Advocated observation and experimentation in science

_____ 10. Tried to harmonize Aristotle's philosophy with the Bible

## Complete the Statement

**Underline the term that accurately completes each of the following statements.**

11. The Battle of Crécy occurred during the (Wars of the Roses/Hundred Years' War).
12. (Romanesque/Gothic) architecture is characterized by thick walls, rounded arches, heavy columns, and small doors and windows.
13. Pope Boniface VIII wrote the (*Summa Theologiae*/*Unam Sanctam*), insisting that submission to the pope is necessary for salvation.
14. The Council of (Pisa/Constance) secured the election of Martin V as the pope, restoring the papacy to Rome.

*(continued on next page)*

## Short Answer

**Write the correct answer to each question in the provided blank.**

15. What was the name for a series of conflicts between noble families in England for the throne?

_______________

16. What term denotes a common spoken language that writers began to use instead of Latin by the twelfth century? _______________

17. Name the organizations whose primary function was to regulate business activity of a given town.

_______________

18. What university subjects composed the trivium? _______________

19. What university subjects composed the quadrivium? _______________

_______________

20. What commercial association promoted trade in northern Europe, especially among German towns?

_______________

21. Who was the most powerful pope in the Roman Church's history? _______________

22. Who taxed the French clergy and convened the Estates-General? _______________

23. Who established circuit courts that traveled throughout England? _______________

24. Who was the "ideal medieval king" who led two crusades? _______________

25. Name the ruling family that built a strong base of power among the southern German states.

_______________

Name ____________________

# Early History of the English Bible

**Answer the questions at the end after reading the following article.**

The history of the English Bible begins with John Wycliffe, who believed that everyone should have the opportunity to read God's Word. In 1382 he and his followers produced the first complete English translation of the Scripture—a translation made from the Latin Vulgate. (Wycliffe knew no Hebrew or Greek.) Although the common people wanted to know what the Bible had to say, the clergy strongly opposed Wycliffe's work. The archbishop of Canterbury called Wycliffe "the very herald and child of anti-Christ, who crowned his wickedness by translating the Scripture into the mother tongue." Nevertheless, the religious and political authorities could not destroy God's Word. Wycliffe's translation survived, and some of its wording even found its way into the King James Version. For example, the phrase "strait is the gate, and narrow is the way" (Matt. 7:14) and the words "beam" and "mote" (Matt. 7:3) come from Wycliffe's translation.

William Tyndale (1492–1536), an able Hebrew and Greek scholar, produced the first English Bible translated directly from the ancient biblical languages. Forced to flee his native England, Tyndale went to Germany, where his New Testament was published in 1525. The authorities in England, however, made every effort to seize or purchase these New Testaments as they were smuggled into the country. On one occasion, a London merchant who was Tyndale's friend sold numerous copies at a high price to the bishop of London. Although the bishop had the copies destroyed, Tyndale used the money he received from the sale to finance a better printing of the New Testament! He also managed to publish part of the Old Testament, but before he could translate and publish all of it, he was captured in Belgium. Condemned as a heretic, he was strangled and then burned at the stake.

Tyndale died, but his work was not in vain. Others used what he had done to produce new translations. A year before Tyndale died, Miles Coverdale (1488–1569) published a translation of the entire Bible. Since he did not know Greek or Hebrew, he relied heavily upon Luther's German translation, the Latin Vulgate, and Tyndale's work. Two years later one of Tyndale's friends, John Rogers, produced the so-called Matthew's Bible. (He published it under the pseudonym of Thomas Matthew.) This was not really a new translation, because Rogers simply combined parts of Coverdale's work with sections of the Old Testament that Tyndale had translated but never published. In 1539 Coverdale himself revised Matthew's Bible. When it was published it measured 16 1/2 by 11 inches and received the name Great Bible because of its size. This was the first version of the English Bible specifically authorized to be read publicly in the churches. For almost thirty years it was the only version that could be used legally in England.

Bible translation work did not cease, however. During the reign of Mary I, some of the most important Protestant leaders fled to Geneva to escape death. While there, these men produced a Bible in 1560 that contained, in their words, "most profitable annotations upon all the hard places." Known as the Geneva Bible, this was the first English version to have numbered verses. This version also used italics to indicate words that were not actually found in the Greek and Hebrew manuscripts. Within a short time, the Geneva Bible became very popular, especially among the Puritans.

In an effort to weaken the popularity of this unauthorized version, the Church of England commissioned a new translation. It came out in 1568 and became known as the Bishop's Bible. In spite of its official status, it never gained wide acceptance. The culmination of all this early translation work occurred at the beginning of the seventeenth century. King James I authorized a group of about fifty scholars to produce a new revision of the Bible. Following the king's orders, these men used the Bishop's Bible as their guide and consulted other English translations

*(continued on next page)*

and certain Hebrew, Greek, and Latin manuscripts—especially the Greek New Testament that had been edited by Erasmus.

To make their work more efficient and to guard against errors, the translators divided themselves into six committees. Each committee was assigned a particular task. For example, one group translated Genesis through II Kings. Once a particular committee completed a portion of its work, it would send it to the others for evaluation and revision.

In 1611 the scholars delivered their work to the king's printer for publication. The King James Version was a masterpiece, but at first many people resented it. For example, the Pilgrims dogmatically rejected it. They had grown to love the familiar phraseology of the older English versions and did not want to change. But with the passage of time, this beautiful translation won the hearts of the English-speaking world.

1. Why did Wycliffe translate Scripture into English? ____________________

2. How did Tyndale die? ____________________

3. What version of the Bible was popular among Puritans? ____________________

4. What does the article show you about the Bible? ____________________

5. Why do you think these men were willing to die for their faith? ____________________

Name ________________________

## The Spanish Armada

**Answer the questions at the end based on the following excerpt from the writings of Robert Carey, a member of the English court.**

The next yeare [1588] the king of Spain's great Armado came upon our coast, thinking to devour us all. Upon the newes sent to court from Plimouth of their certain arrivall, my Lord Cumberland and myselfe tooke post horse, and rode streight to Portsmouth, where we found a frigot that carried us to sea; and having sought for the fleets a whole day, the night after wee fell amongst them: where it was our fortune to light first on the Spanish fleet; and finding ourselves in the wrong, we tackt about, and in short time gott to our own fleet, which was not farre from the other. At our coming aboord our Admirall [a ship], wee stay'd there awhile; but finding the ship much pestered and scant of cabins, we left the Admirall and went aboord Captain Reyman [a ship], where wee stay'd and were very welcome, and much made of.

It was on Thursday that wee came to the fleete. All that day wee followed close the Spanish Armado, and nothing was attempted on either side: the same course wee held all Friday and Saturday, by which time the Spanish fleet cast anchor just before Calais. We likewise did the same, a very small distance behind them, and so continued till Munday morning about two of the clocke; in which time our counsaile [counsel] of warre had provided six old hulkes and stuffed them full of all combustible matter fitt for burning, and on Monday at two in the morning they were lett loose, with each of them a man in her to direct them. The tide serving they brought them very near the Spanish fleet, so that they could not misse to come amongst the midest of them; then they set fire on them, and came off themselves, having each of them a little boate to bring him off. The ships set on fire, came so directly to the Spanish fleet, as they had no way to avoid them, but to cut all their halsers [anchor cables], and so escape; and their haste was such that they left one of their four great galeasses [ships] on ground before Calais, which our men took and had the spoil of, where many of the Spaniards were slaine with the governour thereof, but most of them were saved with wading ashore to Calais.

They being in this disorder, wee made ready to follow them, where began a cruell fight, and wee had such advantage both of wind and tide as wee had a glorious day of them; continuing fight from foure o'clocke in the morning, till almost five or six at night, where they lost a douzen or fourteene of their best shippes, some sunke, and the rest ranne ashore in diverse parts to keep themselves from sinking. After God had given us this great victory, they made all the hast[e] they could away, and wee followed them Tuesday and Wednesday, by which time they were gotten as farre as Flamboroughhead. It was resolved on Wednesday at night, that by four o'clocke on Thursday, wee should have a new fight with them for a farewell; but by two in the morning, there was a flagge of counsaile hung out in our Vice-Admirall [a ship], when it was found that in the whole fleet there was not munition sufficient to make halfe a fight; and therefore it was concluded that we should let them passe, and our fleet to return to the Downes. That night wee parted with them, wee had a mighty storme. Our fleet cast anchor, and endured it; but the Spanish fleet, wanting [lacking] their anchors, were many of them cast ashore on the west of Ireland, where they had all their throates cutt by the kernes [Irish foot soldiers]; and some of them on Scotland, where they were no better used; and the rest (with much adoe) gott into Spaine againe. Thus did God blesse us, and gave victory over this invincible navy; the sea calmed, and all our shippes came to the Downes on Friday in safety.

Edward P. Cheyney. *Readings in English History Drawn from the Original Sources: Intended to Illustrate a Short History of England.* (Boston: Ginn, 1908), 406–8.

*(continued on next page)*

1. What national threat did England encounter in 1588? ______________________

______________________

2. What clever tactic did the English devise to damage Spain's fleet when the Spanish cast anchor near Calais?

______________________

______________________

3. How much damage did the English inflict on the Spanish ships, which became disorganized?

______________________

______________________

4. Why did the English decide against a final attack? ______________________

______________________

5. What providentially timed natural event destroyed much of the Spanish fleet? ______________________

______________________

6. Why did the English ships survive the storm while many Spanish ships were destroyed? ______________________

______________________

______________________

7. What happened to the Spanish who went ashore in Ireland and Scotland? ______________________

______________________

8. How important was this victory for the Protestant cause in England and beyond? ______________________

______________________

______________________

______________________

Name ______________________________

## The St. Bartholomew's Day Massacre

**Answer the questions at the end based on the following excerpt from the writings of John Foxe.**

After a long series of troubles in France, the papists, seeing they could not overcome the protestants by open force, began to devise how they might entrap them by subtlety, and that by two ways: first by a pretended commission sent into the Low Countries, which the prince of Navarre and Conde was to command. This was merely to learn what power and force the admiral had under him, who they were, and what were their names. The second was by a marriage between the prince of Navarre and the king's sister; to which were to be invited all the chief protestants of France. Accordingly they first began with the queen of Navarre, mother to the prince who was to espouse the king's sister. Allured by fair words, she consented to come to Paris. Shortly after she fell sick, and died within five days, not without suspicion of poison.

Notwithstanding, the marriage still proceeded. The admiral, prince of Navarre and Conde, and many other protestant chiefs, were induced by the king's letters and promises to proceed to Paris, and were received with great solemnity. The marriage took place on the 19th of August, 1572, and was solemnized by the cardinal of Bourbonne. Afterwards they resorted to the bishop's palace to dinner. In the evening they were conducted to a palace in the centre of the city, to supper. Four days after this the admiral, coming from the council table, was shot at with a pistol charged with three bullets, and wounded in both his arms. He still remained in Paris, although his friends advised him to flee. Soldiers were appointed in different places of the city to be ready at the command of the king; and upon the watchword being given, they burst out to the slaughter of the protestants, beginning with the admiral himself, who, being wounded, was cast out of the window into the street, where his head being struck off, was embalmed and sent to the pope. The savage people then cut off his arms, and drew his mangled body three days through the streets of Paris, after which they took it to the place of execution, and there hanged it by the heels, to the scorn of the populace.

The martyrdom of this virtuous man had no sooner taken place, than the troops, with rage and violence, ran about slaying all the protestants they knew or could find within the city gates. This continued many days; but the greatest slaughter was in the first three days, in which were said to be murdered above 10,000 men and women, old and young, of all sorts and conditions. The bodies of the dead were carried in carts and thrown into the river, which, with other whole streams in certain places of the city, was reddened with the blood of the slain. In the number of eminent men who fell in this dreadful slaughter were Petrus Ramus, Lambinus, Plateanus, Lomenius, Chapesius, and others.

The brutal deeds of this period were not confined within the walls of Paris, but extended to other cities and quarters of the realm, especially at Lyons, Orleans, Toulouse, and Rouen, where the cruelties were, if possible, even greater than in the capital. Within the space of one month 30,000 religious protestants are said to have been slain. When intelligence of the massacre was received at Rome, the greatest rejoicings took place. The pope and his cardinals went in procession to the church of St. Mark, to give thanks to God; and a medal was struck to commemorate the event. A jubilee was also published, and the ordnance fired from the castle of St. Angelo. To the person who brought the news the cardinal of Lorraine gave 1,000 crowns. Similar rejoicings were also made all over France for this imagined overthrow of the faithful.

The enemies of the truth began now to think that they were the sole lords of men's consciences; and truly, it did seem as if God had abandoned the earth to the ravages of his enemy. But he had otherwise decreed, and thousands who had not bowed the knee to Baal were called forth to glory and virtue.

*(continued on next page)*

The year following died Charles IX of France, the tyrant who had been instrumental in these calamities. He was only in the 28th year of his age, and his death was remarkable and dreadful. When lying on his bed, the blood gushed from various parts of his body. At length, after violent convulsions, and the utterance of the most horrid blasphemies, it issued in such quantities from his mouth that he expired.

John Fox. *Foxe's Book of Martyrs.* (Greenville: Emerald, 2002) 68–71.

1. What happened to the queen of Navarre soon after she arrived in Paris for the wedding? ______________________________

2. What occurred on St. Bartholomew's Day 1572 in Paris, France? ______________________________

3. About how many Protestants were murdered in France within a month? ______________________________

4. How did the pope and the cardinals respond when they heard of the massacre? ______________________________

5. What political leader died an agonizing death the next year? ______________________________

6. Did the massacre destroy Christianity in France? Why or why not? ______________________________

Name ______________________

# Canons and Decrees of the Council of Trent

**Answer the questions at the end based on the following excerpts from the Council of Trent.**

## From Session XXII

On the Sacrifice of the Mass.

Canon I.—If any one saith, that in the mass a true and proper sacrifice is not offered to God; or, that to be offered is nothing else but that Christ is given us to eat; let him be anathema [cursed].

Canon II.—If any one saith, that by those words, Do this for the commemoration of me (Luke xxii. 19), Christ did not institute the apostles priests; or, did not ordain that they, and other priests should offer His own body and blood; let him be anathema.

Canon III.—If any one saith, that the sacrifice of the mass is only a sacrifice of praise and of thanksgiving; or, that it is a bare commemoration of the sacrifice consummated [completed] on the cross, but not a propitiatory sacrifice; or, that it profits him only who receives; and that it ought not to be offered for the living and the dead for sins, pains, satisfactions, and other necessities; let him be anathema. . . .

Canon IX.—If any one saith, that the rite of the Roman Church . . . is to be condemned; or, that the mass ought to be celebrated in the vulgar tongue [common language] only; or, that water ought not to be mixed with the wine that is to be offered in the chalice, for that it is contrary to the institution of Christ; let him be anathema.

## From Session XXV

Decree Concerning Purgatory.

Whereas the Catholic Church, instructed by the Holy Ghost, has, from the sacred writings and the ancient tradition of the Fathers, taught, in sacred councils, and very recently in this œcumenical Synod, that there is a Purgatory, and that the souls there detained [kept] are helped by the suffrages of the faithful, but principally by the acceptable sacrifice of the altar; the holy Synod enjoins on bishops that they diligently endeavour that the sound doctrine concerning Purgatory, transmitted by the holy Fathers and sacred councils, be believed, maintained, taught, and every where proclaimed by the faithful of Christ.

On the Invocation, Veneration, and Relics, of Saints, and on Sacred Images.

The holy Synod enjoins on all bishops, and others who sustain the office and charge of teaching, that . . . they especially instruct the faithful diligently concerning the intercession and invocation of saints; the honour (paid) to relics; and the legitimate use of images: teaching them, that the saints, who reign together with Christ, offer up their own prayers to God for men; that it is good and useful suppliantly to invoke them, and to have recourse to their prayers, aid, (and) help for obtaining benefits from God, through His Son, Jesus Christ our Lord, who is our alone Redeemer and Saviour; but that they think impiously, who deny that the saints, who enjoy eternal happiness in heaven, are to be invocated; or who assert either that they do not pray for men; or, that the invocation of them to pray for each of us even in particular, is idolatry.

. . .

Moreover, [the Synod declares] that the images of Christ, of the Virgin Mother of God, and of the other saints, are to be had and retained particularly in temples, and that due honour and veneration are to be given them; not that any divinity, or virtue, is believed to be in them, on account of which they are to be worshipped; or that anything is to be asked of them; or, that trust is to be reposed in images, as was of old done by the Gentiles who placed their hope in idols; but because the honour which is shown them is referred to the prototypes which those

*(continued on next page)*

images represent; in such wise that by the images which we kiss, and before which we uncover the head, and prostrate ourselves, we adore Christ; and we venerate the saints, whose similitude [likeness] they bear.

Decree Concerning Indulgences.

Whereas the power of conferring Indulgences was granted by Christ to the Church; and she has, even in the most ancient times, used the said power, delivered unto her of God; the sacred holy Synod teaches, and enjoins, that the use of Indulgences, for the Christian people most salutary, and approved of by the authority of sacred Councils, is to be retained in the Church; and It condemns with anathema those who either assert, that they are useless; or who deny that there is in the Church the power of granting them. In granting them, however, It desires that, in accordance with the ancient and approved custom in the Church, moderation be observed; lest, by excessive facility, eccles[i]astical discipline be enervated. And being desirous that the abuses which have crept therein, and by occasion of which this honourable name of Indulgences is blasphemed by heretics, be amended and corrected, It ordains generally by this decree, that all evil gains for the obtaining thereof,—whence a most prolific cause of abuses amongst the Christian people has been derived,—be wholly abolished.

J. Waterworth, trans. *The Canons and Decrees of the Sacred and Œcumenical Council of Trent: Celebrated Under the Sovereign Pontiffs, Paul III, Julius III and Pius IV.* (Chicago: Christian Symbolic, 1848), 158–59, 232–35, 277–78.

1. Contrast the council's teaching on the mass with the teaching of Hebrews 7:27 and 9:24–28.

   ______________________________________________

   ______________________________________________

2. On what basis did the council teach the concept of purgatory? ______________________

   ______________________________________________

3. Compare the council's teaching on purgatory with the teaching of Hebrews 9:27; 2 Corinthians 5:8; and Luke 16:22–24. ______________________

   ______________________________________________

   ______________________________________________

4. Although the Roman Church claims the authority to grant indulgences, who alone has authority to forgive sins, according to Mark 2:10 and Acts 4:10–12? ______________________

5. Contrast the council's view of Mary with Mary's view of herself in Luke 1:46–48. ______________________

   ______________________________________________

   ______________________________________________

   ______________________________________________

Name ______________________

# Chapter Review

## Matching

**Choose the best answer and place the letter in the blank beside the corresponding description.**

A. Sandro Botticelli
B. John Calvin
C. Baldassare Castiglione
D. Miguel de Cervantes
E. Erasmus
F. Johannes Gutenberg
G. John Huss
H. Martin Luther
I. Niccolo Machiavelli
J. Philipp Melanchthon
K. Thomas More
L. Henry of Navarre
M. Francesco Petrarch
N. William Shakespeare
O. John Wycliffe

_____ 1. “Morning Star of the Reformation”

_____ 2. Added the element of movement to Renaissance art

_____ 3. Granted some religious toleration through the Edict of Nantes

_____ 4. Wrote the Augsburg Confession

_____ 5. Author of *Utopia*

_____ 6. German reformer who preached justification by faith alone

_____ 7. Wrote *The Institutes of the Christian Religion*

_____ 8. Published a Greek New Testament in 1516

_____ 9. English playwright; wrote *King Lear*, *Hamlet, Othello*, and *Macbeth*

_____ 10. Wrote a controversial essay titled *The Prince*

_____ 11. Bohemian reformer who was burned at the stake

_____ 12. Foremost Spanish writer of the late Renaissance; author of *Don Quixote*

_____ 13. Printed a Bible using movable-type printing

*(continued on next page)*

## Complete the Statement

**Underline the term that accurately completes each of the following statements.**

14. The Medici family achieved much influence in Renaissance (Venice/Florence).
15. (Albrecht Dürer/Hans Holbein) was a portrait painter who became the court painter of Henry VIII of England.
16. (Albrecht Dürer/Hans Holbein) made many woodcarvings and engravings, which were used to illustrate printed books.
17. (Raphael/Donatello) painted *The School of Athens.*
18. The (Jesuits/Huguenots) promoted the Counter Reformation.
19. The (Diet of Worms/Peace of Augsburg) allowed each prince to choose whether his territory would be Lutheran or Roman Catholic.
20. (Puritans/Separatists) removed themselves from the Church of England.
21. (Humanism/Learning) puts an overemphasis on human worth and ability, leading man to glorify himself instead of God.
22. (Henry VIII/Edward VI) was a frail boy when he became king and was influenced by those who were sympathetic to the Protestant Reformation.
23. (Michelangelo/Donatello) painted the ceiling of the Sistine Chapel.

## Essay

**Write the correct answer to each question in the provided blank.**

24. How does the Renaissance compare with the Reformation? ______________________________

______________________________________________________________________

______________________________________________________________________

______________________________________________________________________

______________________________________________________________________

______________________________________________________________________

______________________________________________________________________

25. How did the Renaissance oppose biblical principles and promote ideas and values that a faithful Christian must reject? ______________________________

______________________________________________________________________

______________________________________________________________________

______________________________________________________________________

Name ______________________

# Early Africa

**Locate each term on the map and place the corresponding number in the appropriate blank.**

_______ Atlantic Ocean

_______ Benin

_______ Ghana

_______ Indian Ocean

_______ Kilwa

_______ Lake Chad

_______ Mali

_______ Mecca

_______ Mediterranean Sea

_______ Red Sea

_______ Sahara

_______ Timbuktu

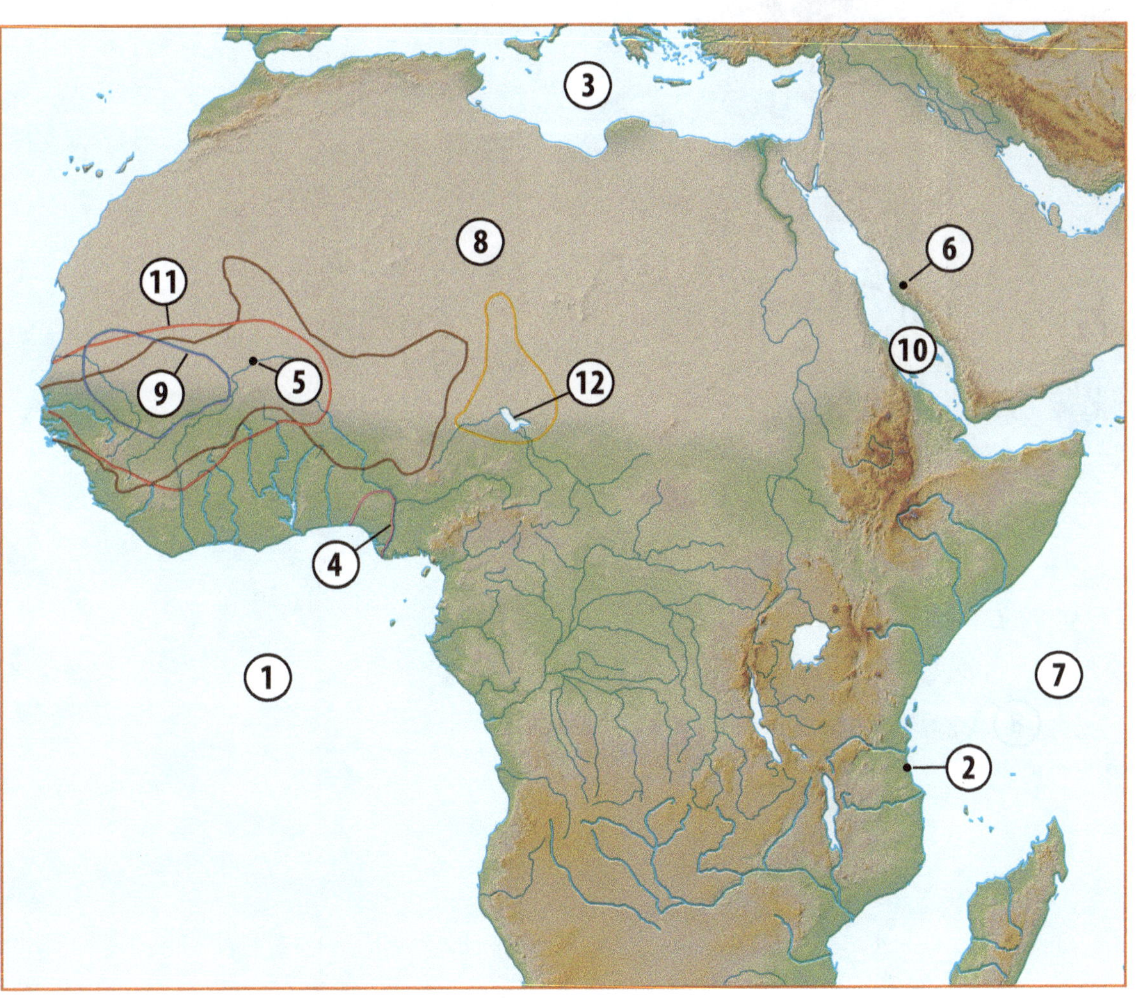

Name ____________________

# India

**Locate each term on the map and place the corresponding number in the appropriate blank.**

_______ Afghanistan

_______ Arabian Sea

_______ Bay of Bengal

_______ Deccan Plateau

_______ Delhi

_______ Himalayas

_______ Indian Ocean

_______ Indus River

_______ Krishna River

_______ Vijayanagara

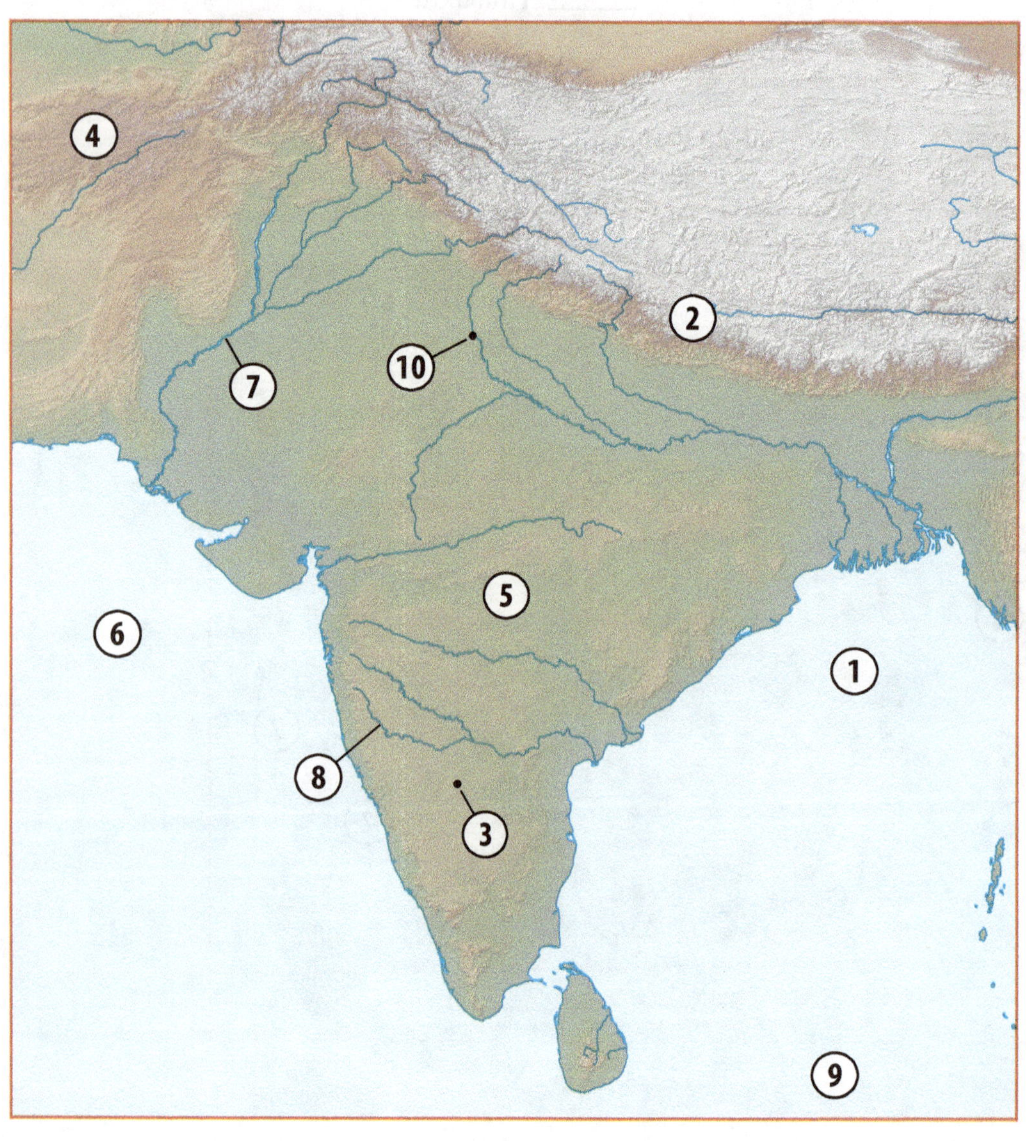

Name ______________________

## Sikh Scripture

**Answer the questions at the end after referring to the student text and reading the following excerpts from the opening verses of the *Granth Sahib.***

### One Universal Creator God.

### The Name is Truth.

Creative Being Personified. No Fear. No Hatred.

Image of the Undying, Beyond Birth, Self-existent.

By Guru's Grace ~

Chant and Meditate:

True in the Primal Beginning. True Throughout the Ages.

True Here and Now. O Nanak, Forever and Ever True. || 1 ||

By thinking, He cannot be reduced to thought, even by thinking hundreds of thousands of times. By remaining silent, inner silence is not obtained, even by remaining lovingly absorbed deep within. The hunger of the hungry is not appeased, even by piling up loads of worldly goods. Hundreds of thousands of clever tricks, but not even one of them will go along with you in the end. So how can you become truthful? And how can the veil of illusion be torn away? O Nanak, it is written that you shall obey . . . His Command, and walk in the Way of His Will. || 1 || By His Command, bodies are created; His Command cannot be described. By His Command, souls come into being; by His Command, glory and greatness are obtained. By His Command, some are high and some are low; by His Written Command, pain and pleasure are obtained. Some, by His Command, are blessed and forgiven; others, by His Command, wander aimlessly forever. Everyone is subject to His Command; no one is beyond His Command. O Nanak, one who understands His Command, does not speak in ego. || 2 || Some sing of His Power—who has that Power? Some sing of His Gifts, and know His Sign and Insignia. Some sing of His Glorious Virtues, Greatness and Beauty. Some sing of knowledge obtained of Him, through difficult philosophical studies. Some sing that He fashions the body, and then again reduces it to dust. Some sing that He takes life away, and then again restores it.

Some sing that He seems so very far away. Some sing that He watches over us, face to face, ever-present. There is no shortage of those who preach and teach. Millions upon millions offer millions of sermons and stories. The Great Giver keeps on giving, while those who receive grow weary of receiving. Throughout the ages, consumers consume. The Commander, by His Command, leads us to walk on the Path. O Nanak, He blossoms forth, Carefree and Untroubled. || 3 || True is the Master, True is His Name—speak it with infinite love. People beg and pray, "Give to us, give to us", and the Great Giver gives His Gifts.

So what offering can we place before Him, by which we might see . . . His Court? What words can we speak to evoke His Love? In the . . . ambrosial hours before dawn, chant the True Name, and contemplate His Glorious Greatness. By the karma of past actions, the robe of this physical body is obtained. By His Grace, the Gate of Liberation is found. O Nanak, know this well: the True One Himself is All. || 4 || He cannot be established, He cannot be created. He Himself is Immaculate and Pure. Those who serve Him are honored. O Nanak, sing of the Lord, the Treasure of Excellence. Sing, and listen, and let your mind be filled with love. Your pain shall be sent far away, and peace shall come to your home. The Guru's Word is the Sound-current of the [cosmos]; the Guru's Word is the Wisdom of the Vedas [Hindu scripture]; the Guru's Word is all-pervading.

*(continued on next page)*

The Guru is Shiva [Hindu deity], the Guru is Vishnu [Hindu deity] and Brahma [Hindu creator god]; the Guru is Paarvati [Hindu goddess of fertility] and Lakhshmi [Hindu goddess of wealth]. Even knowing God, I cannot describe Him; He cannot be described in words. The Guru has given me this one understanding: there is only the One, the Giver of all souls. May I never forget Him! || 5 || If I am pleasing to Him, then that is my pilgrimage and cleansing bath. Without pleasing Him, what good are ritual cleansings? I gaze upon all the created beings: without the karma of good actions, what are they given to receive? Within the mind are gems, jewels and rubies, if you listen to the Guru's Teachings, even once. The Guru has given me this one understanding: there is only the One, the Giver of all souls. May I never forget Him! || 6 || Even if you could live throughout the four ages [Hindu epochs], or even ten times more, and even if you were known throughout the nine continents and followed by all, with a good name and reputation, with praise and fame throughout the world—still, if the Lord does not bless you with His Glance of Grace, then who cares? What is the use? Among worms, you would be considered a lowly worm, and even contemptible sinners would hold you in contempt. O Nanak, God blesses the unworthy with virtue, and bestows virtue on the virtuous. No one can even imagine anyone who can bestow virtue upon Him. || 7 || Listening— . . . the spiritual teachers, the heroic warriors, the yogic masters. Listening—the earth, its support and the [atmosphere]. Listening—the oceans, the lands of the world and the nether regions of the underworld. Listening—Death cannot even touch you. O Nanak, the devotees are forever in bliss. Listening—pain and sin are erased. || 8 || Listening—Shiva, Brahma and Indra [Hindu deities]. Listening—even foul-mouthed people praise Him. Listening—the technology of Yoga [deep meditation] and the secrets of the body. Listening—the Shaastras [precepts], the Simritees [secondary Hindu scriptures] and the Vedas. O Nanak, the devotees are forever in bliss.

http://www.gurbanifiles.org/translations/English%20Translation%20of%20Siri%20Guru%20Granth%20Sahib.pdf

1. According to the opening words, how should a Sikh worship using the Sikh scriptures? ____________

______________________________

2. When should this worship begin? ______________________________

______________________________

3. According to this text, what is the source of wisdom, and how is this related to Hinduism? ____

______________________________

4. To what is this statement referring? "By the karma of past actions, the robe of this physical body is obtained. By His Grace, the Gate of Liberation is found." ______________________________

______________________________

5. What Hindu gods are mentioned in this passage? ______________________________

______________________________

Name ____________________

## Chapter Review

### Matching

**Choose the best answer and place the letter in the blank beside the corresponding statement or description.**

| | | |
|---|---|---|
| A. Akbar | F. Genghis Khan | K. Marco Polo |
| B. Aurangzeb | G. Ivan I | L. Shah Jahan |
| C. Babur | H. Ivan III | M. Sunni Ali |
| D. Batu Khan | I. Kublai Khan | N. Tamerlane |
| E. Cambaluc | J. Mansa Musa | O. Temujin |

_____ 1. Title meaning "universal ruler"

_____ 2. Established the Mughal dynasty

_____ 3. Became the leader of his tribe at age thirteen and gradually united all the Mongol tribes

_____ 4. During his rule Moscow was freed from Mongol domination.

_____ 5. Interacted with other religions and concluded that Islam did not possess exclusive truth

_____ 6. Famous ruler of Mali who made an elaborate pilgrimage to Mecca

_____ 7. Led the Mongols into Europe

_____ 8. His conquests reached from India to Asia Minor, but his empire collapsed shortly after his death.

_____ 9. Established the first foreign dynasty to rule all China

_____ 10. Dedicated Muslim who attempted to seize control of all India

### Short Answer

**Write the correct term for each statement in the provided blank.**

11. Adopted an antiforeigner spirit that led to the closing of China to outside influences for hundreds of years

____________________

12. European name for invaders of Hungary and Poland ____________________

13. Language of the East African city-states ____________________

14. African kingdom that fell to Islamic jihad ____________________

*(continued on next page)*

15. City that was described as "one of the most beautiful and well-constructed towns in the world" ______

16. Religion that sought to maintain control over the "Five Thieves"—lust, rage, greed, attachment, and conceit ______

17. Name of the first of five successive Muslim dynasties in India ______

18. The Mongol dynasty in China ______

19. Mausoleum that became a stunning example of Mughal architecture ______

20. Name of the Mongol empire in India ______

21. Capital of Mali that became an important center of trade ______

22. Name for the strongest Mongol state in Western Asia ______

23. Perhaps the most important forest kingdom in western Africa ______

24. Used the promotion of Hinduism to expand the territory under their control ______

25. Overthrew the Mali Empire ______

Name ____________________

# Columbus's First Voyage

**Answer the questions below after reading the following excerpts from two of Columbus's letters.**

Because, O most Christian, and very high, very excellent, and puissant [powerful] Princes, King and Queen [Ferdinand and Isabella] of the Spains and of the islands of the Sea, our Lords, in this present year of 1492, after your Highnesses had given an end to the war with the Moors who reigned in Europe, and had finished it in the very great city of Granada, where in this present year, on the second day of the month of January, by force of arms, I saw the royal banners of your Highnesses placed on the towers of Alfambra [Alhambra, a Muslim stronghold], which is the fortress of that city, and I saw the Moorish King come forth from the gates of the city and kiss the royal hands of your Highnesses, and of the Prince my Lord, and presently in that same month, acting on the information that I had given to your Highnesses touching the lands of India, and respecting a Prince who is called Gran Can, which means in our language King of Kings, how he and his ancestors had sent to Rome many times to ask for learned men of our holy faith to teach him, and how the Holy Father [the pope] had never complied, insomuch that many people believing in idolatries were lost by receiving doctrine of perdition: YOUR HIGHNESSES, as Catholic Christians and Princes who love the holy Christian faith, and the propagation of it, and who are enemies to the sect of Mahoma [Muhammad] and to all idolatries and heresies, resolved to send me, Cristóbal Colon [Christopher Columbus], to the said parts of India to see the said princes, and the cities and lands, and their disposition, with a view that they might be converted to our holy faith; and ordered that I should not go by land to the eastward, as had been customary, but that I should go by way of the west, whither up to this day, we do not know for certain that any one has gone.

Thus, after having turned out all the Jews from all your kingdoms and lordships, in the same month of January, your Highnesses gave orders to me that with a sufficient fleet I should go to the said parts of India, and for this they made great concessions to me, and ennobled me, so that henceforward I should be called Don, and should be Chief Admiral of the Ocean Sea, perpetual Viceroy and Governor of all the islands and continents that I should discover and gain, and that I might hereafter discover and gain in the Ocean Sea, and that my eldest son should succeed, and so on from generation to generation for ever.

I left the city of Granada on the 12th day of May, in the same year of 1492, being Saturday, and came to the town of Palos, which is a seaport; where I equipped three vessels well suited for such service; and departed from that port, well supplied with provisions and with many sailors, on the 3d day of August of the same year.

1. What military event in 1492 enabled Ferdinand and Isabella to send Columbus out to explore?

   ____________________

2. According to Columbus, why did these rulers send him to find a route to India? ____________________

   ____________________

   ____________________

3. Rather than travel east to India, in what direction was Columbus instructed to travel? Would he travel by land or by sea? ____________________

*(continued on next page)*

Most High and Powerful Lords: In obedience to what your Highnesses command me, I shall state what occurs to me for the peopling and management of the Spanish Island [Hispaniola] and of all others, whether already discovered or hereafter to be discovered, submitting myself, however, to any better opinion.

In the first place, in regard to the Spanish Island: that there should go there settlers up to the number of two thousand who may want to go so as to render the possession of the country safer and cause it to be more profitable and helpful in the intercourse and traffic with the neighboring islands. . . .

Likewise, in order to secure the better and prompter settlement of the said island, that the privilege of getting gold be granted exclusively to those who actually settle and build dwelling-houses in the settlement where they may be, in order that all may live close to each other and more safely. . . .

Likewise, that a church be built, and that priests or friars be sent there for the administration of the sacraments, and for divine worship and the conversion of the Indians.

Likewise, that no settler be allowed to go and gather gold unless with a permit from the governor or mayor of the town in which he lives, to be given only upon his promising under oath to return to the place of his residence and faithfully report all the gold which he may have gathered, this to be done once a month, or once a week, as the time may be assigned to him, the said report to be entered on the proper registry by the clerk of the town in the presence of the mayor, and if so deemed advisable, in the presence of a friar or priest selected for the purpose.

Likewise, that all the gold so gathered be melted forthwith, and stamped with such a stamp as the town may have devised and selected, and that it be weighed and that the share of that gold which belongs to your Highnesses be given and delivered to the mayor of the town, the proper record thereof being made by the clerk and by the priest or friar, so that it may not pass through only one hand and may so render the concealing of the truth impossible. . . .

Likewise, that one per cent. of all the gold gathered be set apart and appropriated for building churches, and providing for their proper furnishing and ornamentation, and to the support of the priests or friars having them in their charge, and, if so deemed advisable, for the payment of some compensation to the mayors and clerks of the respective towns, so as to cause them to fulfil their duties faithfully, and that the balance be delivered to the governor and treasurer sent there by your Highnesses.

Edward Gaylord Bourne, ed. *Original Narratives of the Voyages of Columbus*, in *The Northmen: Columbus and Cabot, 985–1503*. Original Narratives of Early American History (New York: Charles Scribner's Sons, 1906), 89–90, 273–75.

4. According to Columbus, what were his chief goals for exploration? ______________________

______________________

______________________

5. Evaluate Columbus's goals. ______________________

______________________

______________________

______________________

Name ______________________

# Aztec Religion

**Answer the questions at the end after reading the following excerpt from the writings of Hernando Cortés.**

There are, in all districts of this great city [Tenochtitlán], many temples or houses for [the Aztecs'] idols. They are all very beautiful buildings, and in the important ones there are priests of their sect who live there permanently; and, in addition to the houses for the idols, they also have very good lodgings. All these priests dress in black and never comb their hair from the time they enter the priesthood until they leave; and all the sons of the persons of high rank, both the lords and honored citizens also, enter the priesthood and wear the habit from the age of seven or eight years until they are taken away to be married; this occurs more among the first-born sons, who are to inherit, than among the others. They abstain from eating things, and more at some times of the year than at others; and no woman is granted entry nor permitted inside these places of worship.

Amongst these temples there is one, the principal one [the Temple Major], whose great size and magnificence no human tongue could describe, for it is so large that within the precincts, which are surrounded by a very high wall, a town of some five hundred inhabitants could easily be built. All round inside this wall there are very elegant quarters with very large rooms and corridors where their priests live. There are as many as forty towers, all of which are so high that in the case of the largest there are fifty steps leading up to the main part of it; and the most important of these towers is higher than that of the cathedral of Seville. They are so well constructed in both their stone and woodwork that there can be none better in any place, for all the stonework inside the chapels where they keep their idols is in high relief, with figures and little houses, and the woodwork is likewise of relief and painted with monsters and other figures and designs. All these towers are burial places of chiefs, and the chapels therein are each dedicated to the idol which he venerated.

There are three rooms within this great temple for the principal idols, which are of remarkable size and stature and decorated with many designs and sculptures, both in stone and in wood. Within these rooms are other chapels, and the doors to them are very small. Inside there is no light whatsoever; there only some of the priests may enter, for inside are the sculptured figures of the idols, although, as I have said, there are also many outside.

The most important of these idols, and the ones in whom they have most faith, I had taken from their places and thrown down the steps; and I had those chapels where they were cleaned, for they were full of the blood of sacrifices; and I had images of Our Lady [Mary] and of other saints put there, which caused Mutezuma [Montezuma] and the other natives some sorrow. First they asked me not to do it, for when the communities learnt of it they would rise against me, for they believed that those idols gave them all their worldly goods, and that if they were allowed to be ill treated, they would become angry and give them nothing and take the fruit from the earth leaving the people to die of hunger. . . .

. . . Mutezuma and many of the chieftains of the city were with me until the idols were removed, the chapel cleaned and the images set up, and I urged them not to sacrifice living creatures to the idols, as they were accustomed, for, as well as being most abhorrent to God, Your Sacred Majesty's laws forbade it and ordered that he who kills shall be killed. And from then on they ceased to do it, and in all the time I stayed in that city I did not see a living creature killed or sacrificed.

Anthony Pagden, trans. and ed. *Hernán Cortés: Letters from Mexico*, rev. ed. (New Haven: Yale Univ. Press, 1986), 105–7. © 1971 Anthony Pagden. Used by permission.

*(continued on next page)*

The figures of the idols in which these people believe are very much larger than the body of a big man. They are made of dough from all the seeds and vegetables which they eat, ground and mixed together, and bound with the blood of human hearts which those priests tear out while still beating. And also after they are made they offer them more hearts and anoint their faces with the blood. Everything has an idol dedicated to it, in the same manner as the pagans who in antiquity honored their gods. So they have an idol whose favor they ask in war and another for agriculture; and likewise for each thing they wish to be done well they have an idol which they honor and serve.

1. Briefly describe the Aztec temples in Tenochtitlán. __________

2. What did Cortés do with the idols in these temples? __________

3. Briefly describe the appearance of the idols and the materials used to make them. __________

4. Which of Cortés's statements indicate that the Aztecs sacrificed animals and humans in their worship?

5. Why did the Aztecs have many gods? __________

6. Evaluate Aztec religion in light of Leviticus 20:1–5 and Isaiah 44:6–20. __________

Name ____________________

## Devastation of the Indies (1542)

**Answer the questions at the end after reading the following excerpt from the writings of Bartolemé de Las Casas.**

The Indies were discovered in the year one thousand four hundred and ninety-two. In the following year a great many Spaniards went there with the intention of settling the land. Thus, forty-nine years have passed since the first settlers penetrated the land, the first so claimed being the large and most happy isle called Hispaniola, which is six hundred leagues in circumference. Around it in all directions are many other islands, some very big, others very small, and all of them were, as we saw with our own eyes, densely populated with native peoples called Indians. . . . And of all the infinite universe of humanity, these people are the most guileless, the most devoid of wickedness and duplicity, the most obedient and faithful to their native masters and to the Spanish [Spaniards] whom they serve. They are by nature the most humble, patient, and peaceable, holding no grudges, free from embroilments, neither excitable nor quarrelsome. These people are the most devoid of rancors, hatreds, or desire for vengeance of any people in the world. And because they are so weak and complaisant, they are less able to endure heavy labor and soon die of no matter what malady. The sons of nobles among us, brought up in the enjoyments of life's refinements, are no more delicate than are these Indians, even those among them who are of the lowest rank of laborers. They are also poor people, for they not only possess little but have no desire to possess worldly goods. . . .

Yet into this sheepfold, into this land of meek outcasts there came some Spaniards who immediately behaved like ravening wild beasts, wolves, tigers, or lions that had been starved for many days. And Spaniards have behaved in no other way during the past forty years, down to the present time, for they are still acting like ravening beasts, killing, terrorizing, afflicting, torturing, and destroying the native peoples, doing all this with the strangest and most varied new methods of cruelty, never seen or heard of before, and to such a degree that this Island of Hispaniola once so populous (having a population that I estimated to be more than three million), has now a population of barely two hundred persons.

The island of Cuba is nearly as long as the distance between Valladolid and Rome; it is now almost completely depopulated. San Juan [Puerto Rico] and Jamaica are two of the largest, most productive and attractive islands; both are now deserted and devastated. . . . All the people were slain or died after being taken into captivity and brought to the Island of Hispaniola to be sold as slaves. . . . More than thirty other islands in the vicinity of San Juan are for the most part and for the same reason depopulated, and the land laid waste. On these islands I estimate there are 2,100 leagues of land that have been ruined and depopulated, empty of people. . . .

The common ways mainly employed by the Spaniards who call themselves Christian and who have gone there to [exterminate] those pitiful nations and wipe them off the earth is by unjustly waging cruel and bloody wars. Then, when they have slain all those who fought for their lives or to escape the tortures they would have to endure, that is to say, when they have slain all the native rulers and young men (since the Spaniards usually spare only the women and children, who are subjected to the hardest and bitterest servitude ever suffered by man or beast), they enslave any survivors. With these infernal methods of tyranny they debase and weaken countless numbers of those pitiful Indian nations.

Their reason for killing and destroying such an infinite number of souls is that the [Spaniards] have an ultimate aim, which is to acquire gold, and to swell themselves with riches in a very brief time and thus rise to a high estate disproportionate to their merits. It should be kept in mind that their insatiable greed and ambition, the greatest ever seen in the world, is the cause of their villainies. And also, those lands are so rich and felicitous, the native peoples so

*(continued on next page)*

meek and patient, so easy to subject, that our Spaniards have no more consideration for them than beasts. And I say this from my own knowledge of the acts I witnessed. . . .

After the wars and the killings had ended, when usually there survived only some boys, some women, and children, these survivors were distributed among the [Spaniards] to be slaves. The *repartimiento* or distribution was made according to the rank and importance of the [Spaniard] to whom the Indians were allocated, one of them being given thirty, another forty, still another, one or two hundred, and besides the rank of the [Spaniard] there was also to be considered in what favor he stood with the tyrant they called Governor. The pretext was that these allocated Indians were to be instructed in the articles of the Christian Faith. As if those [Spaniards] who were as a rule foolish and cruel and greedy and vicious could be caretakers of souls! And the care they took was to send the men to the mines to dig for gold, which is intolerable labor, and to send the women into the fields of the big ranches to hoe and till the land, work suitable for strong men. Nor to either the men or the women did they give any food except herbs and legumes, things of little substance. The milk in the breasts of the women with infants dried up and thus in a short while the infants perished. And since men and women were separated, there could be no marital relations. And the men died in the mines and the women died on the ranches from the same causes, exhaustion and hunger. And thus was depopulated [the islands] which had been densely populated.

Bartolemé de Las Casas. *Brief Account of the Devastation of the Indies.* Translated by Herma Briffault. New York: Seabury, 1974.

1. How did Las Casas describe the native population of the "Indies"? ______________________

______________________________________________________________

______________________________________________________________

2. To what predators did Las Casas compare the Spanish? ______________________

3. What led to the rapid depopulation of these islands? ______________________

______________________________________________________________

______________________________________________________________

4. What did the Spanish call themselves? Did Las Casas consider this claim to be legitimate?

______________________________________________________________

5. According to Las Casas, why did the Spanish kill so many Indians? ______________________

______________________________________________________________

______________________________________________________________

6. What did the Spanish do with any Indians who survived the Spanish attacks? ______________

______________________________________________________________

7. What biblical principles did the Spanish violate in their treatment of the Indian populations?

______________________________________________________________

______________________________________________________________

______________________________________________________________

______________________________________________________________

Name ______________________________

## Chapter Review

### Matching

**Choose the best answer and place the letter in the blank beside the corresponding description.**

A. Vasco Núñez de Balboa
B. Christopher Columbus
C. Francisco Vásquez de Coronado
D. Hernando Cortés
E. Vasco da Gama
F. Hernando de Soto
G. Bartolomeu Dias
H. Prester John
I. Prince Henry
J. Bartolomé de Las Casas
K. Ferdinand Magellan
L. Francisco Pizarro
M. Marco Polo

_____ 1. Reached Africa's southern tip; called it "the Cape of Storms"

_____ 2. Conquistador in Mexico; defeated the Aztecs

_____ 3. Catholic friar who opposed abuse of Indians in the Americas

_____ 4. Rumored African Christian king

_____ 5. Traveled through the Isthmus of Panama to the Pacific Ocean; named the "South Sea"

_____ 6. Conquistador who founded Lima, Peru, and conquered the Incas

_____ 7. First European to reach India by sailing around Africa

_____ 8. Left Spain in 1492 and sailed west to reach China and Japan

_____ 9. Sought golden cities in Florida

_____ 10. Traveled in the American West to find seven cities of gold

### Short Answer

**Write the correct answer to each question in the provided blank.**

11. What naval force did the English defeat in 1588? ______________________________

12. How did Jacques Cartier contribute to French exploration? ______________________________

______________________________

______________________________

13. What caused scurvy, a disease that many sailors suffered from? ______________________________

14. Under what economic system did European explorers find wealth in the New World to benefit the European mother country? ______________________________

*(continued on next page)*

15. What type of company became common in the Age of Exploration and paid investors dividends?

_______________________________________________

16. What term denotes a proposed business venture posted in a public place? _______________

17. What was the caravel? _______________________________________________

_______________________________________________

18. How did Prince Henry the Navigator contribute to Portuguese exploration? _______________

_______________________________________________

19. For what purpose were the astrolabe, quadrant, and cross-staff used in sailing? _______________

_______________________________________________

20. What term denotes a single naval trip that encompasses the entire globe? _______________

## Matching

**Choose the best answer and place the letter in the blank beside the corresponding description.**

| | | |
|---|---|---|
| A. Afonso de Albuquerque | E. Jacques Cartier | I. Montezuma |
| B. Atahualpa | F. Samuel de Champlain | J. John Smith |
| C. John Cabot | G. Henry Hudson | K. Francis Xavier |
| D. Pedro Cabral | H. Jacques Marquette | |

_____ 21. "Father of New France" and founder of Quebec

_____ 22. Explorer for the Dutch; traveled in what is today New York

_____ 23. English explorer who helped settlers build a village called Jamestown in 1607

_____ 24. Viceroy who organized Portuguese plantations by trade routes

_____ 25. Italian who led England's first expedition to North America

_____ 26. French Jesuit missionary-explorer along the Mississippi River

_____ 27. Jesuit missionary to Japan

_____ 28. Ruler of the Incas when the invading Spanish arrived

_____ 29. Established a Portuguese trading post in India

_____ 30. Ruler of the Aztecs when invading conquistadors arrived

Name ______________________

## The Edict of Nantes

**Answer the questions below after reading the following excerpt from the Edict of Nantes issued by the French king, Henry IV, in 1598.**

We forbid all our subjects, of whatever estate or quality they may be, from renewing the memory of those things, attacking, resenting, injuring, or provoking one another by reproaches for what has occurred, for whatever cause and pretext there may be; from disputing these things, contesting, quarreling, or outraging or offending by word or deed; but they shall restrain themselves and live peaceably together like brothers, friends, and common citizens, under the penalty of being punished as infractors of the peace and disturbers of the public repose. We command that the Roman, Catholic, and Apostolic religion shall be reinstated and re-established in all places and parts of this our kingdom and the lands under our obedience where its exercise has been interrupted, that it may be peaceably and freely exercised without any disturbance or impediment. Expressly forbidding every person of whatever estate, quality, or condition they may be, under the above-mentioned penalties, from troubling, disturbing, or molesting ecclesiastics in the celebration of divine service, in the enjoyment and collection of the tithes, fruits, and revenues of their benefices, and all other rights and duties belonging to them. . . . And to leave no occasion for troubles and differences among our subjects, we have permitted and do permit those of the so-called Reformed religion to live and dwell in all cities and places of this our kingdom and the lands of our obedience, without being questioned, vexed, or molested, nor constrained to do anything with regard to religion contrary to their conscience, nor on account of it to be searched out in their houses and the places where they wish to dwell, bearing themselves otherwise according to what is in our present edict.

http://www.huguenot-museum-germany.com/huguenots/edicts/01-edict-nantes-1598-english.pdf

1. How were Frenchmen instructed to live together? ______________________

______________________

2. What would happen to those that did not abide by the Edict of Nantes? ______________________

______________________

3. What type of freedom did the Edict provide? ______________________

4. What two religions are mentioned in the Edict? ______________________

______________________

5. Do you think the Edict of Nantes was good for France? Why or why not? ______________________

______________________

______________________

______________________

Name ______________________

## Europe (1648)

**Locate each term on the map and place the corresponding number in the appropriate blank.**

| | | |
|---|---|---|
| ______ Atlantic Ocean | ______ Great Britain | ______ Portugal |
| ______ Austria | ______ France | ______ Prussia |
| ______ Black Sea | ______ Hungary | ______ Rome |
| ______ Bohemia | ______ Mediterranean Sea | ______ Russia |
| ______ Brandenburg | ______ Ottoman Empire | ______ Spain |
| ______ Danube River | ______ Papal States | ______ Sweden |
| ______ Denmark | ______ Poland | |

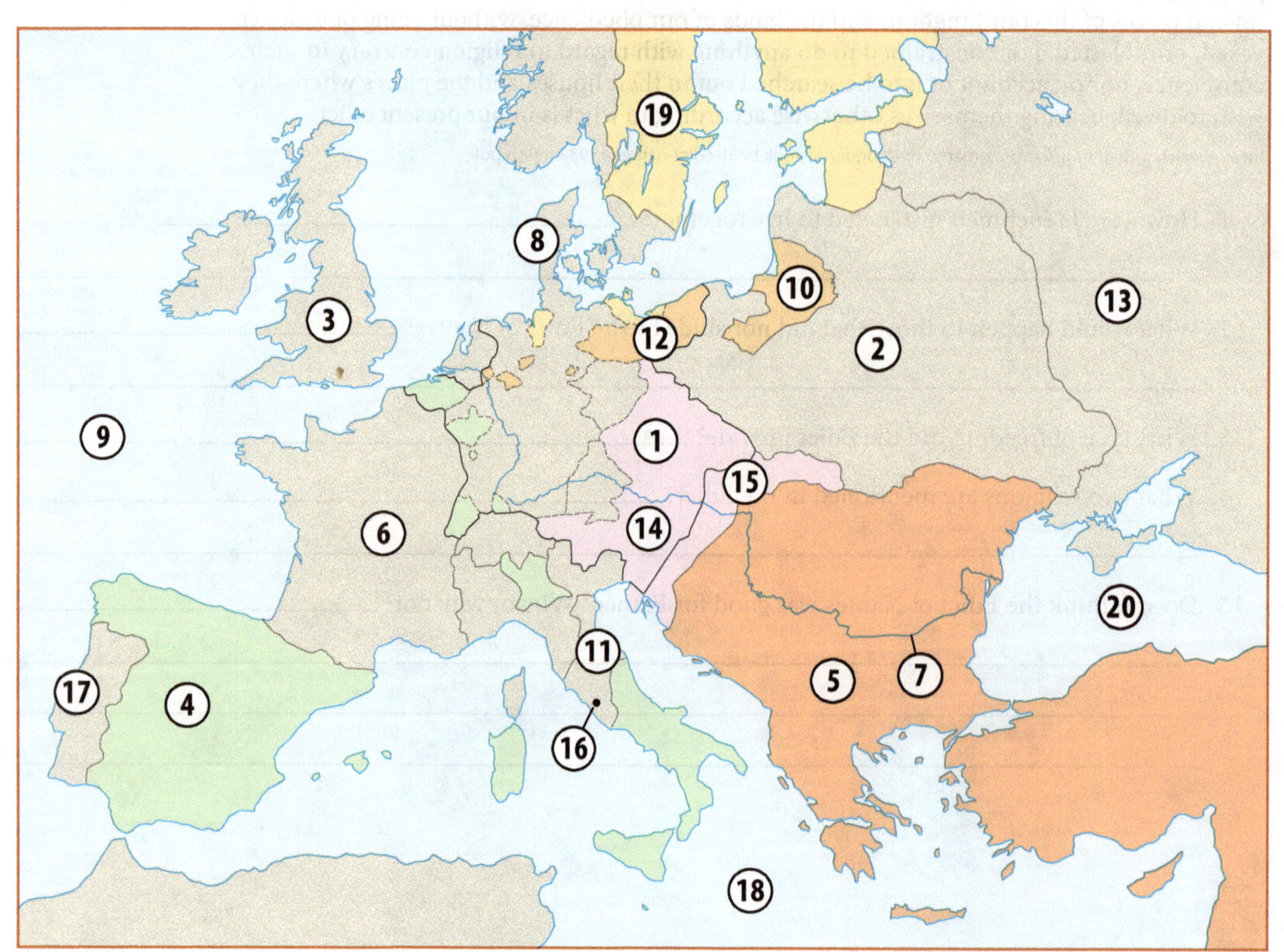

Name ______________________

# Revocation of the Edict of Nantes

**Answer the questions at the end after reading the following excerpt from the writings of Louis de Rouvroy.**

The revocation of the edict of Nantes, without the slightest pretext or necessity, and the various proscriptions [bans] that followed it, were the fruits of a frightful plot . . . which depopulated a quarter of the realm, ruined its commerce, weakened it in every direction, gave it up for a long time to the public and avowed pillage of the dragoons, authorized torments and punishments by which so many innocent people of both sexes were killed by thousands; ruined a numerous class; tore in pieces a world of families; armed relatives against relatives, so as to seize their property and leave them to die of hunger; banished our manufactures to foreign lands, made those lands flourish and overflow at the expense of France, and enabled them to build new cities; gave to the world the spectacle of a prodigious [large] population proscribed [banned], stripped, fugitive, wandering, without crime, and seeking shelter far from its country; sent to the galleys, nobles, rich old men, people much esteemed for their piety, learning, and virtue, people well off, weak, delicate, and solely on account of religion; in fact, to heap up the measure of horror, filled all the realm with perjury and sacrilege, in the midst of the echoed cries of these unfortunate victims of error, while so many others sacrificed their conscience to their wealth and their repose, and purchased both by simulated abjuration [pretended recanting of their Huguenot beliefs], from which without pause they were dragged to adore what they did not believe in, and to receive the divine body of the Saint of Saints [during mass] while remaining persuaded that they were only eating bread which they ought to abhor! Such was the general abomination born of flattery and cruelty. From torture to abjuration, and from that to the communion, there was often only twenty-four hours' distance; and executioners were the conductors of the converts and their witnesses. Those who in the end appeared to have been reconciled, more at leisure did not fail by their flight or their behavior, to contradict their pretended conversion.

The King received from all sides news and details of these persecutions and of these conversions. It was by thousands that those who had abjured and taken the communion were counted; ten thousand in one place; six thousand in another,—all at once and instantly. The King congratulated himself on his power and his piety. He believed himself to have renewed the days of the preaching of the Apostles, and attributed to himself all the honor. The bishops wrote panegyrics [flattering statements] of him, the Jesuits made the pulpit resound with his praises. All France was filled with horror and confusion; and yet there never was so much triumph and joy—never such profusion of laudations! The monarch doubted not of the sincerity of this crowd of conversions; the converters took good care to persuade him of it and beatify him beforehand. He swallowed their poison in long draughts. He had never yet believed himself so great in the eyes of man, or so advanced in the eyes of God, in the reparation of his sins and of the scandals of his life. He heard nothing but eulogies [praises], while the good and true Catholics and the true bishops groaned in spirit to see the orthodox act toward error and heretics as heretical tyrants and heathens had acted against the truth, the confessors, and the martyrs. They could not, above all, endure this immensity of perjury and sacrilege. They bitterly lamented the durable and irremediable odium [long-lasting and irreversible disgust] that detestable measure cast upon the true religion, while our neighbors, exulting to see us thus weaken and destroy ourselves, profited by our madness, and built designs upon the hatred we should draw upon ourselves from all the Protestant Powers.

But to these speaking truths, the King was inaccessible. Even the conduct of Rome in this matter could not open his eyes. That Court which formerly had not been ashamed to extol the [Saint Bartholomew's Day Massacre], to thank God for it by public processions, to employ the

*(continued on next page)*

greatest masters to paint this execrable [disgusting] action in the Vatican,—Rome, I say, would not give the slightest approbation [approval] to this onslaught on the Huguenots.

Duke of Saint-Simon [Louis de Rouvroy]. *Memoirs of Louis XIV and the Regency*, trans. Bayle St. John, vol. 3 (Akron: M. Walter Dunne, 1901), 13–15.

1. According to Rouvroy, what effect did the revocation of the Edict of Nantes have on French society?

2. How did the revocation strengthen France's enemies?

3. What were the various responses to the revocation among French Catholics?

4. Besides Louis's Catholic beliefs and his desire for religious unification, what other reason does Rouvroy give for the king's decision to revoke the edict?

5. Following the persecution of the Huguenots, what actions stirred Louis's already-inflated pride?

6. Although Louis evidently assumed that he had acted in accord with the Church of Rome by allowing this persecution, how, according to Rouvroy, did Rome react?

Name ______________________

# Louis XIV

**Answer the questions below after reading the following excerpts from the writings of Louis de Rouvroy.**

Louis XIV was made for a brilliant Court. In the midst of other men, his figure, his courage, his grace, his beauty, his grand mien [appearance], even the tone of his voice and the majestic and natural charm of all his person, distinguished him till his death as the King Bee, and showed that if he had only been born a simple private gentleman, he would equally have excelled in *fêtes* [parties], pleasures, and gallantry, and would have had the greatest success in love. The intrigues and adventures which early in life he had been engaged in—when the Comtesse de Soissons lodged at the Tuileries [a palace in Paris], as superintendent of the Queen's household, and was the center figure of the Court group—had exercised an unfortunate influence upon him: he received those impressions with which he could never after successfully struggle. From this time, intellect, education, nobility of sentiment, and high principle, in others, became objects of suspicion to him, and soon of hatred. The more he advanced in years, the more this sentiment was confirmed in him. He wished to reign by himself. His jealousy on this point unceasingly became weakness. He reigned, indeed, in little things; the great he could never reach: even in the former, too, he was often governed. The superior ability of his early ministers and his early generals soon wearied him. He liked nobody to be in any way superior to him. Thus he chose his ministers, not for their knowledge, but for their ignorance; not for their capacity [ability], but for their want [lack] of it. He liked to form them, as he said; liked to teach them even the most trifling things. It was the same with his generals. He took credit to himself for instructing them; wished it to be thought that from his cabinet he commanded and directed all his armies. Naturally fond of trifles, he unceasingly occupied himself with the most petty details of his troops, his household, his mansions; would even instruct his cooks, who received, like novices, lessons they had known by heart for years. This vanity, this unmeasured and unreasonable love of admiration, was his ruin. His ministers, his generals, his mistresses, his courtiers, soon perceived his weakness. They praised him with emulation and spoiled him. Praises, or to say truth, flattery, pleased him to such an extent, that the coarsest was well received, the vilest even better relished. It was the sole means by which you could approach him.

1. What kind of people did Louis XIV hate and treat with suspicion? ______________________

______________________

2. Why did he choose ministers who lacked knowledge? ______________________

______________________

3. What was the only way a person could approach Louis and gain his favor? ______________________

______________________

He early showed a disinclination [dislike] for Paris. The troubles that had taken place there during the minority [Louis's youth] made him regard the place as dangerous; he wished, too, to render himself venerable [esteemed] by hiding himself from the eyes of the multitude; all these considerations fixed him at St. Germains soon after the death of the Queen, his mother. It was to that place he began to attract the world by *fêtes* and gallantries, and by making it felt that he wished to be often seen.

His love for Madame de la Vallière, which was at first kept secret, occasioned frequent excursions to Versailles, then a little card castle, which had been built by Louis XIII—annoyed, and to

*(continued on next page)*

his suite still more so, at being frequently obliged to sleep in a wretched inn there, after he had been out hunting in the forest of Saint Leger. . . .

These excursions of Louis XIV by degrees gave birth to those immense buildings he erected at Versailles; and their convenience for a numerous court, so different from the apartments at St. Germains, led him to take up his abode there entirely shortly after the death of the Queen. He built an infinite number of apartments, which were asked for by those who wished to pay their court to him; whereas at St. Germains nearly everybody was obliged to lodge in the town, and the few who found accommodation at the *château* were strangely inconvenienced. . . .

He was exceedingly jealous of the attention paid him. Not only did he notice the presence of the most distinguished courtiers, but those of inferior degree also. He looked to the right and to the left, not only upon rising but upon going to bed, at his meals, in passing through his apartments, or his gardens of Versailles, where alone the courtiers were allowed to follow him; he saw and noticed everybody; not one escaped him, not even those who hoped to remain unnoticed. He marked well all absentees from the Court, found out the reason of their absence, and never lost an opportunity of acting toward them as the occasion might seem to justify. . . . When their names were in any way mentioned, "I do not know them," the King would reply haughtily. Those who presented themselves but seldom were thus characterized: "They are people I never see"; these decrees were irrevocable.

Duke of Saint-Simon [Louis de Rouvroy]. *Memoirs of Louis XIV and the Regency*, trans. Bayle St. John, vol. 2 (Akron: M. Walter Dunne, 1901), 359–60, 365–66.

4. What French city did Louis dislike? Why? ______________________________

______________________________________________________________

5. How did Louis entertain his many visitors at court? ______________________

______________________________________________________________

6. How did Louis respond to those in his court who did not pay him enough attention or spend enough time at Versailles? ______________________________

______________________________________________________________

______________________________________________________________

Name ______________________

# Peter the Great and Westernization

**Answer the questions below after reading the following excerpts from the writings of Jean Rousset de Missy.**

The Tsar [Peter the Great] labored at the reform of fashions, or, more properly speaking, of dress. Until that time the Russians had always worn long beards, which they cherished and preserved with much care. . . . With these long beards they wore the hair very short, except the ecclesiastics, who, to distinguish themselves, wore it very long. The Tsar, in order to reform that custom, ordered that gentlemen, merchants, and other subjects, except priests and peasants, should each pay a tax of one hundred rubles a year if they wished to keep their beards; the commoners had to pay one kopeck each. Officials were stationed at the gates of the towns to collect that tax, which the Russians regarded as an enormous sin on the part of the Tsar and as a thing which tended to the abolition of their religion. . . . [T]here were many old Russians who, after having their beards shaved off, saved them preciously, in order to have them placed in their coffins, fearing that they would not be allowed to enter heaven without their beards. As for the young men, they followed the new custom with the more readiness, as it made them appear more agreeable to the fair sex.

1. How did Peter make the Russian men remain clean-shaven? ______________________

2. Why did some Russian men save their beards after they were cut off? ______________________

______________________

From the reform in beards we may pass to that of clothes. Their garments, like those of the Orientals, were very long, reaching to the heel. The Tsar issued an ordinance abolishing that costume, commanding all the boyars (nobles) and all those who had positions at the court to dress after the French fashion, and likewise to adorn their clothes with gold or silver according to their means. . . . As for the rest of the people, the following method was employed. A suit of clothes cut according to the new fashion was hung at the gate of the city, with a decree enjoining upon all except peasants to have their clothes made on this model, under penalty of being forced to kneel and have all that part of their garments which fell below the knee cut off, or pay two grives every time they entered the town with clothes in the old style. Since the guards at the gates executed their duty in curtailing the garments in a sportive spirit, the people were amused and readily abandoned their old dress, especially in Moscow and its environs, and in the towns which the Tsar oftenest visited. The dress of the women was changed, too. English hairdressing was substituted for the caps and bonnets hitherto worn; bodices, stays, and skirts, for the former undergarments.

James Harvey Robinson and Charles A. Beard. *Readings in Modern European History: A Collection of Extracts from the Sources Chosen with the Purpose of Illustrating Some of the Chief Phases of the Development of Europe During the Last Two Hundred Years*, vol. 1, *The Eighteenth Century: The French Revolution and the Napoleonic Period.* (Boston: Ginn, 1908), 61–63.

3. What standard of dress did Peter develop? How did he ensure its enforcement? ______________________

______________________

______________________

4. Did Peter successfully transform Russia into a Western society? (You may need to consult outside resources to fully answer this question.) ______________________

______________________

______________________

Name ____________________

# Chapter Review

## Complete the Statement

**Underline the term that accurately completes each of the following statements.**

1. The French and Indian War in America was called the (War of the Austrian Succession/ Seven Years' War) in Europe.
2. The Treaty of Utrecht ended the War of the (Spanish/Austrian) Succession.
3. The (Romanov/Habsburg) family were rulers of Austria and Spain.
4. The (Hohenzollern/Bourbon) family united the German states into one country.
5. The chief minister to Louis XIII was (Jules Mazarin/Cardinal Richelieu).

## Matching

**Choose the best answer and write the letter in the blank beside the corresponding description.**

| | | |
|---|---|---|
| A. Catherine II | F. Frederick II | K. Louis XV |
| B. Charles I | G. Henry IV | L. William Pitt |
| C. Charles II | H. James II | M. Maria Theresa |
| D. Frederick I | I. Joseph II | |
| E. Frederick William | J. Louis XIV | |

_____ 6. Called "the Great Elector"

_____ 7. Began absolutism in France after the French civil wars

_____ 8. Raised Austria's taxes and dissolved monasteries

_____ 9. Prussian ruler who earned the title "the Great"

_____ 10. Nearly bankrupted France with wars and extensive building programs

_____ 11. Reestablished the Stuart monarchy

_____ 12. Expelled from power in a move known as the Glorious Revolution

_____ 13. Acquired the title "King in Prussia" for future Prussian rulers

_____ 14. Protected by the Pragmatic Sanction; became ruler of Austria in 1740

_____ 15. Beheaded in 1649 after the end of England's civil war

*(continued on next page)*

## Essay

**Write the correct answer to each question.**

16. Both England and France underwent civil wars. Compare the results of these wars, including how they affected the power of each nation's king. ______

17. How was Louis XIV an outstanding example of absolutism? ______

## Short Answer

**Write the correct answer to each question.**

18. Why did some nations of Europe form the Grand Alliance? ______

19. What name was given to those who supported Parliament during the English Civil War? ______

20. Why did France, a Catholic country, help the Protestants during the Thirty Years' War? ______

21. Whom did Louis XIV appoint as his minister of finance? ______

22. What was the goal of the Great Northern War? ______

23. France lost all territory on the mainland of North America as a result of what agreement? ______

24. Which Russian ruler was a cruel tyrant and built the beautiful St. Basil's Cathedral? ______

25. Who led the forces of Parliament during the English Civil War? ______

Name ______________________

## *The Spirit of Laws*

In *Readings in Modern European History,* James Harvey Robinson and Charles A. Beard state, "Montesquieu believed that the English owed their liberty to the fact that the three powers of government, namely the legislative, the executive, and the judiciary, were not in the same hands, as in some of the European States. This theory of the three powers, and of the necessity of keeping them separate, exercised a great influence upon those who drew up the Constitution of the United States."

**Answer the questions at the end after reading the following excerpt from the writings of Montesquieu.**

In every government there are three sorts of powers. . . .

By virtue of the first [legislative], the prince, or magistrate, enacts temporary or perpetual laws, and amends or abrogates [ends] those that have been already enacted. By the second [executive], he makes peace or war, sends or receives embassies, establishes the public security, and provides against invasions. By the third [judicial], he punishes criminals, or determines the disputes that arise between individuals. . . .

The political liberty of the subject is a tranquillity of mind due to the assurance each person has of his safety. In order to have this liberty, it is requisite that the government be so constituted that no man need be afraid of another.

When the legislative and executive powers are united in the same person, or in the same body of magistrates, there can be no liberty, because apprehensions may arise lest the same monarch or senate should enact tyrannical laws, and then execute them in a tyrannical manner.

Again, there is no liberty if the judiciary power be not separated from the legislative and executive. Were it joined with the legislative, the life and liberty of the subject would be exposed to arbitrary control; for the judge would be then the legislator. Were it joined to the executive power, the judge might behave with violence and oppression.

There would be an end of everything, were the same man, or the same body, whether of the nobles or of the people, to exercise those three powers,—that of enacting laws, that of executing the public resolutions, and that of trying the suits of individuals.

Most kingdoms in Europe enjoy a moderate government, because the prince who is invested with the two first powers leaves the third to his subjects. In Turkey, where these three powers are united in the sultan's person, the subjects groan under the most dreadful oppression.

In the republics of Italy, where these three powers are united, there is less liberty than in our monarchies. Hence their government is obliged to have recourse to as violent methods for its support as even that of the Turks; witness the state inquisitors, and the lion's mouth into which every informer may at all hours throw his written accusations.

In what a situation must the poor subject be, under those republics! The same body of magistrates are possessed, as executors of the laws, of the whole power they have given themselves in the quality of legislators. They may plunder the State by their general determinations; and, as they have likewise the judiciary power in their hands, every private citizen may be ruined by their particular decisions.

The whole power is here united in one body; and though there is no external pomp that indicates a despotic sway, yet the people feel the effects of it every moment.

*(continued on next page)*

Hence it is that many of the princes of Europe, whose aim has been arbitrary power, have constantly set out with uniting in their own persons all the branches of magistracy and all the great offices of State.

James Harvey Robinson and Charles A. Beard. *Readings in Modern European History: A Collection of Extracts from the Sources Chosen with the Purpose of Illustrating Some of the Chief Phases of the Development of Europe During the Last Two Hundred Years*, vol. 1, *The Eighteenth Century: The French Revolution and the Napoleonic Period.* (Boston: Ginn, 1908), 191–92.

1. What are the responsibilities of the three separate branches of government? ______________

______________________________________________

______________________________________________

2. According to Montesquieu, how does separation of powers benefit citizens? Apply 1 Timothy 2:1–2 to the benefits derived from separation of powers. ______________

______________________________________________

______________________________________________

3. According to Montesquieu, what are the consequences of placing government responsibilities in a single person or in a political group? ______________

______________________________________________

4. What governments does Montesquieu use as illustrations of absolute rule by an individual or a group?

______________________________________________

5. Restate the final paragraph in your own words. ______________

______________________________________________

______________________________________________

Name ____________________

# Benjamin Franklin's View of Jesus

**Benjamin Franklin's correspondence provides a glimpse into the thinking of many who embraced the Enlightenment. Answer the questions at the end after reading the following excerpts from the correspondence of Ezra Stiles and Benjamin Franklin.**

From Ezra Stiles, President of Yale College, to B. Franklin. . . .

Yale College, 28 January, 1790.

Sir,

We have lately received Governor Yale's portrait from his family in London, and deposited it in the College Library, where is also deposited one of Governor Saltonstall's. I have also long wished that we might be honored with that of Dr. Franklin. In the course of your long life, you may probably have become possessed of several portraits of yourself. Shall I take too great a liberty in humbly asking a donation of one of them to Yale College? . . .

You know, Sir, that I am a Christian, and would to Heaven all others were such as I am, except my imperfections and deficiencies of moral character. As much as I know of Dr. Franklin, I have not an idea of his religious sentiments. I wish to know the opinion of my venerable friend concerning Jesus of Nazareth. He will not impute this to impertinence [bold disrespect] or improper curiosity, in one, who for so many years has continued to love, estimate, and reverence his abilities and literary character, with an ardor and affection bordering on adoration. If I have said too much, let the request be blotted out, and be no more; and yet I shall never cease to wish you that happy immortality, which I believe Jesus alone has purchased for the virtuous and truly good of every religious denomination in Christendom, and for those of every age, nation, and mythology, who reverence the Deity, are filled with integrity, righteousness, and benevolence. Wishing you every blessing, I am, dear Sir, your most obedient servant,

Ezra Stiles.

To Ezra Stiles. . . .

Philadelphia, 9 March, 1790.

Reverend and Dear Sir,

I received your kind letter of January 28th, and am glad you have at length received the portrait of Governor Yale from his family, and deposited it in the College Library. He was a great and good man, and had the merit of doing infinite service to your country by his munificence to that institution. The honor you propose doing me by placing mine in the same room with his, is much too great for my deserts; but you always had a partiality for me, and to that it must be ascribed [credited]. I am however too much obliged to Yale College, the first learned society that took notice of me and adorned me with its honors, to refuse a request that comes from it through so esteemed a friend. But I do not think any one of the portraits you mention, as in my possession, worthy of the situation and company you propose to place it in. You have an excellent artist lately arrived. If he will undertake to make one for you, I shall cheerfully pay the expense; but he must not delay setting about it, or I may slip through his fingers, for I am now in my eighty-fifth year, and very infirm [weak]. . . .

You desire to know something of my religion. It is the first time I have been questioned upon it. But I cannot take your curiosity amiss, and shall endeavour in a few words to gratify it. Here is my creed. I believe in one God, the creator of the universe. That he governs it by his Providence. That he ought to be worshipped. That the most acceptable service we render to him is doing good to his other children. That the soul of man is immortal, and will be treated with

*(continued on next page)*

justice in another life respecting its conduct in this. These I take to be the fundamental points in all sound religion, and I regard them as you do in whatever sect I meet with them.

As to Jesus of Nazareth, my opinion of whom you particularly desire, I think his system of morals and his religion, as he left them to us, the best the world ever saw or is like to see; but I apprehend it has received various corrupting changes, and I have, with most of the present Dissenters [Unitarians] in England, some doubts as to his Divinity; though it is a question I do not dogmatize upon, having never studied it, and think it needless to busy myself with it now, when I expect soon an opportunity of knowing the truth with less trouble. I see no harm, however, in its being believed, if that belief has the good consequence, as probably it has, of making his doctrines more respected and more observed; especially as I do not perceive, that the Supreme takes it amiss, by distinguishing the unbelievers in his government of the world with any peculiar marks of his displeasure.

I shall only add, respecting myself, that, having experienced the goodness of that Being in conducting me prosperously through a long life, I have no doubt of its continuance in the next, though without the smallest conceit of meriting such goodness. My sentiments on this head you will see in the copy of an old letter enclosed, which I wrote in answer to one from an old religionist [perhaps George Whitefield], whom I had relieved in a paralytic case by electricity, and who, being afraid I should grow proud upon it, sent me his serious though rather impertinent caution. I send you also the copy of another letter, which will show something of my disposition relating to religion. With great and sincere esteem and affection, I am, &c.

B. Franklin.

Benjamin Franklin. *The Works of Benjamin Franklin: Containing Several Political and Historical Tracts Not Included in Any Former Edition, and Many Letters Official and Private Not Hitherto Published*, vol. 10. (London: Benjamin Franklin Stevens, 1882), 421–25.

1. What two requests does Ezra Stiles make of Benjamin Franklin? ____________________

____________________

2. Why did Franklin consider himself obligated to grant Stiles's requests? ____________________

____________________

3. According to his own explanation, what were Franklin's religious beliefs? ____________________

____________________

____________________

____________________

4. Contrast Franklin's view of Jesus with the teachings of John 10:24–33 and Revelation 22:6. ____________________

____________________

____________________

____________________

____________________

Name ______________________

# Voltaire and the Bible

**Answer the questions at the end after reading the following excerpts from Voltaire's *The Philosophy of History.***

## From Chapter XXIII

[The Jewish] nation was composed of no more than a single family, who, in the space of two hundred years, produced a race of two millions of people; for to furnish six hundred thousand warriors, who according to Genesis came out of Egypt, they must have consisted of at least two millions of souls.

This multiplication, contrary to the order of nature, is one of those miracles which God deigned to operate in favor of the Jews.

It is in vain for a multitude of learned men to be astonished that the king of Egypt should have commanded the two midwives to destroy all the male children of the Hebrews,—that the king's daughter, who resided at Memphis, should go and bathe herself at a great distance from Memphis, in a branch of the Nile where nobody ever bathed on account of crocodiles; it is in vain for them to make objections to the age of eighty, which Moses had already attained, before he undertook to conduct a whole people out of bondage.

They dispute about the ten plagues of Egypt. They say that the magicians of the kingdom could not perform the same miracles as the messenger of God; and that if God gave them this power, he seems to have acted against himself. They suppose that as Moses had changed all the waters into blood, there remained no more water for the magicians to perform the same metamorphosis upon.

They ask how could Pharaoh pursue the Jews with a great number of horsemen, after all the horses had died, by the fifth and sixth plagues? They ask why six hundred warriors should run away when God was at their head, and they might have engaged the Egyptians to advantage, all the first born of whom being struck dead? They ask again, why God did not give fertile Egypt to his cherished people, instead of making them wander forty years in shocking deserts?

There is but a single answer to all these innumerable objections; and this answer is, God would have it so. The Church believes it, and we should believe it. It is in this respect that this history differs from others. Every people have their prodigies; but everything is prodigious with the Jewish nation; and it should have been so, as this people were conducted by God himself. It is plain that the history of God should not resemble that of man. Wherefore we shall not relate any of those supernatural facts, which should be mentioned only in the holy Scripture. Still less should we dare attempt their explanation. Let us only examine those few that may be subject to criticism.

## From Chapter XXIV

What can we think of an old man [i.e., Moses] of eighty years of age, who by himself alone undertakes to conduct a whole people over whom he had no authority? His arm cannot fight nor his tongue articulate. He is described as a cripple and a stammerer. He conducts his followers for forty years successively through horrid deserts. He wants to give them a settlement, but he gives them none. If we were to pursue his steps in the deserts of Sur, Sin, Horeb, Sinai, Pharan, and of Cades-Barnea, and observe his retrograde motions towards the very spot from which he set out, could we believe that he was a great commander? It is stated that he was at the head of six hundred thousand warriors, and he could neither provide clothing nor subsistence for them. God does everything. God remedies everything. He nourishes, He clothes the people, by working miracles. Moses, then, is nothing of himself, and his impotence shows that he can

*(continued on next page)*

be guided by nothing but the hand of the Almighty. We therefore consider him as a man, and not the minister of God. His personality, in this capacity, is an object of interesting enquiry.

He wants to go into the country of the Canaanites, on the west of the river Jordan, in the land of Jericho, which is in fact the only fruitful spot in the whole province; and instead of taking this road, he turns eastward, towards Esion-gaber and the Black Sea, a savage barren country on which not a single shrub or bush grows, and which is without a rivulet, without springs, save a few small wells of brackish and unwholesome water.

Voltaire. *Collected Works of Voltaire: The Complete Romances, Including "Candide," and "The Ignorant Philosopher"* (New York: Greystone, n.d.), 410–12.

1. Contrast Voltaire's sarcastic comment that the nation of Israel expanded to two million people over a two-hundred-year period with the accounts in Exodus 1:7 and 12:40. ______

2. Voltaire asks how Pharaoh could pursue the Jews with horsemen since Egypt's horses supposedly died in the fifth and sixth plagues. How does that assertion hold up when compared to Exodus 9:1–12, where those plagues are described? ______

3. Contrast Voltaire's description of Moses with the accounts in Exodus 3:10 and Deuteronomy 34:7.

______

4. How do Voltaire's comments illustrate Romans 1:18–22 and 2 Peter 3:14–16? ______

5. How does Voltaire's view of history reflect the ideas and attitudes of the Enlightenment? ______

Name ____________________

# Eyewitness Account of a Whitefield Meeting

**Answer the questions at the end after reading the following excerpt from the writings of Nathan Cole, who worked in Connecticut as a farmer and a carpenter.**

Now it pleased God to send Mr. Whitefield into this land; and my hearing of his preaching at Philadelphia, like one of the old apostles, and many thousands flocking to hear him preach the Gospel, and great numbers were converted to Christ, I felt the Spirit of God drawing me by conviction; I longed to see and hear him and wished he would come this way. I heard he was come to New York and the Jerseys and great multitudes flocking after him under great concern for their souls which brought on my concern more and more, hoping soon to see him; but next I heard he was at Long Island, then at Boston, and next at Northampton. Then on a sudden, in the morning about 8 or 9 of the clock there came a messenger and said Mr. Whitefield preached at Hartford and Wethersfield yesterday and is to preach at Middletown this morning at ten of the clock. I was in my field at work. I dropped my tool that I had in my hand and ran home to my wife, telling her to make ready quickly to go and hear Mr. Whitefield preach at Middletown, then ran to my pasture for my horse with all my might, fearing that I should be too late. Having my horse, I with my wife soon mounted the horse and went forward as fast as I thought the horse could bear; and when my horse got much out of breath, I would get down and put my wife on the saddle and bid her ride as fast as she could and not stop or slack for me except I bade her, and so I would run until I was much out of breath and then mount my horse again, and so I did several times to favour my horse. We improved every moment to get along as if we were fleeing for our lives, all the while fearing we should be too late to hear the sermon, for we had twelve miles to ride double in little more than an hour and we went round by the upper housen parish. And when we came within about half a mile or a mile of the road that comes down from Hartford, Wethersfield, and Stepney to Middletown, on high land I saw before me a cloud of fog arising. I first thought it came from the great river, but as I came nearer the road I heard a noise of horses' feet coming down the road, and this cloud was a cloud of dust made by the horses' feet. It arose some rods into the air over the tops of hills and trees; and when I came within about 20 rods of the road, I could see men and horses slipping along in the cloud like shadows, and as I drew nearer it seemed like a steady stream of horses and their riders, scarcely a horse more than his length behind another, all of a lather and foam with sweat, their breath rolling out of their nostrils every jump. Every horse seemed to go with all his might to carry his rider to hear news from heaven for the saving of souls. It made me tremble to see the sight, how the world was in a struggle. I found a vacancy between two horses to slip in mine and my wife said "[Oh,] our clothes will be all spoiled, see how they look," for they were so covered with dust that they looked almost all of a colour, coats, hats, shirts, and horse. We went down in the stream but heard no man speak a word all the way for 3 miles but every one pressing forward in great haste; and when we got to Middletown old meeting house, there was a great multitude, it was said to be 3 or 4,000 of people, assembled together. We dismounted and shook off our dust, and the ministers were then coming to the meeting house. I turned and looked towards the Great River and saw the ferry boats running swift backward and forward bringing over loads of people, and the oars rowed nimble and quick. Everything, men, horses, and boats seemed to be struggling for life. The land and banks over the river looked black with people and horses; all along the 12 miles I saw no man at work in his field, but all seemed to be gone. When I saw Mr. Whitefield come upon the scaffold, he looked almost angelical; a young, slim, slender youth, before some thousands of people with a bold undaunted countenance. [Whitefield was then in his midtwenties.] And my hearing how God was with him everywhere as he came along, it solemnized my mind and put me into a trembling fear before he began to preach; for he looked as if he was clothed with authority from the Great God, and a sweet solemn solemnity sat upon his

*(continued on next page)*

brow, and my hearing him preach gave me a heart wound. By God's blessing, my old foundation was broken up, and I saw that my righteousness would not save me.

Nathan Cole. "George Whitefield Comes to Middletown," in George Whitefield's Journals. (n.p.: Banner of Truth Trust, 1960), 561–62.

1. What was Nathan Cole doing when he heard that Whitefield would be preaching soon at a nearby town? What did Cole do when he received this information? ______________________________

______________________________

2. What difficulties did Cole and his wife face in trying to reach Middletown in time to hear the sermon?

______________________________

______________________________

______________________________

______________________________

3. How large was the crowd that assembled? ______________________________

______________________________

4. What physical descriptions of Whitefield does Cole record? ______________________________

______________________________

5. What realization overwhelmed and convicted Cole? ______________________________

______________________________

6. Are people today as eager to hear the gospel as the New England colonists are in this account? Explain your answer. ______________________________

______________________________

______________________________

______________________________

______________________________

Name ______________________________

# Chapter Review

## Matching

**Choose the best answer and place the letter in the blank beside the corresponding description.**

A. Johann Sebastian Bach
B. Francis Bacon
C. Copernicus
D. William Harvey
E. Edward Jenner
F. Johannes Kepler
G. John Locke
H. Isaac Newton
I. Paracelsus
J. Joseph Priestley
K. Baruch Spinoza
L. Andreas Vesalius
M. Voltaire

_____ 1. Found that the planets' orbits are elliptical

_____ 2. Unitarian minister and contributor to the field of science

_____ 3. Studied the heart and the circulation of the blood

_____ 4. Studied anatomy; wrote *On the Fabric of the Human Body*

_____ 5. French supporter of the Enlightenment and critic of society

_____ 6. Composer of music

_____ 7. Advocated pantheism

_____ 8. Social contract theory of government

_____ 9. Developed a vaccination for smallpox

_____ 10. Applied mathematics to the study of the universe

## Complete the Statement

**Underline the term that accurately completes each of the following statements.**

11. Antoine Lavoisier is the Father of Modern (Astronomy/Chemistry).
12. (Pantheism/Empiricism) is the belief that everything in the universe is all part of one great substance called "god."
13. (Nikolaus von Zinzendorf/August Francke) trained Pietist pastors and missionaries at the University of Halle, Germany.
14. (George Whitefield/John Wesley) made several preaching tours in the American colonies.
15. The paintings of El Greco are examples of (mannerist/neoclassical) art.
16. (Francis Bacon/Galileo Galilei) is probably the best-known astronomer in history.

*(continued on next page)*

17. (Robert Boyle/Paracelsus) published the law of inverse gas pressure which is named after him.

18. (Montesquieu/René Descartes) promoted the idea that men could change their government.

19. (Claudio Monteverdi/Philipp Spener) promoted piety in Germany.

20. (Nikolaus von Zinzendorf/John Locke) was a leader of the Moravians.

## Essay

**Write the correct answer to each question in the provided blank.**

21. What were some of the effects of the Scientific Revolution? ______________________

______________________________________________________________

______________________________________________________________

______________________________________________________________

______________________________________________________________

22. Describe the chief teachings of rationalism. ______________________________

______________________________________________________________

______________________________________________________________

______________________________________________________________

______________________________________________________________

23. What unbiblical ideas did Jean-Jacques Rousseau advocate? ____________________

______________________________________________________________

______________________________________________________________

______________________________________________________________

______________________________________________________________

24. How did Jonathan Edwards contribute to the Great Awakening? __________________

______________________________________________________________

______________________________________________________________

______________________________________________________________

______________________________________________________________

25. Explain the Enlightenment view of government. ____________________________

______________________________________________________________

______________________________________________________________

______________________________________________________________

______________________________________________________________

Name ______________________

# William Pitt and the American Colonies

In *Readings in English History Drawn from the Original Sources*, Edward P. Cheyney states, "When the troubles with the American colonies over the enforcement of the Stamp Act arose, William Pitt, who had been in retirement since 1761, returned to parliament and made [an] address in the House of Commons. He advocated practical reconciliation, while asserting a general abstract right possessed by parliament to exercise control over the colonies."

**Answer the questions at the end after reading the following excerpt from William Pitt's speech given on January 14, 1766.**

Gentlemen:

Sir, I have been charged with giving birth to sedition in America. They have spoken their sentiments with freedom against this unhappy act [the Stamp Act], and that freedom has become their crime. Sorry I am to hear the liberty of speech in this House imputed [regarded] as a crime. But the imputation shall not discourage me. It is a liberty I mean to exercise. No gentleman ought to be afraid to exercise it. It is a liberty by which the gentleman [George Grenville, the prime minister] who calumniates [slanders] it might have profited. He ought to have desisted from his project. The gentleman tells us America is obstinate; America is almost in open rebellion. I rejoice that America has resisted. Three millions of people so dead to all the feelings of liberty as voluntarily to submit to be slaves, would have been fit instruments to make slaves of the rest. I come not here armed at all points, with law cases and acts of parliament, with the statute book doubled down in dog's-ears, to defend the cause of liberty; if I had, I myself would have cited the two cases of Chester and Durham. I would have cited them to have shown that, even under former arbitrary [unreasonably harsh] reigns, parliaments were ashamed of taxing a people without their consent, and allowed them representatives [in government]. . . .

I am no courtier of America. I stand up for this kingdom. I maintain that the parliament has the right to bind,—to restrain America. Our legislative power over the colonies is sovereign and supreme. When it ceases to be sovereign and supreme, I would advise every gentleman to sell his lands, if he can, and embark for that country. When two countries are connected together, like England and her colonies, without being incorporated, the one must necessarily govern; the greater must rule the less; but so rule it as not to contradict the fundamental principles that are common to both. . . .

The Americans have not acted in all things with prudence and temper. The Americans have been wronged. They have been driven to madness by injustice. Will you punish them for the madness you have occasioned? Rather let prudence and temper come first from this side. I will undertake for America that she will follow the example. There are two lines in a ballad of Prior's, of a man's behaviour to his wife, so applicable to you and your colonies that I cannot help repeating them:

"Be to her faults a little blind:

Be to her virtues very kind."

Upon the whole, I will beg leave [permission] to tell the House what is really my opinion. It is, that the Stamp Act be repealed absolutely, totally, and immediately. That the reason for the repeal be assigned, because it was founded on an erroneous principle. At the same time let the sovereign authority of this country over the colonies be asserted in as strong terms as can be devised, and be made to extend to every point of legislation whatsoever; that we may bind their trade, confine their manufactures, and exercise every power whatsoever, except that of taking their money out of their pockets without their consent.

Edward P. Cheyney. *Readings in English History Drawn from the Original Sources: Intended to Illustrate "A Short History of England."* (Boston: Ginn, 1908), 623–25.

*(continued on next page)*

1. What specific liberty does William Pitt say he is exercising when giving his address to Parliament?

2. According to Pitt, in what manner did Parliament usually tax the English people, even during the reign of unreasonable kings?

3. What does he say regarding Parliament's authority over the colonies?

4. According to Pitt, why did the American colonists resist Parliament's abuse of authority?

5. According to Pitt, what would solve England's conflict with the American colonies?

6. Is he correct in asserting that Parliament had the right to exercise authority over the American colonies?

Name ______________________

# Eyewitness Account of the French Revolution

**Answer the questions below after reading the following excerpts from the writings of Arthur Young, an English writer and eyewitness of the French Revolution.**

The 9th [of June 1789]. The business going forward at present in the pamphlet shops of Paris is incredible. I went to the Palais Royal [Royal Palace] to see what new things were published, and to procure a catalogue of all. Every hour produces something new. Thirteen came out to-day, sixteen yesterday, and ninety-two last week. We think sometimes that Debrett's or Stockdale's shops at London are crouded, but they are mere deserts, compared to Desein's, and some others here, in which one can scarcely squeeze from the door to the counter. . . . This spirit of reading political tracts, they say, spreads into the provinces, so that all the presses of France are equally employed. Nineteen-twentieths of these productions are in favour of liberty, and commonly violent against the clergy and nobility; I have to-day bespoke many of this description, that have reputation; but enquiring for such as had appeared on the other side of the question, to my astonishment I find there are but two or three that have merit enough to be known. Is it not wonderful [astonishing], that while the press teems with the most levelling and even seditious [rebellious] principles, that if put in execution would overturn the monarchy, nothing in reply appears, and not the least step is taken by the court to restrain this extreme licentiousness [unrestraint] of publication. It is easy to conceive the spirit that must thus be raised among the people. But the coffee-houses in the Palais Royal present yet more singular and astonishing spectacles; they are not only crouded within, but other expectant crouds are at the doors and windows, listening *a gorge deployé* [attentively] to certain orators, who from chairs or tables harangue each his little audience: the eagerness with which they are heard, and the thunder of applause they receive for every sentiment of more than common hardiness or violence against the present government, cannot easily be imagined. I am all amazement at the ministry permitting such nests and hot-beds of sedition and revolt, which disseminate [spread] amongst the people, every hour, principles that by and by must be opposed with vigour, and therefore it seems little short of madness to allow the propagation at present.

1. What ideas and principles did the pamphlet shops and the coffeehouses promote? ______________________

______________________

2. Against what groups of people were the political pamphlets directed? ______________________

______________________

3. How widespread were revolutionary sentiments and ideas in France during Young's visit? ______________________

______________________

______________________

4. What was the French king's response to the pamphleteers? ______________________

______________________

The 21st [of July 1789 at Strasbourg]. I have spent some time this morning at the *cabinet litteraire* [reading room], reading the gazettes and journals that give an account of the transactions at Paris: and I have had some conversation with several sensible and intelligent men on the present revolution. The spirit of revolt is gone forth into various parts of the kingdom; the price

*(continued on next page)*

of bread has prepared the populace every where for all sorts of violence; at Lyons there have been commotions as furious as at Paris, and the same at a great many other places: Dauphiné is in arms: and Bretagne in absolute rebellion. The idea is, that the people will, from hunger, be driven to revolt; and when once they find any other means of subsistence than that of honest labour, every thing will be to be feared. Of such consequence it is to a country, and indeed to every country, to have a good police of corn; a police that shall by securing a high price to the farmer, encourage his culture enough to secure the people at the same time from famine. ... *Night*—I have been witness to a scene curious to a foreigner; but dreadful to Frenchmen that are considerate. Passing through the square of the *hotel de ville* [town hall], the mob were breaking the windows with stones, notwithstanding an officer and a detachment of horse was in the square. Perceiving that their numbers not only increased, but that they grew bolder and bolder every moment, I thought it worth staying to see what it would end in, and clambered on to the roof of a row of low stalls opposite the building, against which their malice was directed. Here I beheld the whole commodiously [conveniently]. Perceiving that the troops would not attack them, except in words and menaces, they grew more violent, and furiously attempted to beat the door in pieces with iron crows [crowbars]; placing ladders to the windows. In about a quarter of an hour, which gave time for the assembled magistrates to escape by a back door, they burst all open, and entered like a torrent with a universal shout of the spectators. From that minute a shower of casements, sashes, shutters, chairs, tables, sophas, books, papers, pictures, &c., rained incessantly from all the windows of the house, which is seventy or eighty feet long, and which was then succeeded by tiles, skirting boards, bannisters, frame-work, and every part of the building that force could detach. The troops, both horse and foot, were quiet spectators. They were at first too few to interpose, and, when they became more numerous, the mischief was too far advanced to admit of any other conduct than guarding every avenue around, permitting none to go to the scene of action, but letting every one that pleased retire with his plunder; guards being at the same time placed at the doors of the churches, and all public buildings. I was for two hours a spectator at different places of the scene, secure myself from the falling furniture, but near enough to see a fine lad of about 14 crushed to death by something as he was handing plunder to a woman, I suppose his mother, from the horror pictured in her countenance. I remarked several common soldiers, with their white cockades, among the plunderers, and instigating the mob even in sight of the officers of the detachment. There were amongst them people so decently dressed, that I regarded them with no small surprize:—they destroyed all the public archives; the streets for some way around strewed with papers; this has been a wanton mischief; for it will be the ruin of many families unconnected with the magistrates.

Arthur Young. *Arthur Young's Travels in France During the Years 1787, 1788, 1789*. ed. [Matilda] Betham-Edwards. (London: George Bell and Sons, 1906), 153–54, 207–9.

5. What event in Strasbourg did Young witness, perceiving that revolt had spread to this city? ______________

______________________________________________

6. How did the soldiers react to the looters? ______________________________

______________________________________________

______________________________________________

Name ______________________

# Execution of Louis XVI

**Answer the questions at the end after reading the following excerpts from the writings of Jeanne-Louise-Henriette Genet Campan, who was Marie Antoinette's lady-in-waiting.**

A majority of fifty-three pronounced for the death of this weak man, but blameless King; the Duke of Orleans, his near kinsman, and father to the late King of the French, among the number. All efforts to obtain a reconsideration, a reference, or delay, were fruitless; the majority were bent on death, and . . . the executive council was charged with the melancholy commission of carrying the sentence into execution. . . . Garat then told [the king] sorrowfully that he was commissioned to communicate to him the decrees of the Convention. Grouvelle, secretary of the executive council, read them to him. The first declared Louis XVI guilty of treason against the general safety of the state; the second condemned him to death; the third rejected any appeal to the people; and the fourth and last, ordered his execution in twenty-four hours. . . .

[The Abbé Edgeworth records the following:] "The path leading to the scaffold was extremely rough and difficult to pass; the King was obliged to lean on my arm, and, from the slowness with which he proceeded, I feared for a moment that his courage might fail: but what was my astonishment, when arrived at the last step, I felt that he suddenly let go my arm, and I saw him cross with a firm foot the breadth of the whole scaffold, silence, by his look alone, fifteen or twenty drums that were placed opposite to him; and, in a loud voice, heard him pronounce distinctly these memorable words:—'I die innocent of all the crimes laid to my charge; I pardon those who have occasioned my death; and I pray to God that the blood which you are now going to shed may never be visited on France.' He was proceeding, when a man on horseback, in the national uniform, waved his sword and ordered the drums to beat. Many voices were at the same time heard encouraging the executioners, who immediately seized the King with violence, and dragged him under the axe of the guillotine, which with one stroke severed his head from his body."

It was on Monday, the 21st of January, 1793. He was aged thirty-eight years four months and twenty-eight days.

Of the sorrows of the royal family during that fatal day, the Duchess of Angoulême gives the following brief statement. Whose heart will not sympathize with the griefs of these noble mourners, three out of the four of whom were so soon to follow to the tomb the adored and faithful husband, the beloved brother, the pious and devoted father!

"On the morning of this terrible day, the princesses rose at six o'clock. The night before, the Queen had scarcely strength enough to put her son to bed. She threw herself, dressed as she was, upon her own bed, where she was heard shivering with cold and grief all night long! At a quarter past six, the door opened; the princesses believed they were sent for to see the King, but it was only the officers looking for a prayer-book for his mass. They did not, however, abandon the hope of seeing him, till the shouts of joy of the unprincipled populace announced to them that all was over."

It has been said, that as the axe fell, the Abbé Edgeworth took leave of the King in the following memorable words: "Son of St. Louis, ascend to heaven!" but on being questioned in after days, he declared himself unconscious of anything that [happened concerning] himself at that awful moment. . . .

Thus ends the first act of the horrid tragedy, never, we trust, to be repeated, the second of which was the slaughter of all the prisoners save one, and the denouement [conclusion], the terrible retribution wrought on the guilty nation [France] during the devastating wars of that Child of the Revolution, Napoleon the Emperor, in the course of which three millions of native Frenchmen fattened the plains of foreign countries by their gore; and the final subjugation

*(continued on next page)*

[subjection] of France and occupation of the regicidal capital [Paris] by the descendants of the Saxon, the Goth, the Vandal, and the Hun [the Germans], whom the grande nation held ever [always] in such contemptuous loathing.

Verily a great lesson to guilty nations, that their retribution is in this world; and that, in the words of the old tragedian, "Crime begets crime, and of Guilt, guilt is for ever the avenger."

[Jeanne-Louise-Henriette Genet] Campan. *Memoirs of the Court of Marie Antoinette, Queen of France*, new ed., vol. 1. (Philadelphia: Keystone, 1890), 211–12, 217–19.

1. How did Louis XVI behave at his execution? ______

2. How did the king's execution become the beginning, or "first act," of a violent drama? ______

3. How did the execution of Louis begin a chain of events that ended French dominance in Europe? ______

4. Which of Campan's comments about future troubles with the Germans proved prophetic? (See Chapters 17, 20, and 22 in the student text.) ______

5. Compare Campan's comments with the teachings of Psalm 7:15 and Matthew 26:52. Explain how the French illustrated the truth of these principles. ______

Name ______________________

## Napoleon's Empire

**Locate each term on the map and place the corresponding number in the appropriate blank.**

_______ Atlantic Ocean

_______ Austerlitz

_______ Austrian Empire

_______ Black Sea

_______ Confederation of the Rhine

_______ French Empire

_______ Kingdom of Italy

_______ Kingdom of Naples

_______ Leipzig

_______ Mediterranean Sea

_______ Moscow

_______ North Sea

_______ Norway

_______ Ottoman Empire

_______ Prussia

_______ Russian Empire

_______ Spain

_______ Sweden

_______ Trafalgar

_______ Waterloo

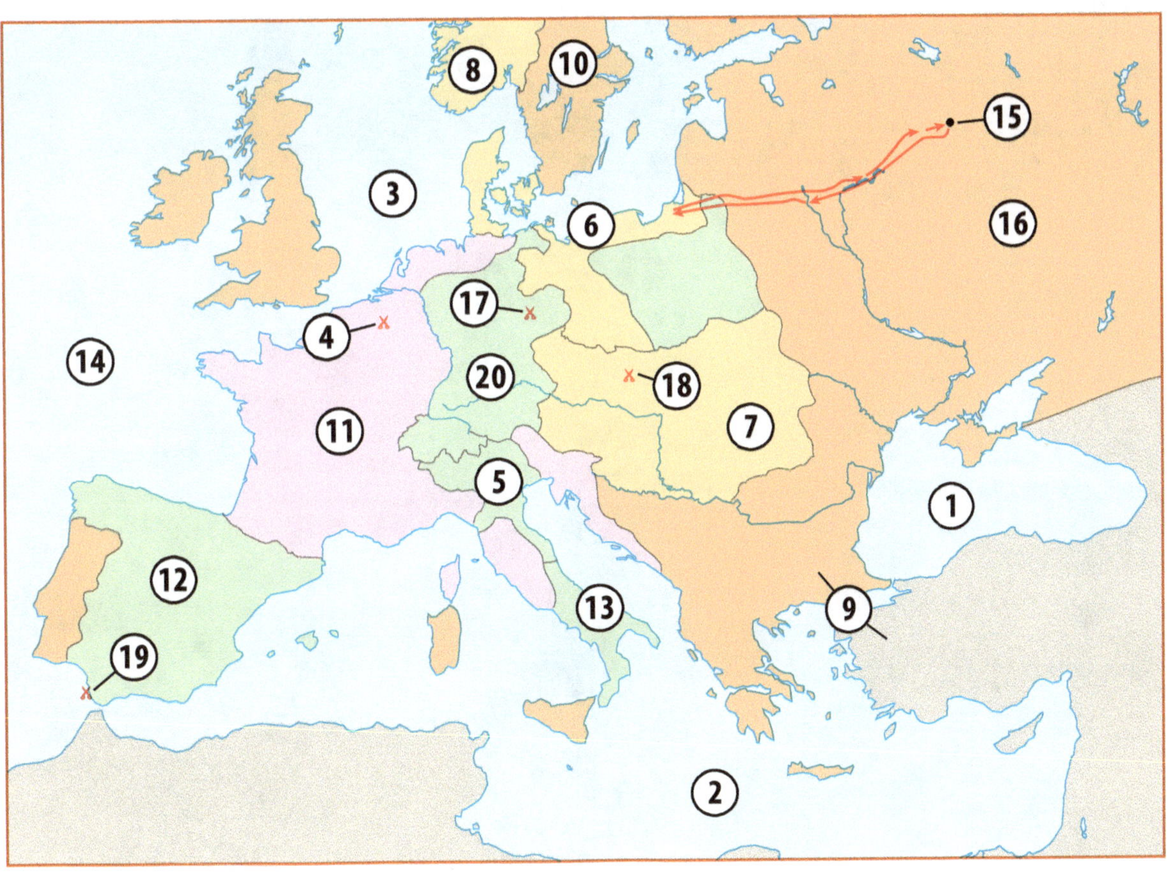

Name ____________________

## Visiting the Battlefield of Waterloo

**Answer the questions at the end after reading the following excerpt from the writings of Charlotte Anne Eaton, an English author who was near Waterloo when Napoleon was defeated.**

From the spot where we now stood [the battlefield of Waterloo] I cast my eyes on every side, and saw nothing but the dreadful and recent traces of death and devastation. The rich harvests of standing corn, which had covered the scene of action we were contemplating, had been beaten into the earth, and the withered and broken stalks dried in the sun, now presented the appearance of stubble, though blacker and far more bare than any stubble land.

In many places the excavations made by the shells had thrown up the earth all around them; the marks of horses' hoofs, that had plunged ancle deep in clay, were hardened in the sun; and the feet of men, deeply stamped into the ground, left traces where many a deadly struggle had been. The ground was ploughed up in several places with the charge of the cavalry, and the whole field was literally covered with soldiers' caps, shoes, gloves, belts, and scabbards, broken feathers battered into the mud, remnants of tattered scarlet cloth, bits of fur and leather, black stocks and havresacs [soldiers' backpacks], belonging to the French soldiers, buckles, packs of cards, books, and innumerable papers of every description. I picked up a volume of Candide [a book by Voltaire]; a few sheets of sentimental love-letters, evidently belonging to some French novel; and many other pages of the same publication were flying over the field in much too muddy a state to be touched. One German Testament, not quite so dirty as many that were lying about, I carried with me nearly the whole day;—printed French military returns, muster rolls, love letters and washing bills; illegible songs, scattered sheets of military music, epistles without number in praise of "l'Empereur, le Grand Napoléon [the Emperor, Napoleon the Great]," and filled with the most confident anticipations of victory under his command, were strewed over the field which had been the scene of his defeat. The quantities of letters and of blank sheets of dirty writing paper were so great that they literally whitened the surface of the earth.

The road to Genappe, descending from the front of the British position, where we were now standing, passes the farm-house of La Haye Sainte, and ascends the opposite height, on the summit of which stands "La Belle Alliance," which was occupied by the French. We walked down the hill to La Haye Sainte—its walls and slated roofs were shattered and pierced through in every direction with cannon shot. We could not get admittance into it, for it was completely deserted by its inhabitants. Three wounded officers of the 42d and 92d regiments were standing here to survey the scene: they had all of them been wounded in the battle of the 16th. One of them had lost an arm, another was on crutches, and the third seemed to be very ill. Their carriage waited for them, as they were unable to walk. After some conversation with them, we proceeded up the hill to the hamlet of La Belle Alliance. The principal house on the left side of the road was pierced through and through with cannon balls, and the offices behind it were a heap of dust from the fire of the British artillery. Notwithstanding the ruinous state of the house, it was filled with inhabitants. Its broken walls, "its looped and windowed wretchedness," might indeed defend them sufficiently well "from seasons such as these," when the soft breezes and the bright beams of summer played around it—but against "the pelting of the storm," it would afford them but a sorry shelter. It was immediately to be repaired; but I rejoiced that it yet remained in its dilapidated state.

The house was filled with vestiges of the battle. Cuirasses, helmets, swords, bayonets, feathers, brass eagles, and crosses of the Legion of Honour, were to be purchased here. The house consisted of three rooms, two in front, and a very small one behind. On the opposite side of the road is a little cottage, forming part of the hamlet of La Belle Alliance; and at a short distance,

*(continued on next page)*

by the way side, is another low-roofed cottage, which was pointed out to us as the place where Buonaparte breakfasted on the morning of the battle.

[Charlotte Anne Eaton]. *Narrative of a Residence in Belgium During the Campaign of 1815: And of a Visit to the Field of Waterloo.* (London: John Murray, 1817), 278–83.

1. What physical details indicated that a major battle had recently occurred? ______

2. What literature had the soldiers carried with them to battle? ______

3. What items did soldiers leave behind on the battlefield? ______

4. How did the French soldiers' letters reveal their optimism? ______

5. How did the farmhouse of La Haye Sainte demonstrate the great destruction of the British artillery? ______

6. How was the French optimism tragically ironic? ______

Name ______________________________

# Chapter Review

## Complete the Statement

**Underline the term that accurately completes each of the following statements.**

1. The (First/Second) Estate consisted of Catholic clergy.
2. Napoleon's armies were defeated in 1813 at (Austerlitz/Leipzig).
3. Marat, Danton, and Robespierre were members of the (Jacobins/Estates-General).
4. The (Consulate/Directory) replaced the National Convention in 1795 as France's new government.
5. Napoleon died in exile in 1821 on the island of (Elba/St. Helena).

## Matching

**Choose the best answer and place the letter in the blank beside the corresponding description.**

A. Bill of Rights
B. Brunswick Manifesto
C. Civil Constitution of the Clergy
D. Code Napoleon
E. Committee of Public Safety
F. Declaration of Independence
G. Declaration of the Rights of Man
H. Mayflower Compact
I. Tennis Court Oath
J. Treaty of Paris

_____ 6. Written by American leaders to explain America's separation from England

_____ 7. Contained the Third Estate's demand for a written constitution

_____ 8. Placed France's clergy and national church under state control

_____ 9. Britain's official recognition of America's independence

_____ 10. Established many of France's laws that still exist today

_____ 11. The first ten amendments to the US Constitution

_____ 12. Authorized France's Tribunal to kill suspected enemies

_____ 13. Called on the French to support and protect their king

_____ 14. Issued to express the natural rights of all Frenchmen

_____ 15. Established civil authority for the Plymouth Colony

*(continued on next page)*

## Short Answer

**Write the correct answer to each question in the provided blank.**

16. What French phrase denotes a sudden and illegal seizure of power? ______________________

17. To what position did the French voters elect Napoleon in 1802? ______________________

______________________

## Essay

**Write the correct answer to each question in the provided blank.**

18. What role did British war commanders play in the defeat of Napoleon Bonaparte? ______________________

______________________

______________________

______________________

19. How did the Russians turn Napoleon's Russian campaign into a disaster for the French? ______________________

______________________

______________________

______________________

20. How did Napoleon Bonaparte betray the original intent of the French Revolution? ______________________

______________________

______________________

______________________

______________________

______________________

______________________

Name ______________________________

# Metternich and European Governments

**Answer the questions at the end after reading the following excerpt from the writings of Prince Klemens von Metternich.**

Let the governments announce this determination to their people, and demonstrate it by facts. Let them reduce the doctrinaires [those inflexibly attached to a theory] to silence within their States, and show their contempt for them abroad. Let them not encourage by their attitude or actions the suspicion of being favorable or indifferent to error; let them not allow it to be believed that experience has lost all its rights to make way for experiments which at the least are dangerous. Let them be precise and clear in all their words, and not seek by concessions to gain over those parties who aim at the destruction of all power but their own, whom concessions will never gain over, but only further embolden in their pretensions to power.

Let them in these troublous times be more than usually cautious in attempting real ameliorations [improvements], not imperatively claimed [demanded] by the needs of the moment, to the end that good itself may not turn against them,—which is the case whenever a government measure seems to be inspired by fear.

Let them not confound concessions made to parties with the good they ought to do for their people, in modifying, according to their recognized needs, such branches of the administration as require it.

Let them give minute attention to the financial state of their kingdoms, so that their people may enjoy, by the reduction of public burdens, the real, not imaginary, benefits of a state of peace.

Let them be just, but strong; beneficent [charitable], but strict.

Let them maintain religious principles in all their purity, and not allow the faith to be attacked and morality interpreted according to the social contract or the visions of foolish sectarians.

Let them suppress secret societies, that gangrene of society.

In short, let the great monarchs strengthen their union, and prove to the world that while it exists, it is beneficent, and insures the political peace of Europe; that it is powerful only for the maintenance of tranquillity at a time when so many attacks are directed against it; that the principles which they profess are paternal [fatherly] and protective, menacing only the disturbers of public tranquillity. . . .

To every great State determined to survive the storm there still remain many chances of salvation, and a strong union between the States on the principles we have announced will overcome the storm itself.

James Harvey Robinson and Charles A. Beard. *Readings in Modern European History: A Collection of Extracts from the Sources Chosen with the Purpose of Illustrating Some of the Chief Phases of the Development of Europe During the Last Two Hundred Years,* vol. 1, *The Eighteenth Century: The French Revolution and the Napoleonic Period.* (Boston: Ginn, 1908), 386–87.

1. According to Metternich, how can a ruler hurt himself by making changes and improvements? ______________

______________________________________________

______________________________________________

*(continued on next page)*

2. According to Metternich, what should a ruler do financially to prevent revolution from spreading into his country? ______

______

______

3. What does Metternich suggest regarding religious principles? In your own words, explain what he means.

______

______

______

______

______

4. What does Metternich consider the "gangrene of society"? ______

5. How does he describe the revolutionary ideas that were spreading throughout Europe? ______

______

______

Name ______________________________

## Europe After the Congress of Vienna (1815)

**Locate each term on the map and place the corresponding number in the appropriate blank.**

_______ Atlantic Ocean

_______ Austrian Empire

_______ Baltic Sea

_______ Black Sea

_______ Crete

_______ Denmark

_______ France

_______ Kingdom of Prussia

_______ Kingdom of the Two Sicilies

_______ Mediterranean Sea

_______ North Sea

_______ Ottoman Empire

_______ Papal States

_______ Portugal

_______ Russian Empire

_______ Spain

_______ Sweden

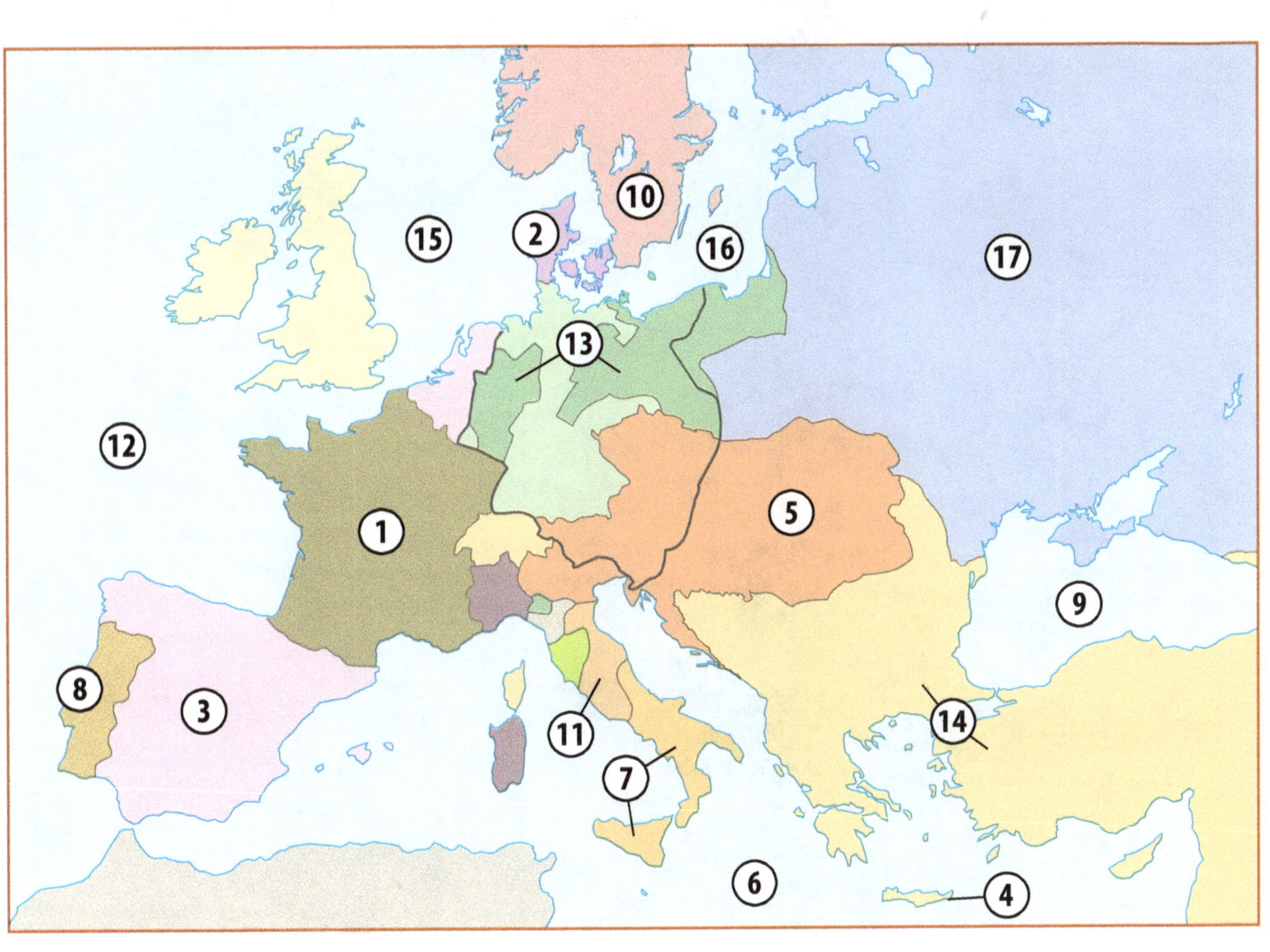

Name ______________________

# Young Italy

**Answer the questions at the end after reading the following excerpt from the writings of Joseph Mazzini, an Italian nationalist who organized and funded revolutionaries.**

Young Italy is a brotherhood of Italians who believe in a law of *progress* and *duty*, and are convinced that Italy is destined to become one nation, convinced also that she possesses sufficient strength within herself to become one, and that the ill success of her former efforts is to be attributed not to the weakness, but to the misdirection of the revolutionary elements within her,—that the secret force lies in constancy and unity of effort. They join this association with the firm intention of consecrating both thought and action to the great aim of reconstituting Italy as one independent sovereign nation of free men and equals. . . .

The aim of the association is *revolution*; but its labors will be essentially educational, both before and after the day of revolution; and it therefore declares the principles upon which the national education should be conducted, and from which alone Italy may hope for safety and regeneration. . . .

Young Italy is *republican* and *unitarian* [seeking unity],—republican, because theoretically every nation is destined, by the law of God and humanity, to form a free and equal community of brothers; and the republican government is the only form of government that insures this future: Because all true sovereignty resides essentially in the nation, the sole progressive and continuous interpreter of the supreme moral law; . . . because the monarchical element being incapable of sustaining itself alone by the side of the popular element, it necessarily involves the existence of the intermediate element of an aristocracy,—the source of inequality and corruption to the whole nation; because both history and the nature of things teach us that elective monarchy tends to generate anarchy, and hereditary monarchy tends to generate despotism; because, when monarchy is not—as in the Middle Ages—based upon the belief, now extinct, in right divine [absolutism], it becomes too weak to be a bond of unity and authority in the State; because the inevitable tendency of the series of progressive transformations taking place in Europe is toward the enthronement of the republican principle, and because the inauguration of the monarchical principle in Italy would carry along with it the necessity of a new revolution shortly after.

Our Italian tradition is essentially republican; our great memories are republican; the whole history of our national progress is republican; whereas the introduction of monarchy amongst us was coeval [simultaneous] with our decay, and consummated our ruin by its constant servility [servitude] to the foreigner and antagonism to the people as well as to the unity of the nation. . . .

If monarchy were once set up as the aim of the Italian insurrection, it would, by a logical necessity, draw along with it all the obligations of the monarchical system, concessions to foreign courts, trust in and respect for diplomacy, and the repression of that popular element, by which alone our salvation can be achieved. By intrusting the supreme authority to monarchists whose interest it would be to betray us, we should infallibly bring the insurrection to naught. . . .

Young Italy is *unitarian*, because, without unity there is no true nation; because, without unity there is no real strength; and Italy, surrounded as she is by powerful, united, and jealous nations, has need of strength above all things; because federalism, by reducing her to the political impotence of Switzerland, would necessarily place her under the influence of one of the neighboring nations; because federalism, by reviving the local rivalries now extinct, would throw Italy back upon the Middle Ages; . . . because federalism, by destroying the unity of the great Italian family, would strike at the root of the great mission Italy is destined to accomplish for humanity; because Europe is undergoing a progressive series of transformations, which are gradually and irresistibly guiding European society to form itself into vast and united masses;

*(continued on next page)*

because the entire work of internal civilization in Italy will be seen, if rightly studied, to have been tending for ages toward unity.

The means by which Young Italy proposes to reach its aim are education and insurrection, to be adopted simultaneously and made to harmonize with each other. Education must ever be directed to teach, by example, word, and pen, the necessity of insurrection. Insurrection, whenever it can be realized, must be so conducted as to render it a means of national education. Education, though of necessity secret in Italy, will be public outside of Italy. . . .

Insurrection, by means of guerrilla bands, is the true method of warfare for all nations desirous of emancipating themselves from a foreign yoke. This method of warfare supplies the want—inevitable at the commencement of the insurrection—of a regular army; it calls the greatest number of elements into the field, and yet may be sustained by the smallest number. It forms the military education of the people and consecrates every foot of the native soil by the memory of some warlike deed. Guerrilla warfare opens a field of activity for every local capacity, forces the enemy into an unaccustomed method of battle, avoids the evil consequences of a great defeat, secures the national war from the risk of treason, and has the advantage of not confining it within any defined and determinate basis of operations. It is invincible, indestructible.

James Harvey Robinson and Charles A. Beard. *Readings in Modern European History: A Collection of Extracts from the Sources Chosen with the Purpose of Illustrating Some of the Chief Phases of the Development of Europe During the Last Two Hundred Years, vol. 2, Europe Since the Congress of Vienna.* (Boston: Ginn, 1909), 115–18.

1. What was the goal of Young Italy? ______________________________

______________________________________________

2. What, according to this excerpt, is Mazzini's opinion of a monarchy? ______________

______________________________________________

3. Why does Mazzini place such a great emphasis on unity? ______________________

______________________________________________

4. What methods does he advocate to achieve Young Italy's goal? __________________

______________________________________________

Name ______________________________

## Chapter Review

### Complete the Statement

**Underline the term that accurately completes each of the following statements.**

1. The Red Shirts was an Italian nationalist group led by (Camillo di Cavour/Giuseppe Garibaldi).
2. (Giuseppe Mazzini/Camillo di Cavour) started a patriotic society called Young Italy.
3. (*Mestizos*/*Caudillos*) were military leaders who established dictatorships.
4. The (June Days/July Revolution) forced Charles X to flee to England.
5. In the 1820s, European powers helped the (Hungarians/Greeks) win independence from the Ottoman Empire.

### Matching

**Choose the best answer and place the letter in the blank beside the corresponding description.**

| | | |
|---|---|---|
| A. Alexander I | E. Charles X | I. Dom Pedro |
| B. Alexander II | F. Franz Josef I | J. Louis Philippe |
| C. Otto von Bismarck | G. Louis XVIII | K. Nicholas I |
| D. Lord Castlereagh | H. Louis Napoleon | L. Victor Emmanuel II |

_____ 6. Austrian emperor who crushed nationalist revolts

_____ 7. Proclaimed himself emperor of the Second French Empire

_____ 8. Czar who abolished serfdom in 1861

_____ 9. Implemented the policy of Russification

_____ 10. First king of united Italy

_____ 11. Prussia's chancellor who unified Germany

_____ 12. France's "citizen king" from 1830 to 1848

_____ 13. King who attempted to restore absolutism in France

_____ 14. Became king of France following the defeat of Napoleon

_____ 15. Czar who attended the Congress of Vienna

*(continued on next page)*

## Short Answer

**Write the correct answer to each question in the provided blank.**

16. What Frenchman represented his defeated country at the Congress of Vienna? ______

17. What unbiblical attitudes did romanticism promote? ______

18. What term denotes compensation that a defeated country pays to other nations for war damages?

______

19. What term denotes Spaniards born in the New World? ______

20. What agreement recognized the independence of Belgium and declared it a perpetually neutral state?

______

21. Who freed Chile and Peru from Spanish domination? ______

22. Who was the most famous neoclassical painter and used themes from classical Greece and Rome?

______

23. What policy warned the European nations that any attempt to establish or reestablish colonies in the Western Hemisphere would be considered an act of aggression? ______

## Essay

**Write the correct answer to each question in the provided blank.**

24. How did musical aims and styles change during the Age of Romanticism? ______

25. In what ways was the 1814 Congress of Vienna ultimately a failure? ______

Name ______________________

## Testimonies About Child Laborers

**Answer the questions at the end after reading the following excerpts from Parliament's 1833 investigation of child laborers' working conditions.**

*Charles Harris, a boy working in the carding room of Mr. Oldacres's mill for spinning worsted yarn, testified as follows:*

I am twelve years old. I have been in the mill twelve months. I attend to a drawing machine. We begin at six o'clock and stop at half past seven. We don't stop work for breakfast. We do sometimes. This week we have not. Nothing has been said to me by Mr. Oldacres or the overlooker, or anybody else, about having any questions asked me. I am sure of that. The engine always stops for dinner. It works at tea time in the hot weather; and then we give over at half past seven instead of eight, which is the general time. We have generally about twelve hours and a half of it. On Saturdays we begin at six and give over at four. I get 2*s.* [shillings] 6*d.* [pence] a week. I have a father and mother, and give them what I earn. I have worked overhours [overtime] for two or three weeks together about a fortnight since. All the difference was, we worked breakfast time and tea time, and did not go away till eight. We are paid for such overhours at the rate of 2*d.* for three hours. I have always that for myself.

What do you do with it?

I save it for clothes sometimes. I put it into a money club for clothes. I have worked nine hours over in one week. I got for that 5½*d.* I gave it [to] my mother, and she made it up to 6*d.* and put it into the money club. She always puts by 6*d.* a week from my wages for that. . . .

*The father of two children in a mill at Lenton deposed as follows:*

My two sons (one ten, the other thirteen) work at Milnes's factory at Lenton. They go at half past five in the morning; don't stop at breakfast or tea time. They stop at dinner half an hour. Come home at a quarter before ten. They used to work till ten, sometimes eleven, sometimes twelve. They earn between them 6*s.* 2*d.* per week. One of them, the eldest, worked at Wilson's for two years, at 2*s.* 3*d.* per week. He left because the overlooker beat him and loosened a tooth for him. I complained, and they turned him away for it. They have been gone to work sixteen hours now; they will be very tired when they come home at half past nine. I have a deal of trouble to get 'em up in the morning. I have been obliged to beat 'em with a strap in their shirts, and to pinch 'em, in order to get them well awake. It made me cry to be obliged to do it.

Did you make them cry?

Yes, sometimes. They will be home soon, very tired; and you will see them.

I [i.e. the government inspector] preferred walking towards the factory to meet them. I saw the youngest only, and asked him a few questions. He said, "I'm sure I shan't stop to talk to you; I want to go home and get to bed; I must be up at half past five again to-morrow morning."

*A family in the same town of Lenton gave the following evidence:*

*The boy.* I am going fourteen; my sister is eleven. I have worked in Milnes's factory two years. She goes there also. We are both in the clearing room. I think we work too long hours; I've been badly with it. We go at half past five; give over at half past nine. I am now just come home. We sometimes stay till twelve. We are obliged to work overhours. I have 4*s.* a week; that is for staying from six to seven. They pay for overhours besides. I asked to come away one night lately, at eight o'clock, being ill; I was told, if I went I must not come again. I am not well now. I can seldom eat any breakfast; my appetite is very bad. I have had a bad cold for a week.

*Father.* I believe him to be ill from being overworked. My little girl came home the other day cruelly beaten. I took her to Mr. Milnes; did not see him, but showed Mrs. Milnes the marks. I thought of taking it before a magistrate, but was advised to let it drop. They might have turned

*(continued on next page)*

both my children away. That man's name is Blagg; he is always strapping the children. I shan't let the boy go there much longer; I shall try to apprentice him; it's killing him by inches; he falls asleep over his food at night. I saw an account of such things in the newspapers, and thought how true it was of my own children.

*Mother*. I have worked in the same mills myself. The same man was there then. I have seen him behave shocking to the children. He would take 'em by the hair of the head and drag 'em about the room. He has been there twelve years. There's many young ones in that hot room. There's six of 'em badly now, with bad eyes and sick headache. This boy of ours has always been delicate from a child. His appetite is very bad now; he does not eat his breakfast sometimes for two or three days together. The little girl bears it well; she is healthy. I would prefer their coming home at seven, without additional wages. The practice of working overhours has been constantly pursued at Milnes's factory.

James Harvey Robinson and Charles A. Beard. *Readings in Modern European History: A Collection of Extracts from the Sources Chosen with the Purpose of Illustrating Some of the Chief Phases of the Development of Europe During the Last Two Hundred Years*, vol. 2, *Europe Since the Congress of Vienna*. (Boston: Ginn, 1909), 282–85. (The bracketed phrase *i.e. the government inspector* is in the original.)

1. What difficulties did these children encounter while working at the mills? ____________________

____________________

____________________

2. How did mill managers misuse the children workers? ____________________

____________________

3. Apply Leviticus 19:13; 25:17; and Psalm 72:4, 12 to these accounts. ____________________

____________________

____________________

Name ______________________________

## *The Communist Manifesto*

**Answer the questions at the end after reading the following excerpt from the writings of Karl Marx and Friedrich Engels.**

A spectre [ghost] is haunting Europe—the spectre of Communism. All the Powers of old Europe have entered into a holy alliance to exorcise [drive out] this spectre: Pope and Czar, Metternich and Guizot, French Radicals and German police-spies.

Where is the party in opposition that has not been decried as Communistic by its opponents in power? Where is the Opposition that has not hurled back the branding reproach of Communism, against the more advanced opposition parties, as well as against its reactionary adversaries?

Two things result from this fact.

I. Communism is already acknowledged by all European Powers to be itself a Power.

II. It is high time that Communists should openly, in the face of the whole world, publish their views, their aims, their tendencies, and meet this nursery tale of the Spectre of Communism with a Manifesto of the party itself.

To this end, Communists of various nationalities have assembled in London, and sketched the following Manifesto, to be published in the English, French, German, Italian, Flemish and Danish languages.

I. Bourgeois [middle class] and Proletarians [poor working class]

The history of all hitherto existing societies is the history of class struggles.

Freeman and slave, patrician and plebeian, lord and serf, guild-master and journeyman, in a word, oppressor and oppressed, stood in constant opposition to one another, carried on an uninterrupted, now hidden, now open fight, a fight that each time ended, either in a revolutionary re-constitution of society at large, or in the common ruin of the contending classes.

In the earlier epochs of history, we find almost everywhere a complicated arrangement of society into various orders, a manifold gradation of social rank. In ancient Rome we have patricians, knights, plebeians, slaves; in the Middle Ages, feudal lords, vassals, guild-masters, journeymen, apprentices, serfs; in almost all of these classes, again, subordinate gradations.

The modern bourgeois society that has sprouted from the ruins of feudal society has not done away with class antagonisms. It has but established new classes, new conditions of oppression, new forms of struggle in place of the old ones. Our epoch, the epoch of the bourgeoisie, possesses, however, this distinctive feature: it has simplified the class antagonisms. Society as a whole is more and more splitting up into two great hostile camps, into two great classes, directly facing each other: Bourgeoisie and Proletariat.

From the serfs of the Middle Ages sprang the chartered burghers of the earliest towns. From these burgesses the first elements of the bourgeoisie were developed. . . .

The bourgeoisie, historically, has played a most revolutionary part.

The bourgeoisie, wherever it has got the upper hand, has put an end to all feudal, patriarchal, idyllic relations. It has pitilessly torn asunder the motley feudal ties that bound man to his "natural superiors," and has left remaining no other nexus [connection] between man and man than naked self-interest, than callous "cash payment." It has drowned the most heavenly ecstasies of religious fervour, of chivalrous enthusiasm, of philistine sentimentalism, in the icy water of egotistical [selfish] calculation. It has resolved personal worth into exchange value, and in place of the numberless and indefeasible chartered freedoms, has set up that single,

*(continued on next page)*

unconscionable freedom—Free Trade. In one word, for exploitation, veiled by religious and political illusions, naked, shameless, direct, brutal exploitation.

*The Communist Manifesto* by Karl Marx and Friedrich Engels. Public domain.

1. Whom do Marx and Engels accuse of trying to drive out the "spectre of Communism"? ______

______

2. According to Marx and Engels, what is the main theme of history? ______

______

3. According to Marx and Engels, how does class warfare always end? ______

______

4. What examples do they give in support of their view of history? ______

______

5. According to Marx and Engels, what motivates the bourgeoisie? ______

______

6. Do Marx and Engels offer any specific evidence to support their accusations against the bourgeoisie?

______

Name ______________________________

## *The Descent of Man*

**Answer the questions below after reading the following excerpts from the writings of Charles Darwin.**

With savages, the weak in body or mind are soon eliminated; and those that survive commonly exhibit a vigorous state of health. We civilized men, on the other hand, do our utmost to check the process of elimination; we build asylums for the imbecile, the maimed, and the sick; we institute poor-laws; and our medical men exert their utmost skill to save the life of every one to the last moment. There is reason to believe that vaccination has preserved thousands who from a weak constitution would formerly have succumbed to small-pox. Thus the weak members of civilized societies propagate their kind. No one who has attended to the breeding of domestic animals will doubt that this must be highly injurious to the race of man. It is surprising how soon a want of care, or care wrongly directed, leads to the degeneration of a domestic race; but, excepting in the case of man himself, hardly any one is so ignorant as to allow his worst animals to breed. . . .

The greater number of naturalists who have taken into consideration the whole structure of man, including his mental faculties, have followed Blumenbach and Cuvier, and have placed man in a separate Order, under the title of the Bimana [two handed], and therefore on an equality with the orders of the Quadrumana [four handed], Carnivora, etc. Recently many of our best naturalists have recurred to the view first propounded by Linnæus, so remarkable for his sagacity, and have placed man in the same Order with the Quadrumana, under the title of the Primates. The justice of this conclusion will be admitted; for, in the first place, we must bear in mind the comparative insignificance for classification of the great development of the brain in man, and that the strongly marked differences between the skulls of man and the Quadrumana . . . apparently follow from their differently developed brains. In the second place, we must remember that nearly all the other and more important differences between man and the Quadrumana are manifestly adaptive in their nature, and relate chiefly to the erect position of man; such as the structure of his hand, foot, and pelvis, the curvature of his spine, and the position of his head. . . .

It would be beyond my limits, and quite beyond my knowledge, even to name the innumerable points of structure in which man agrees with the other Primates. Our great anatomist and philosopher, Prof. Huxley, has fully discussed this subject, and concludes that man in all parts of his organization differs less from the higher apes than these do from the lower members of the same group. Consequently there "is no justification for placing man in a distinct order."

In an early part of this work I brought forward various facts, showing how closely man agrees in constitution with the higher mammals; and this agreement must depend on our close similarity in minute structure and chemical composition. I gave, as instances, our liability to the same diseases, and to the attacks of allied parasites; our tastes in common for the same stimulants, and the similar effects produced by them, as well as by various drugs, and other such facts.

As small unimportant points of resemblance between man and the Quadrumana are not commonly noticed in systematic works, and as, when numerous, they clearly reveal our relationship, I will specify a few such points. The relative position of our features is manifestly the same; and the various emotions are displayed by nearly similar movements of the muscles and skin, chiefly above the eyebrows and round the mouth. Some few expressions are, indeed, almost the same, as in the weeping of certain kinds of monkeys and in the laughing noise made by others, during which the corners of the mouth are drawn backward, and the lower eyelids wrinkled. The external ears are curiously alike. In man the nose is much more prominent than in most monkeys.

*(continued on next page)*

1. According to Darwin, what is the natural end of the weak and sick? What does he call those who, in essence, allow "weak members of civilized societies" to breed? ______________________

______________________

2. With what types of animals does Darwin compare man? ______________________

3. How does the Bible contrast man with other created beings? (See Gen. 1:25–28 and Ps. 8:3–8.) ______________________

______________________

______________________

From the fundamental differences between certain languages, some philologists have inferred that when man first became widely diffused, he was not a speaking animal; but it may be suspected that languages, far less perfect than any now spoken, aided by gestures, might have been used, and yet have left no traces on subsequent and more highly developed tongues. Without the use of some language, however imperfect, it appears doubtful whether man's intellect could have risen to the standard implied by his dominant position at an early period.

Whether primeval man, when he possessed but few arts, and those of the rudest kind, and when his power of language was extremely imperfect, would have deserved to be called man, must depend on the definition which we employ. In a series of forms graduating insensibly from some ape-like creature to man as he now exists, it would be impossible to fix on any definite point when the term "man" ought to be used. But this is a matter of very little importance. So, again, it is almost a matter of indifference whether the so-called races of man are thus designated, or are ranked as species or sub-species; but the latter term appears the more appropriate. Finally, we may conclude that when the principle of evolution is generally accepted, as it surely will be before long, the dispute between the monogenists and polygenists will die a silent and unobserved death.

4. According to Darwin, what is the origin and history of language? ______________________

______________________

______________________

5. How does the Bible describe man's early use of language in Genesis 2? ______________________

______________________

______________________

With respect to [intellectual] differences . . . between man and woman, it is probable that sexual selection has played a highly important part. I am aware that some writers doubt whether there is any such inherent difference; but this is at least probable from the analogy of the lower animals which present other secondary sexual characters. No one disputes that the bull differs in disposition from the cow, the wild boar from the sow, the stallion from the mare, and, as is well known to the keepers of menageries, the males of the larger apes from the females. Woman seems to differ from man in mental disposition, chiefly in her greater tenderness and less selfishness; and this holds good even with savages, as shown by a well-known passage in Mungo Park's Travels, and by statements made by many other travellers. Woman, owing to her maternal instincts, displays these qualities toward her infants in an eminent degree; therefore it is likely that she would often extend them toward her fellow-creatures. Man is the rival of other men; he delights in competition, and this leads to ambition which passes too easily into selfishness. These latter qualities seem to be his natural and unfortunate birthright. It is generally admitted that with woman the powers of intuition, of rapid perception, and perhaps

*(continued on next page)*

of imitation, are more strongly marked than in man; but some, at least, of these faculties are characteristic of the lower races, and therefore of a past and lower state of civilization. The chief distinction in the intellectual powers of the two sexes is shown by man's attaining to a higher eminence, in whatever he takes up, than can woman—whether requiring deep thought, reason, or imagination, or merely the use of the senses and hands. If two lists were made of the most eminent men and women in poetry, painting, sculpture, music (inclusive both of composition and performance), history, science, and philosophy, with half a dozen names under each subject, the two lists would not bear comparison. We may also infer, from the law of the deviation from averages, so well illustrated by Mr. Galton, in his work on "Hereditary Genius," that if men are capable of a decided pre-eminence over women in many subjects, the average of mental power in man must be above that of woman. . . .

Now, when two men are put into competition, or a man with a woman, both possessed of every mental quality in equal perfection, save that one has higher energy, perseverance, and courage, the latter will generally become more eminent in every pursuit, and will gain the ascendency. He may be said to possess genius—for genius has been declared by a great authority to be patience; and patience, in this sense, means unflinching, undaunted perseverance. But this view of genius is perhaps deficient; for without the higher powers of the imagination and reason, no eminent success can be gained in many subjects. These latter faculties, as well as the former, will have been developed in man, partly through sexual selection—that is, through the contest of rival males, and partly through natural selection—that is, from success in the general struggle for life; and as in both cases the struggle will have been during maturity, the characters gained will have been transmitted more fully to the male than to the female offspring. It accords in a striking manner with this view of the modification and reinforcement of many of our mental faculties by sexual selection, that, first, they notoriously undergo a considerable change at puberty, and, secondly, that eunuchs remain throughout life inferior in these same qualities. Thus man has ultimately become superior to woman. It is, indeed, fortunate that the law of the equal transmission of characters to both sexes prevails with mammals; otherwise it is probable that man would have become as superior in mental endowment to woman, as the peacock is in ornamental plumage to the peahen. . . .

As before remarked of bodily strength, although men do not now fight for their wives, and this form of selection has passed away, yet, during manhood, they generally undergo a severe struggle in order to maintain themselves and their families; and this will tend to keep up or even increase their mental powers, and, as a consequence, the present inequality between the sexes. . . .

The main conclusion arrived at in this work, namely, that man is descended from some lowly organized form, will, I regret to think, be highly distasteful to many. But there can hardly be a doubt that we are descended from barbarians. The astonishment which I felt on first seeing a party of Fuegians on a wild and broken shore will never be forgotten by me, for the reflection at once rushed into my mind—such were our ancestors. These men were absolutely naked and bedaubed with paint, their long hair was tangled, their mouths frothed with excitement, and their expression was wild, startled, and distrustful. They possessed hardly any arts, and, like wild animals, lived on what they could catch; they had no government, and were merciless to every one not of their own small tribe. He who has seen a savage in his native land will not feel much shame if forced to acknowledge that the blood of some more humble creature flows in his veins. For my own part, I would as soon be descended from that heroic little monkey who braved his dreaded enemy in order to save the life of his keeper, or from that old baboon, who, descending from the mountains, carried away in triumph his young comrade from a crowd of astonished dogs—as from a savage who delights to torture his enemies, offers up bloody sacrifices, practices infanticide without remorse, treats his wives like slaves, knows no decency, and is haunted by the grossest superstitions.

Charles Darwin. *The Descent of Man and Selection in Relation to Sex*, 2 vols. (New York: P. F. Collier and Son, 1902), 180–81, 200–202, 240, 725–28, 796–97.

*(continued on next page)*

6. According to Darwin, how are men superior to women? ____________________

7. How does the Bible describe women in Proverbs 31:10–28 and 1 Peter 3:1–7? ____________________

8. What is Darwin's "main conclusion"? What does he describe to justify this conclusion? ____________________

9. Does Darwin's writing support the concept of racism (the imagined superiority of one ethnic group over another)? ____________________

Name ______________________

# Chapter Review

## Complete the Statement

**Underline the term that accurately completes each of the following statements.**

1. Marxism refers to capitalists, industrialists, and middle-class property owners as the (proletariat/bourgeoisie).
2. (Robert Fulton/Henry Ford) produced the famous Model T automobile.
3. (Charles Dickens/John Dalton) attacked social injustice in his novels by portraying the ugly effects of industrialism.
4. The labors of (John McAdam/William Gladstone) centered on transportation and road construction.
5. The Reform Bill of 1832 addressed problems in (welfare/voting rights).

## Matching

**Choose the best answer and place the letter in the blank beside the corresponding description.**

| | | |
|---|---|---|
| A. Richard Arkwright | F. John Kay | K. Charles Townshend |
| B. Henry Bessemer | G. George Mueller | L. Richard Trevithick |
| C. Samuel Clemens | H. Robert Owen | M. Eli Whitney |
| D. Benjamin Disraeli | I. Robert Raikes | N. William Wilberforce |
| E. James Hargreaves | J. Wilhelm Roentgen | |

_____ 6. Started Sunday schools to teach children to read and write

_____ 7. Father of the Industrial Revolution; invented a spinning frame

_____ 8. Established a utopian community in New Harmony, Indiana

_____ 9. Advocated crop rotation and fertilizer

_____ 10. Devised a cotton gin for separating seeds from cotton

_____ 11. Developed an efficient process for making steel

_____ 12. Built a steam-powered locomotive

_____ 13. Physicist who discovered x-rays

_____ 14. Used pen name Mark Twain

_____ 15. Founded orphanages in England

*(continued on next page)*

## Short Answer

**Write the correct answer to each question in the provided blank.**

16. Which scientist proposed the theory of relativity? ____________________

17. Who was the first to operate a steamboat as a commercial success? ____________________

18. Which famous novelist described life in Russia during the Napoleonic Wars? ____________________

19. Which evangelist joined with Ira Sankey to hold evangelistic campaigns? ____________________

20. What form of artistic expression believed that life should be portrayed as it really was? ____________________

21. Which husband-and-wife team found new radioactive elements? ____________________

22. List four issues that the Chartist movement advocated. ____________________

____________________

____________________

23. According to Adam Smith's book *Wealth of Nations*, how should a nation's government influence the nation's economy? ____________________

____________________

## Essay

**Write the correct answer to each question in the provided blank.**

24. How did the factory system change society and the worker's lifestyle? ____________________

____________________

____________________

____________________

____________________

25. Contrast Karl Marx's view of history with the biblical view found in Daniel 2:36–44. ____________________

____________________

____________________

____________________

____________________

____________________

____________________

Name ______________________________

# Imperialism in the Far East 1914

**Locate the following on the map. Color the countries (marked by an asterisk) based on imperialism by the following countries: Great Britain, France, Germany, Netherlands, Japan, and the United States.**

| | | |
|---|---|---|
| ______ Borneo* | ______ Formosa* | ______ Korea* |
| ______ Burma* | ______ French Indochina* | ______ New Guinea* |
| ______ Ceylon* | ______ India* | ______ Pacific Ocean |
| ______ China | ______ Indian Ocean | ______ Philippines* |
| ______ East China Sea | ______ Japan | ______ South China Sea |

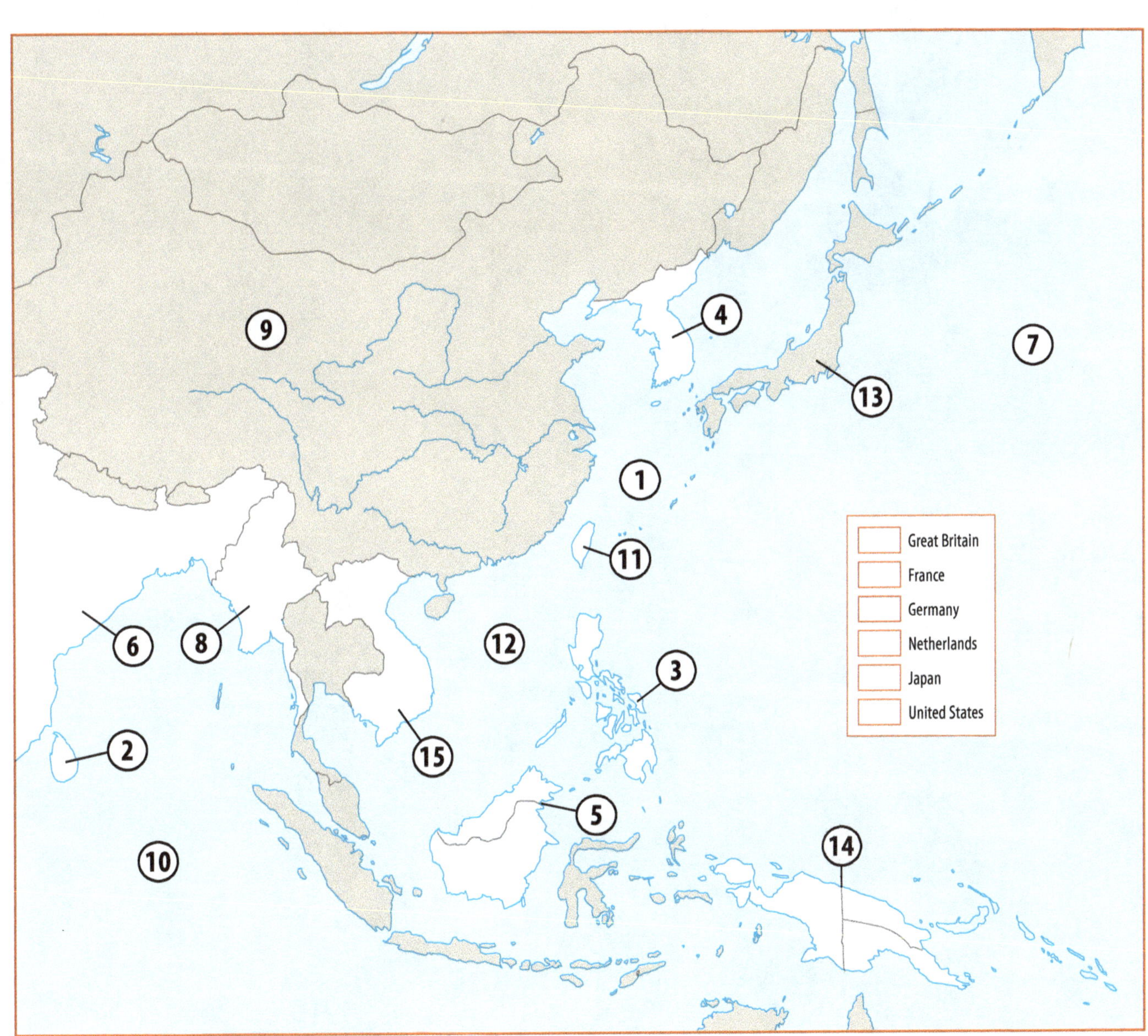

Name ______________________________

## The Middle Passage

Olaudah Equiano (ca. 1745–97) was an African who was kidnapped, brought to the African coast, and then sold to European slave traders. In his autobiography he recounts his experience of the infamous Middle Passage—the slaves' transatlantic voyage from Africa to the Americas, during which slaves underwent harsh trials and often died from the unspeakable conditions aboard ship. Equiano eventually gained his freedom and became an abolitionist. Later he became a Christian during the Methodist revivals.

**Answer the questions at the end after reading the following excerpt from the writings of Olaudah Equiano.**

One day, when we had a smooth sea and moderate wind, two of my wearied countrymen who were chained together (I was near them at the time), preferring death to such a life of misery, somehow made through the nettings and jumped into the sea: immediately another quite dejected fellow, who, on account of his illness, was suffered [allowed] to be out of irons, also followed their example; and I believe many more would very soon have done the same if they had not been prevented by the ship's crew, who were instantly alarmed. Those of us that were the most active were in a moment put down under the deck, and there was such a noise and confusion amongst the people of the ship as I never heard before, to stop [the ship], and get the boat out to go after the slaves. However two of the wretches were drowned, but they got the other, and afterwards flogged him unmercifully for thus attempting to prefer death to slavery. In this manner we continued to undergo more hardships than I can now relate, hardships which are inseparable from this accursed trade. Many a time we were near suffocation from the want [lack] of fresh air, which we were often without for whole days together. This, and the stench of the necessary tubs, carried off [killed] many. During our passage I first saw flying fishes, which surprised me very much: they used frequently to fly across the ship, and many of them fell on the deck. I also now first saw the use of the quadrant; I had often with astonishment seen the mariners make observations with it, and I could not think what it meant. They at last took notice of my surprise; and one of them, willing to increase it, as well as to gratify my curiosity, made me one day look through it. The clouds appeared to me to be land, which disappeared as they passed along. This heightened my wonder; and I was now more persuaded than ever that I was in another world, and that every thing about me was magic. At last we came in sight of the island of Barbadoes, at which the whites on board gave a great shout, and made many signs of joy to us. We did not know what to think of this; but as the vessel drew nearer we plainly saw the harbour, and other ships of different kinds and sizes; and we soon anchored amongst them off Bridge Town. Many merchants and planters now came on board, though it was in the evening. They put us in separate parcels, and examined us attentively. They also made us jump, and pointed to the land, signifying we were to go there. We thought by this we should be eaten by these ugly men, as they appeared to us; and, when soon after we were all put down under the deck again, there was much dread and trembling among us, and nothing but bitter cries to be heard all the night from these apprehensions, insomuch that at last the white people got some old slaves from the land to pacify us. They told us we were not to be eaten, but to work, and were soon to go on land, where we should see many of our country people. This report eased us much; and sure enough, soon after we were landed, there came to us Africans of all languages. We were conducted immediately to the merchant's yard, where we were all pent up together like so many sheep in a fold, without regard to sex or age. As every object was new to me every thing I saw filled me with surprise. What struck me first was that the houses were built with stories, and in every other respect different from those in Africa: but I was still more astonished on seeing people on horseback. I did not know what this could mean; and indeed I thought these people were full of nothing but magical arts. While I was in this astonishment one of my fellow

*(continued on next page)*

prisoners spoke to a countryman of his about the horses, who said they were the same kind they had in their country. I understood them, though they were from a distant part of Africa, and I thought it odd I had not seen any horses there; but afterwards, when I came to converse with different Africans, I found they had many horses amongst them, and much larger than those I then saw. We were not many days in the merchant's custody before we were sold after their usual manner, which is this:—On a signal given, (as the beat of a drum) the buyers rush at once into the yard where the slaves are confined, and make choice of that parcel they like best. The noise and clamour with which this is attended, and the eagerness visible in the countenances of the buyers, serve not a little to increase the apprehensions of the terrified Africans, who may well be supposed to consider them as the ministers of that destruction to which they think themselves devoted. In this manner, without scruple [moral restraint], are relations and friends separated, most of them never to see each other again. I remember in the vessel in which I was brought over, in the men's apartment, there were several brothers, who, in the sale, were sold in different lots; and it was very moving on this occasion to see and hear their cries at parting. O, ye nominal Christians! might not an African ask you, learned you this from your God, who says unto you, Do unto all men as you would men should do unto you? Is it not enough that we are torn from our country and friends to toil for your luxury and lust of gain? Must every tender feeling be likewise sacrificed to your avarice [greed]? Are the dearest friends and relations, now rendered more dear by their separation from their kindred, still to be parted from each other, and thus prevented from cheering the gloom of slavery with the small comfort of being together and mingling their sufferings and sorrows? Why are parents to lose their children, brothers their sisters, or husbands their wives? Surely this is a new refinement in cruelty, which, while it has no advantage to atone for it, thus aggravates distress, and adds fresh horrors even to the wretchedness of slavery.

*The Interesting Narrative of the Life of Olaudah Equiano, or Gustavus Vassa, the African: Written by Himself* by Olaudah Equiano. Public domain.

1. In what conditions were Africans transported to the Americas? ____________________

2. What did some Africans do to escape the slave ship? ____________________

3. How does Equiano apply Matthew 7:12 to the slave trade? ____________________

4. How does Equiano describe Europeans involved in the slave trade? ____________________

Name ______________________

## Livingstone and African Slavery

**Answer the questions below after reading the following excerpts from the writings of David Livingstone.**

*June 19th,* 1866.—We passed a woman tied by the neck to a tree, and dead. The people of the country explained that she had been unable to keep up with the other slaves in a gang, and her master had determined that she should not become the property of any one else if she recovered after resting for a time. I may mention here that we saw others tied up in a similar manner, and one lying in the path shot or stabbed, for she was in a pool of blood. The explanation we got invariably was that the Arab who owned these victims was enraged at losing his money by the slaves becoming unable to march, and vented his spleen [expressed his anger] by murdering them; but I have nothing more than common report in support of attributing this enormity [wickedness] to the Arabs. . . .

*June 27th.*—To-day we came upon a man dead from starvation, as he was very thin. One of our men wandered and found a number of slaves with slave-sticks on, abandoned by their master from want [lack] of food; they were too weak to be able to speak or say where they had come from; some were quite young. We crossed the Tulosi, a stream coming from south, about twenty yards wide.

At Chenjewala's the people are usually much startled when I explain that the numbers of slaves we see dead on the road have been killed partly by those who sold them; for I tell them that if they sell their fellows, they are like the man who holds the victim while the Arab performs the murder.

Chenjewala blamed Machemba, a chief above him on the Rovuma, for encouraging the slave-trade; I told him I had traveled so much among them that I knew all the excuses they could make: each head man blamed some one else.

"It would be better if you kept your people, and cultivated more largely," said I. "Oh, Machemba sends his men and robs our gardens after we have cultivated," was the reply. One man said that the Arabs who come and tempt them with fine clothes are the cause of their selling: this was childish, so I told them they would very soon have none to sell; their country was becoming jungle, and all their people who did not die in the road would be making gardens for Arabs at Kilwa and elsewhere. [Kilwa was a town on Africa's eastern coast.]

*June 28th.*—When we got about an hour from Chenjewala's we came to a party in the act of marauding; the owners of the gardens made off for the other side of the river, and waved to us to go against the people of Machemba, but we stood on a knoll with all our goods on the ground, and waited to see how matters would turn out. Two of the marauders came to us, and said they had captured five people. I suppose they took us for Arabs, as they addressed Musa [Livingstone's guide]. . . .

[*September 13th.*] In the course of this day's march we were pushed close to the Lake by Mount Gomé, and, being now within three miles of the end of the Lake, we could see the whole plainly. There we first saw the Shiré emerge, and there also we first gazed on the broad waters of Nyassa.

Many hopes have been disappointed here. Far down on the right bank of the Zambesi lies the dust of her whose death changed all my future prospects; and now, instead of a check being given to the slave-trade by lawful commerce on the Lake, slave-dhows [slave ships] prosper!

An Arab slave-party fled on hearing of us yesterday. It is impossible not to regret the loss of good Bishop Mackenzie, who sleeps far down the Shiré, and with him all hope of the Gospel being introduced into Central Africa. The silly abandonment of all the advantages of the Shiré

*(continued on next page)*

route by the bishop's successor I shall ever bitterly deplore; but all will come right some day, though I may not live to participate in the joy, or even see the commencement of better times.

In the evening we reached the village of Cherekalongwa, on the brook Pamchololo, and were very jovially received by the head man with beer. He says that Mukaté, Kabinga, and Mponda alone supply the slave-traders now by raids on the Manganja, but they go south-west to the Maravi, who, impoverished by a Mazitu raid, sell each other as well. . . .

*September 16th.*—At Mukaté's. . . . We had a long discussion about the slave-trade. The Arabs have told the chief that our object in capturing slaves is to get them into our own possession, and make them of our own religion. The evils which we have seen—the skulls, the ruined villages, the numbers who perish on the way to the coast and on the sea, the wholesale murders committed by the Waiyau to build up Arab villages elsewhere—these things Mukaté often tried to turn off [dismiss] with a laugh, but our remarks are safely lodged in many hearts. Next day, as we went along, our guide spontaneously delivered their substance to the different villages along our route. Before we reached him, a head man, in convoying me a mile or two, whispered to me, "Speak to Mukaté to give his forays up."

It is but little we can do; but we lodge a protest in the heart against a vile system, and time may ripen it. Their great argument is, "What could we do without Arab cloth?" My answer is, "Do what you did before the Arabs came into the country." At the present rate of destruction of population, the whole country will soon be a desert.

1. What two non-European peoples engaged in the African slave trade? ____________________

2. How did the Africans support the slave trade? ____________________

3. What does God's Word teach about kidnapping and enslaving others (1 Tim. 1:9–10)? ____________________

____________________

4. According to the Arabs, what did Livingstone and his party plan to do with the African people? ____________________

____________________

5. What evidence does Livingstone record to expose the slave trade's dreadful impact on Africa? ____________________

____________________

*September 19th.*—When we had proceeded a mile this morning we came to three or four hundred people making salt on a plain impregnated with it. They lixiviate the soil [mix it with water] and boil the water, which has filtered through a bunch of grass in a hole in the bottom of a pot, till all is evaporated and a mass of salt left. We held along the plain till we came to Mponda's, a large village, with a stream running past. . . . Mponda is a blustering sort of person, but immensely interested in every thing European. He says that he would like to go with me. "Would not care though he were away ten years."—I say that he may die in the journey.—"He will die here as well as there, but he will see all the wonderful doings of our country." He knew me, having come to the boat to take a look *incognito* when we were here formerly.

We found an Arab slave-party here, and went to look at the slaves; seeing this, Mponda was alarmed lest we should proceed to violence in his town, but I said to him that we went to look only. Eighty-five slaves were in a pen formed of dura stalks. . . . The majority were boys of about eight or ten years of age; others were grown men and women. Nearly all were in the taming-stick; a few of the younger ones were [tied up]. . . . Several pots were on the fires cooking dura and beans. A crowd went with us, expecting a scene; but I sat down, and asked a few questions about the journey, in front. The slave-party consisted of five or six half-caste coast Arabs, who said that they came from Zanzibar; but the crowd made such a noise that we could not hear ourselves speak. I asked if they had any objections to my looking at the slaves; the owners pointed out the different slaves, and said that after feeding them, and accounting for the losses

*(continued on next page)*

Slaves in Tanzania

in the way to the coast, they made little by the trip. I suspect that the gain is made by those who ship them to the ports of Arabia, for at Zanzibar most of the younger slaves we saw went at about seven dollars a head. I said to them it was a bad business altogether. . . .

*July* 28*th*[, 1867].—Prayers, with the [Anglican] Litany. Slavery is a great evil wherever I have seen it. A poor old woman and child are among the captives; the boy, about three years old, seems a mother's pet: his feet are sore from walking in the sun. He was offered for two fathoms, and his mother for one fathom: he understood it all, and cried bitterly, clinging to his mother. She had, of course, no power to help him: they were separated at Karungu afterward.

[The above is an episode of every-day occurrence in the wake of the slave-dealer. "Two fathoms," mentioned as the price of the boy's life—the more valuable of the two—means four yards of unbleached calico, which is a universal article of barter throughout the greater part of Africa: the mother was bought for two yards. The reader must not think that there are no lower prices; in the famines which succeed the slave-dealer's raids, boys and girls are at times to be purchased by the dealer for a few handfuls of maize.]

[*February* 25*th,* 1868.] No better authority for what has been done or left undone by Mohammedans [Muslims] in this country can be found than Mohamad bin Saleh; for he is very intelligent, and takes an interest in all that happens, and his father was equally interested in this country's affairs. He declares that no attempt was ever made by Mohammedans to proselytize the Africans: they teach their own children to read the Koran, but them only: it is never translated, and to servants who go to the mosque it is all dumb-show [unintelligible]. Some servants imbibe [absorb] Mohammedan bigotry about eating, but they offer no prayers. Circumcision, to make *halel*, or fit to slaughter the animals for their master, is the utmost advance any have made. As the Arabs in East Africa never feel themselves called on to propagate the doctrines of Islam among the heathen Africans, the statement of Captain Burton that they would make better missionaries to the Africans than Christians, because they would not insist on the abandonment of polygamy, possesses the same force as if he had said Mohammedans would catch more

*(continued on next page)*

birds than Christians, because they would put salt on their tails. The indispensable requisite or qualification for any kind of missionary is that he have some wish to proselytize: this the Arabs do not possess in the slightest degree.

As they never translate the Koran, they neglect the best means of influencing the Africans, who invariably wish to understand what they are about. When we were teaching adults the alphabet, they felt it a hard task. "Give me medicine; I shall drink it to make me understand it," was their earnest entreaty [request]. When they have advanced so far as to form clear conceptions of Old Testament and Gospel histories, they tell them to their neighbors; and, on visiting distant tribes, feel proud to show how much they know: in this way the knowledge of Christianity becomes widely diffused [spread]. Those whose hatred to its self-denying doctrines has become developed by knowledge, propagate slanders; but still they speak of Christianity, and awaken attention. The plan, therefore, of the Christian missionary in imparting knowledge is immeasurably superior to that of the Moslem in dealing with dumb-show. I have, however, been astonished to see that none of the Africans imitate the Arab prayers: considering their great reverence of the Deity, it is a wonder that they do not learn to address prayers to Him except on very extraordinary occasions.

David Livingstone. *The Last Journals of David Livingstone, in Central Africa: From Eighteen Hundred and Sixty-Five to His Death; Continued by a Narrative of His Last Moments and Sufferings, Obtained from His Faithful Servants Chuma and Susi*, ed. Horace Waller. (New York: Harper and Brothers, 1875), 59, 64, 91–92, 94–97, 182, 223–24. (The bracketed section "The above . . . maize" is in the original.)

6. What price did the slave traders put on the three-year-old boy? ______

7. What disaster often followed the slave dealers' raids and lowered the cost of a slave to a few handfuls of maize (corn)? ______

8. According to Livingstone, how much did the Muslims teach the Africans about Islam? ______

9. How did Africans spread knowledge of God's Word in Africa? ______

Name ______________________________

## *Imperialism in Africa 1914*

***Locate the following on the map. Color the countries based on imperialism by the following countries: Belgium, Great Britain, France, Germany, Italy, Portugal, and Spain.***

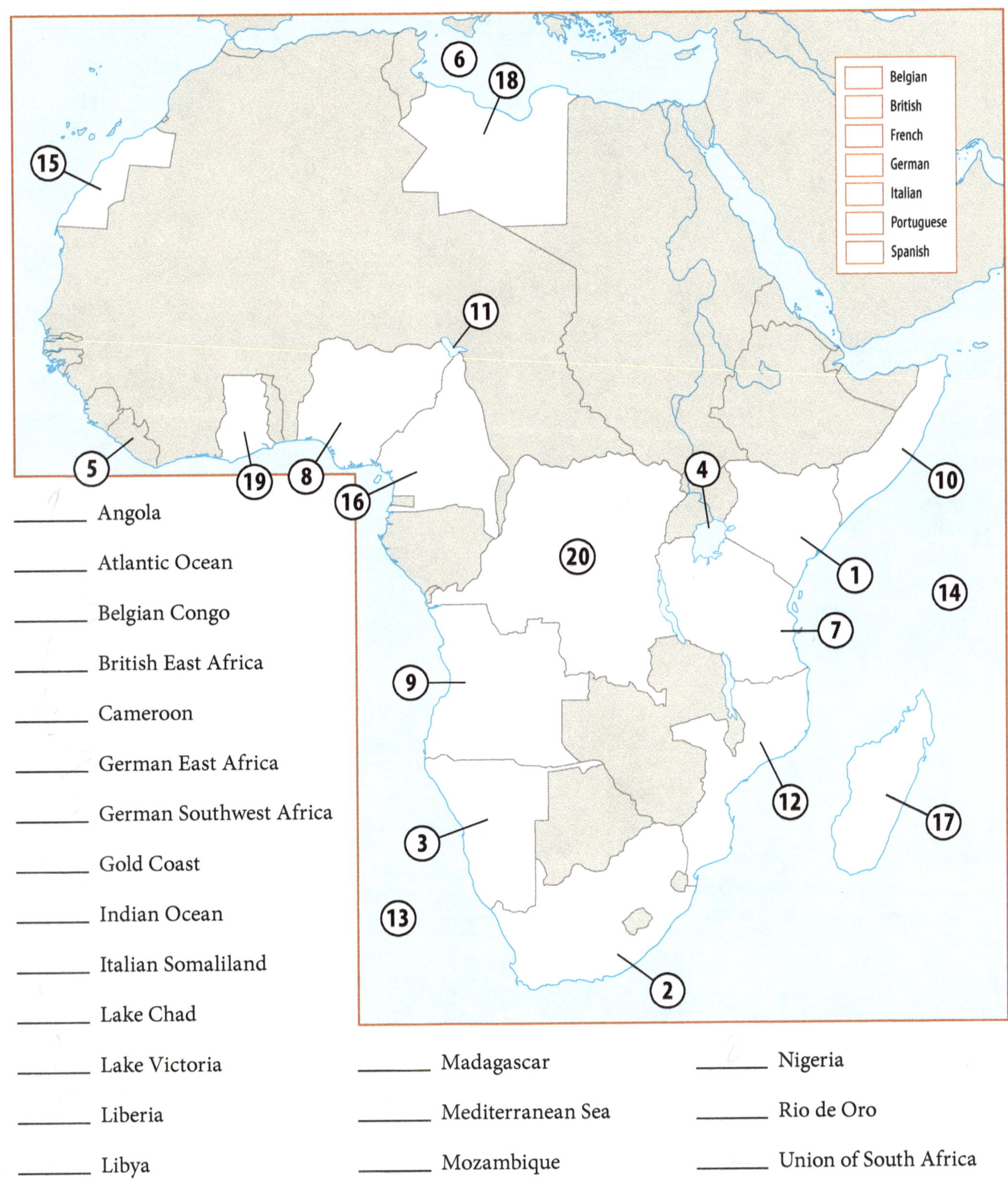


_______ Angola

_______ Atlantic Ocean

_______ Belgian Congo

_______ British East Africa

_______ Cameroon

_______ German East Africa

_______ German Southwest Africa

_______ Gold Coast

_______ Indian Ocean

_______ Italian Somaliland

_______ Lake Chad

_______ Lake Victoria

_______ Liberia

_______ Libya

_______ Madagascar

_______ Mediterranean Sea

_______ Mozambique

_______ Nigeria

_______ Rio de Oro

_______ Union of South Africa

Name ______________________________

# Chapter Review

## Complete the Statement

**Underline the term that accurately completes each of the following statements.**

1. The (British North American Act/Quebec Act) permitted the French Canadians to retain their language, law, and customs and to freely practice their Roman Catholic religion.
2. The (Crimean War/Boer War) was the first major international conflict after the defeat of Napoleon.
3. The (Boxer Rebellion/Sepoy Mutiny) came about because of Hindu and Muslim beliefs.
4. King Leopold II colonized (the Congo/Algeria) for Belgium.

## Matching

**Choose the best answer and place the letter in the blank beside the corresponding description.**

| | | |
|---|---|---|
| A. William Carey | E. Louis Philippe | I. Hudson Taylor |
| B. Robert Clive | F. Matthew Perry | J. Mary Slessor |
| C. James Cook | G. Karl Peters | K. Henry Stanley |
| D. Leopold II | H. Cecil Rhodes | |

_____ 5. Missionary to China

_____ 6. Founded a German colony in Southwest Africa

_____ 7. Explored Australia for England

_____ 8. Found Livingstone in 1871 at Lake Tanganyika

_____ 9. Translated the Bible into Indian languages, including Bengali

_____ 10. Missionary to Africa

_____ 11. Aggressive British imperialist in southern Africa

_____ 12. Achieved military victories that made India a British colony

_____ 13. Forcefully persuaded Japan to open trade with the United States

_____ 14. Belgium's king who allowed African nationals to be severely mistreated

*(continued on next page)*

## Short Answer

**Write the correct answer to each question in the provided blank.**

15. Name the ruling family in Japan when the Treaty of Kanagawa was signed. ____________________

16. What 1907 agreement indicated strong Western control of the Near East, especially of Iran and Afghanistan? ____________________

17. What is the importance of the Russo-Japanese War (1904–5)? ____________________

## Essay

**Write the correct answer to each question in the provided blank.**

18. How did Japan and China respond differently to Western imperialism? How did those responses affect those nations? ____________________

19. How did the Ages of Exploration and Imperialism confirm that man is sinful? Provide examples from the chapter. ____________________

20. How did the Ages of Exploration and Imperialism enlarge the African slave trade? How did the Islamic slave trade differ from the European slave trade? ____________________

Name ______________________________

## Rival Alliances (1914)

**Locate each term on the map and place the corresponding number in the appropriate blank.**

| | |
|---|---|
| _______ Albania | _______ Great Britain |
| _______ Austria-Hungary | _______ Greece |
| _______ Bulgaria | _______ Italy |
| _______ France | _______ Ottoman Empire |
| _______ Germany | _______ Spain |

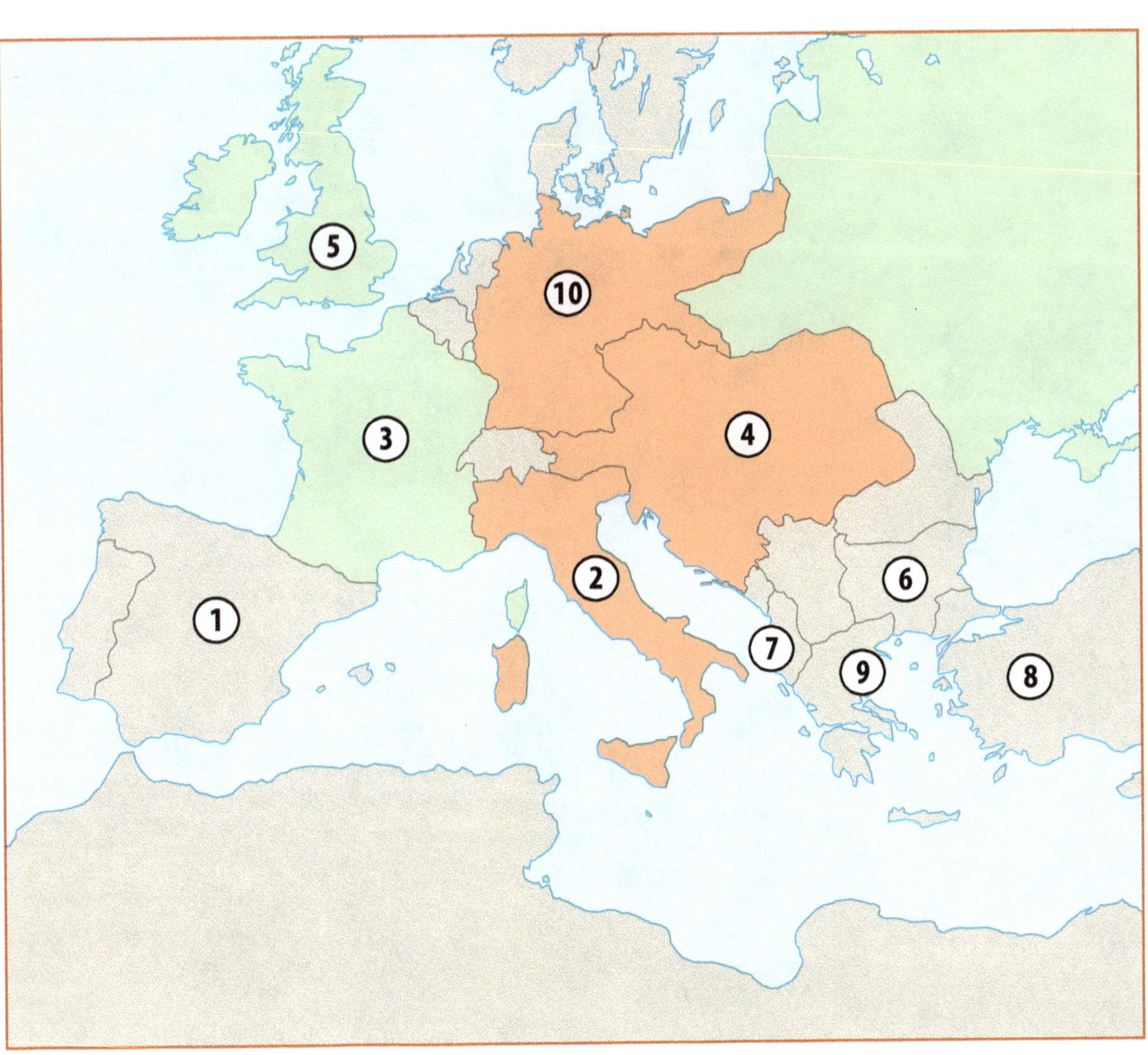

Name ____________________

# Armenian Genocide

**Answer the questions below after reading the following excerpts from the writings of Jacques de Morgan.**

This was the end of the year 1895. Officers were sent out from Yildiz-Kiosk, and executions in the provinces marked the passage of the Imperial messengers.

To describe the atrocities then committed would require the publication of a large volume. A passage from the work of Pastor Lepsius is sufficient to give an idea of the unexpected woes that suddenly fell on the Armenians:

"In the village of Hoh, in the Kharput district, the Christians were gathered together inside a mosque. Eighty young men were chosen from among them and led outside the village to be slaughtered. Hundreds of Armenians were tortured because they refused to sign addresses to the Sultan accusing their relatives and neighbors of high treason. One of them refusing to swear to a statement which would have delivered the honest people of his village to the executioner, was ordered by the judges to be tortured. All night long this lasted; first he was bastinadoed [beaten] on the soles of his feet in a room adjoining which were the womenfolk of his family. They tied him up, flogged him, tore out his beard hair by hair, burned his flesh with red-hot iron, and still he refused to swear as was demanded of him.

"'I am a Christian,' he said, 'I cannot stain my soul with innocent blood . . . In the name of divine mercy, finish me.'

"It was important for Abdul-Hamid to have documents in hand to show that the Armenians were revolutionaries, so as to justify his acts to the representatives of France, Britain, and the United States, and to legitimize these heinous crimes by passing them off as acts of justice dictated by reasons of State.

"In 1890 the Sultan, already preparing to exterminate the Armenians, had the genial idea to arm the Kurds on the borders of Armenia and give them the name of Hamidian Cavalry. He let loose, as can be well imagined, these bandits against the Christians, and then encouraged by the hesitant attitude of the ambassadors, in 1894 he ordered a trial massacre at Sassoun, an experiment which lasted three weeks. The regular army itself was ordered to do the killing.

"In one place, three to four hundred women, and in another two hundred, after being delivered up to the soldiers, were despatched [killed] by the sword or the bayonet.

"In another place, about sixty women and girls were shut up for several days in a small church, delivered to the soldiers, and then finally slaughtered; a river of blood flowed from the church door. Elsewhere, on a mountain, some thousands of fugitives held out for ten days or so, but in vain. A woman ran out on a high rock and cried: 'Sisters, you must choose: either fall into the hands of these Turks or else follow me,' and holding in her arms her one-year-old child, she cast herself down. Her companions followed her, and the Sultan decorated the officer in command of the murderers, and sent a silver banner to the Kurdish chieftains."

From 1894 to 1896 more than 200,000 Armenians were put to death, 100,000 were made Moslems by force, and more than 100,000 women and girls were ravished and sent into harems. Armenia being devastated, there was no harvest, and the remainder of the inhabitants suffered a terrible famine. Fleeing to the mountains and hiding in inaccessible spots, the peasants watched their homes sacked and burned, thousands of their villages being reduced to ashes.

From Europe there went up a tremendous cry of indignation [outrage] as the groanings of the victims reached the ears of the western world, but no power dared to intervene with the energy that was called for; to have despatched [sent] an expeditionary force to the Turkish coasts would have brought about a European war, and so they all held off.

*(continued on next page)*

1. Why did Abdul-Hamid try to force the Armenians to say they were rebellious to the Turks? ________________

________________

________________

2. What role did the Kurds play in the Armenian genocide? ________________

________________

________________

3. What was the European response to the genocide? ________________

________________

On account of the war [World War I] that had just been declared on the Entente Powers, all the young Christians of the [Ottoman] Empire were called to the colors [drafted], but they were not sent to the front. They were divided into sections of several hundreds each, and used for the building and upkeep of roads; then, when they had finished this work, a large number were executed.

The towns and villages with only old people, women, and children left in them, and incapable of any defense, were occupied by the troops. Most of the men and male children were slain, and the remainder were ordered to gather into columns of 1,000 to 2,000 each, to go off into exile. These formalities were accompanied by summonses to adopt the Moslem religion, also by every kind of violence on the part of the soldiers. The property of the evicted inhabitants was distributed or sold to Moslems for next to nothing.

The columns started out, accompanied by soldiers and by Kurdish horsemen who, on the way, indulged in every conceivable brutality, killing as fancy took them, and selling the women as slaves in the small towns and villages they passed through.

Even these sales were conducted methodically. In each town the women and young girls were lined up in front of the Konak (government building) and offered to purchasers; on the following day the remainder of the column resumed the march. Many of the unfortunates exhausted by fatigue and hunger fell by the wayside; most of these rose no more, a spear or bayonet-thrust put an end to their sufferings.

Many of these columns were entirely massacred, especially at a place called Kemagh-Boghaz on the Euphrates below Erzindjan. Others, their ranks greatly thinned, reached Mesopotamia, where most of them gradually died off in the bleak desert climate, homeless and starving. . . .

To give a better realization . . . of all the horror of these mass executions and pillaging, allow me to add to the above report a few authentic documents covering each phase of these frightful dramas. They may all be summed up in four acts, viz: the execution of the young men, the massacres, the caravan, [and] the desert.

A witness stated: "One day we met a number of workmen. 'They are going to kill them all off,' our traveling companion (a gendarme) said to me. From the top of a hill our driver pointed out to me with his whip about four hundred workmen whom they had lined up on the edge of a sloping piece of ground. We know what happened. In another place, while the gendarmes shot, Turkish workmen finished off the victims with knives and stones." . . .

In one town in Armenia, a Danish hospital-nurse was one night awakened by shooting, and realizing that numbers were being shot down before the departure of the caravan, she wrote: "I felt really relieved to think that those victims were at last beyond human cruelty. Fortunate are those who are killed!"

Fortunate victims, indeed! for the lot of the survivors, those whom death did not take, was frightful. The caravan decimated by hunger, exhaustion, and the cruelty of their guards, had to

*(continued on next page)*

go on and on. Sometimes the cries of women and children fill the air. Strength fails, hideous hunger adds its scourge. The unfortunates devour straw, grass, whenever they can. "I looked at them," said one witness, "and wild animals could not have been worse; they rushed on the guards carrying food, and the guards struck them with clubs, hard enough sometimes to kill them. It was difficult to realize that these were human beings."

While the caravan plods along a road strewn with the corpses from the preceding convoy, sometimes through reeking air, the local mob, conscious that here they can prey at will, follow along like a pack of wolves, biting and tearing. The mob kill and steal.

When they pass near the river, mothers throw their children in the water and themselves after them. Or else the gendarmes throw in all the children under twelve or fifteen, and any who can swim, they shoot in the water.

Even at the end of the seemingly interminable march, their martyrdom is not over for the unhappy survivors, for the desert climate is terrible for these people accustomed to mountain air. Among them are to be seen some who from what remains of their clothing appear to have been men of position, educated women speaking European languages, chiefly English and French, people who have known the intellectual and material well-being of civilization! . . .

"Of the between 2,000 and 3,000 peasants of Upper Armenia brought to Aleppo," said a German professor in the school of that city, "there remain forty or fifty skeletons. With distorted features, they succumb to blows, to hunger, and thirst. Europeans are forbidden to give bread to the starving creatures. Forty or fifty phantoms were heaped together in one court; they are the demented ones, they no longer know how to eat. When offered bread they refused it unconcernedly. They merely groan as they await death. Every day over a hundred corpses are taken out of Aleppo. Young girls, women, children, almost naked on the ground, lie between the dying and coffins already prepared, and breathe their last feeble sighs."

In every province of Armenia the massacres were terrible, but those that took place at Mouch surpassed in barbarity the atrocities in any other town. A witness of this awful drama stated: "Day broke, it was the 2nd of July, 1915, a day of suffering and calamity, a day of terror for the unhappy Armenians. Early in the morning, Kurds and regular soldiers overran the town shouting, and entered the Armenian quarters. They began by killing those who were still there since the departure of thirteen hundred people who had gone off in caravan the day before and been wiped out. Most of the inhabitants, no longer doubting the fate that awaited them, had gathered in the houses in the center of the town, where they seemed a little safer. There, families were grouped together forty, fifty, even a hundred persons huddled together in narrow rooms, with doors and windows and all entrances barricaded.

"Soon howls of approaching men drew nearer; the band of madmen invaded the streets, shooting as they came, and armed with hatchets they attacked the doors which flew in splinters. Then followed an indescribable slaughter. Cries of terror and agony were mingled with the noise of hatchet-blows and with the calls urging on the murderers. The streets ran with blood, and bodies were piling up in front of the houses, while the Turks continued to shout: 'Vour! Vour!' ('Strike! Strike!') The Kurds yelled and howled for blood, as these wild beasts went from house to house swinging their blood-covered hatchets.

"The unhappy Armenians, crazed with fear, pressed against one another, were crushed and suffocated. The cries and shrieks of the women were heard, as children were trampled to death by those who strove to save them.

"A young woman handed one of the executioners her child she was holding in her arms. 'Take him,' she begged, 'I give him to you, only do not kill him.' The soldier seized the child, threw it down and cut off its head with one stroke; then turning to the unhappy mother, with one more blow with his axe he cleaved her skull."

Jacques de Morgan. *The History of the Armenian People: From the Remotest Times to the Present Day*, trans. Ernest F. Barry. (n.p.: Hairenik Association, 1918), 304–5, 308–11.

*(continued on next page)*

4. What role did Armenians play in World War I? ______________________________________________

______________________________________________________________________________

5. How did the "soldiers and . . . Kurdish horsemen" (Muslims) treat Armenian survivors who were marched off to exile? ______________________________________________________________

______________________________________________________________________________

______________________________________________________________________________

6. What role did the Kurds play in the massacre at Mouch? ____________________________________

______________________________________________________________________________

______________________________________________________________________________

7. How did a Muslim soldier respond when an Armenian mother handed him her son and pleaded for his life? ____________________________________________________________________________

______________________________________________________________________________

Name ______________________

# Eyewitness Account of World War I

In *The Harvard Volunteers in Europe*, M. A. DeWolfe Howe notes that "early in the War, André Chéronet Champollion, '02 [Harvard alumnus of the class of 1902], a naturalized American citizen of French descent, enlisted in the French Army. He was a grandson of the late Austin Corbin and a great-grandson of Jean François Champollion, the eminent Egyptologist who deciphered the Rosetta Stone. . . . On March 1, 1915, he went to the front. . . . [The following] letter, dated March 20, was written only three days before he fell at Bois-le-Prêtre, in France, killed by a bullet in the forehead."

**Answer the questions at the end after reading the following letter by André Chéronet Champollion.**

AT THE FRONT, March 20, 1915.

Six days ago we left the village of "Dunghurst" at two in the morning and got back to the trenches at about eight, that is, six hours later. When we first entered the long communication-trench, things seemed pretty quiet. Only a shot and an explosion at long intervals could be heard. We had travelled along the communication-trench about half an hour, and were about to enter our shelters in the second line trenches when not far away came two fairly loud bomb explosions in quick succession. Then the earth seemed all of a sudden to reel. There was a commotion like the bursting asunder of a volcano. Two hundred yards off, above the trees, a column of huge rocks, lumps of earth, tree-trunks, and probably numerous human limbs, rose slowly and majestically. The upper fragments, as they rose, seemed to advance menacingly in our direction, as if they must surely hit us when they returned to earth. They seemed suspended in the air for an indefinite space of time, as if there was no hurry at all about their falling back. They seemed to cross and criss-cross in all directions, now obscuring half the sky. Gradually the mass assumed the shape of the upper portion of an elm tree, and then began to subside. Then could be heard the smashing sound of the tree branches as this mass of rock and earth fell back with the crushing force of an avalanche. Everybody ducked and plunged head first into the shelters.

Almost immediately there came the sound of thousands of heavy rain drops on a stiff canvass or the snapping of innumerable small whips; all this punctuated by a peculiar bizz, bizz, whizz sound like someone whistling in surprise. I could not help making the inward remark, "I knew war was tough, but look here, boys, isn't this a bit too rough?" It seemed that the Germans had exploded a mine under one of our trenches, then opened a violent fusillade [burst of gunfire] to capture what remained of it. Being second line troops just arrived from resting up, we were not required to fight. We consequently were huddled together in a bomb-proof shelter, packed all day like sardines, but quite satisfied to remain where we were, while above our heads shot and shell seemed to pass for several hours with unexampled violence. That night also was "stormy," but since then, that is for the last five days, there has been little else but sniping and desultory [random] firing by the artillery. In the above action we lost sixty men killed and two hundred wounded, but the enemy failed to capture the trench and lost a few yards of one they had held the day before.

The day after the explosion I saw many dead and wounded men carried out of the trenches on stretchers. Some of the wounded seemed more mauled than some of the dead. Behind a hedge at the end of the communication-trench, which hedge is erected to conceal our movements, I counted twenty-five dead men lined up for burial. Their faces were usually concealed by part of their uniforms, but their arms assumed every imaginable attitude, gestures of prayer, attitudes of men pleading, some even seemed threatening. Here and there big red gashes and splotches indicated where they had been hit. A few men are hit every day by the desultory artillery fire and the sniping.

*(continued on next page)*

All the trees in this wood show signs of the punishment they have received. Whole acres are shaved down, trees two feet in diameter have been broken in two like matches by 210 mm. shells. Almost all have lost branches. Their trunks are all scarred by bullet holes and scratches.

In the second line trenches we live the lives of convicts at hard labor. Either we have to dig more trenches or carry heavy logs, iron bars, bales of hay, etc., from the outside, along the communication-trench to where we are "lodged," a distance of about half a mile. As the communication-trenches are always congested with men coming and going, this work is all the more irksome.

We live like swine. There is no water, so we never wash or even brush our teeth. We are not allowed to drink water. We simply live in filth. At night we are huddled together in a small bomb-proof or covered trench. Though we are pretty well protected from the weather and bullets, we have hardly room enough to turn around in. We use candles to light up this [area], but nevertheless everything gets lost or hopelessly dirty. We eat from the pail, and can get or send for all the red or white wine we want. In the morning, besides tepid [lukewarm] coffee, we are given a swig of rum which warms our stomach and starts the blood going. This small pleasure and continued pipe smoking are about our only joys—but hold—there is also our mail, which we get fairly regularly.

M. A. DeWolfe Howe, ed. *The Harvard Volunteers in Europe: Personal Records of Experience in Military, Ambulance, and Hospital Service.* (Cambridge: Harvard Univ. Press, 1916), 14, 18–22.

1. What did the Germans do that surprised the French troops? ______________________________

______________________________

2. How does Champollion describe the violence he witnessed? ______________________________

______________________________

______________________________

3. What difficult conditions did the soldiers endure? ______________________________

______________________________

______________________________

______________________________

4. How does Champollion's death, which occurred shortly after this letter was written, illustrate James 4:14?

______________________________

______________________________

______________________________

Name ______________________________

# U-boat Attack: April 1916

**Answer the questions at the end after reading the following account by Edgar von Spiegel, a U-boat commander.**

The steamer appeared to be close to us and looked colossal. I saw the captain walking on his bridge, a small whistle in his mouth. I saw the crew cleaning the deck forward, and I saw, with surprise and a slight shudder, long rows of wooden partitions right along all decks, from which gleamed the shining black and brown backs of horses.

"Oh [no], horses! What a pity, those lovely beasts!"

"But it cannot be helped," I went on thinking. "War is war, and every horse the fewer on the Western front is a reduction of England's fighting power." I must acknowledge, however, that the thought of what must come was a most unpleasant one, and I will describe what happened as briefly as possible. . . .

"Stand-by for firing a torpedo!" I called down to the control-room. . . .

"FIRE!"

A slight tremor went through the boat—the torpedo had gone. . . .

The death-bringing shot was a true one, and the torpedo ran towards the doomed ship at high speed. I could follow its course exactly by the light streak of bubbles which was left in its wake. . . .

. . . I saw that the bubble-track of the torpedo had been discovered on the bridge of the steamer, as frightened arms pointed towards the water and the captain put his hands in front of his eyes and waited resignedly. Then a frightful explosion followed, and we were all thrown against one another by the concussion, and then, like Vulcan, huge and majestic, a column of water two hundred metres high and fifty metres broad, terrible in its beauty and power, shot up to the heavens.

"Hit abaft the second funnel," I shouted down to the control-room. . . .

All [the steamer's] decks lay visible to me. From all the hatchways a storming, despairing mass of men were fighting their way on deck—grimy stokers, officers, soldiers, grooms, cooks. They all rushed, ran, screamed for boats, tore and thrust one another from the ladders leading down to them, fought for the life-belts and jostled one another on the sloping deck. All amongst them, rearing, slipping horses were wedged. The starboard boats could not be lowered on account of the list; everyone therefore ran across to the port boats, which, in the hurry and panic, had been lowered with great stupidity either half-full or overcrowded. The men left behind were wringing their hands in despair and running to and fro along the decks; finally they threw themselves into the water so as to swim to the boats.

Then—a second explosion, followed by the escape of white hissing steam from all hatchways and scuttles. A boiler must have burst. The white steam drove the horses mad. I saw a beautiful long-tailed dapple-grey horse take a mighty leap over the berthing rails and land into a fully-laden boat. At that point I could not bear the sight any longer, and I lowered the periscope and dived deep.

Edgar von Spiegel. *U. Boat 202: The War Diary of a German Submarine*. Trans. by Barry Domvile. (London: Andrew Melrose, 1919), 40–44.

*(continued on next page)*

1. What did Spiegel see on the Allied vessel that made him reluctant to attack it? ______

______

2. How does this account reveal an inconsistency in the way Spiegel values life? ______

______

______

______

3. Since World War I involved numerous deadly new weapons (including the machine gun, the airplane, long-range cannons, and poisonous gas), why do you think unrestricted submarine warfare was so offensive to the people of the world? ______

______

______

Name ______________________________

# Robert Lansing and the League of Nations

**Answer the questions at the end after reading the following excerpt from the writings of Robert Lansing.**

President Wilson's decision to go to Paris and to engage in person in the negotiations was strongly influenced by his belief that it was the only sure way of providing in the treaty of peace for the organization of a League of Nations. While his presence in Paris was probably affected to an extent by other considerations, as I have pointed out, it is to be presumed that he was anxious to participate directly in the drafting of the plan of organization of the League and to exert his personal influence on the delegates in favor of its acceptance by publicly addressing the Conference. This he could hardly have done without becoming a delegate. It would seem, therefore, that the purpose of creating a League of Nations and obtaining the incorporation of a plan of organization in the treaty to be negotiated had much to do with the President's presence at the peace table. . . .

A union of the nations for the purpose of preventing wars of aggression and conquest seemed to him the most practical, if not the only, way of accomplishing this supreme object, and he urged it with earnestness and eloquence in his public addresses relating to the bases of peace.

There was much to be said in favor of the President's point of view. Unquestionably the American people as a whole supported him in the belief that there ought to be some international agreement, association, or concord which would lessen the possibility of future wars. An international organization to remove in a measure the immediate causes of war, to provide means for the peaceable settlement of disputes between nations, and to draw the governments into closer friendship appealed to the general desire of the peoples of America and Europe. The four years and more of horror and agony through which mankind had passed must be made impossible of repetition, and there seemed no other way than to form an international union devoted to the maintenance of peace by composing, as far as possible, controversies which might ripen into war. . . .

The outbreak of the war and the dreadful waste and suffering which followed impelled the societies and associations then organized to redoubled effort and induced the formation of new organizations. People everywhere began to realize that their objects were real and not merely sentimental or academic, that they were seeking practical means to remove the conditions which had made the Great War possible. Public opinion became more and more pronounced as the subject was more widely discussed in the journals and periodicals of the day and at public meetings, the divergence of views being chiefly in regard to the means to be employed by the proposed organization and not as to the creation of the organization, the necessity for which appeared to be generally conceded. . . .

[Lansing records the text of a letter that he wrote to President Woodrow Wilson on May 25, 1916, explaining his objections to the League of Nations. Lansing believed that such a league would subject America to other nations by obligating America to be involved in foreign matters, even at its own expense. Lansing then proceeds to describe how this letter negatively affected the president's relations with him.]

The President, thus early advised of my unqualified opposition to any plan which was similar in principle to the one advocated by the League to Enforce Peace, naturally concluded that I would look with disfavor on an international guaranty which by implication, if not by declaration, compelled the use of force to give it effect. Doubtless he felt that I would not be disposed to aid in perfecting a plan which had as its central idea a guaranty of that nature. Disliking

*(continued on next page)*

opposition to a plan or policy which he had originated or made his own by adoption, he preferred to consult those who without debate accepted his judgment and were in sympathy with his ideas. Undoubtedly the President by refraining from asking my advice spared himself from listening to arguments against the guaranty and the use of force which struck at the very root of his plan, for I should, if I had been asked, have stated my views with entire frankness.

The other reason for not consulting me, as I now realize, but did not at the time, was that I belonged to the legal profession. It is a fact, which Mr. Wilson has taken no trouble to conceal, that he does not value the advice of lawyers except on strictly legal questions, and that he considers their objections and criticisms on other subjects to be too often based on mere technicalities and their judgments to be warped by an undue regard for precedent. This prejudice against the legal profession in general was exhibited on more than one occasion during our sojourn at Paris. . . .

In the carrying out of his scheme and in creating an organization to give effect to the guaranty I believed that I saw as an unavoidable consequence an exaltation of force and an overlordship of the strong nations. Under such conditions it would be impossible to preserve within the organization the equality of nations, a precept of international law which was the universally recognized basis of intercourse between nations in time of peace. This I considered most unwise and a return to the old order, from which every one hoped that the victory over the Central Empires had freed the world.

Robert Lansing. *The Peace Negotiations: A Personal Narrative.* (Boston: Houghton Mifflin, 1921), 28–31, 41, 45.

1. Why did President Wilson promote a league of nations? ______________________________

______________________________

______________________________

2. Why did Wilson avoid asking Lansing for advice concerning the League? ______________________________

______________________________

______________________________

3. What group of people did Wilson avoid consulting about his proposed league? ______________________________

______________________________

4. Why did Lansing seek to prevent the United States from joining the League? ______________________________

______________________________

______________________________

______________________________

5. Who turned out to be correct about the effectiveness of the League of Nations—Lansing or Wilson?

______________________________

Name ______________________

# Chapter Review

## Complete the Statement

**Underline the term that accurately completes each of the following statements.**

1. The Treaty of (St. Germain/Sèvres) required Austria to give territory to Italy and recognize the independence of Czechoslovakia, Hungary, Poland, and Yugoslavia.
2. In the (Kellogg-Briand/Locarno) Pact, Germany recognized its present borders with France and Belgium as permanent.
3. (Georges Clemenceau/Vittorio Orlando) was France's representative at the Paris Peace Conference.
4. The (Reinsurance Treaty/Treaty of Brest-Litovsk) took Russia out of World War I.
5. (Bismarck's System/The Schlieffen Plan) was an effort to keep France isolated diplomatically from the rest of Europe.

## Matching

**Choose the best answer and place the letter in the blank beside the corresponding description.**

A. Andrew Carnegie
B. Charles Dawes
C. Francis Ferdinand
D. Ferdinand Foch
E. David Lloyd George
F. Paul von Hindenburg
G. Nicholas II
H. Alfred Nobel
I. John J. Pershing
J. Baron Manfred Richthofen
K. Wilhelm II
L. Woodrow Wilson
M. Alvin C. York

_____ 6. Established a peace prize

_____ 7. Defeated Russian forces at the Battle of Tannenberg

_____ 8. Stopped Germany's 1918 offense before American forces arrived

_____ 9. Germany's kaiser who forced Bismarck to resign as chancellor

_____ 10. Leader of the American Expeditionary Force

_____ 11. American steel manufacturer and philanthropist

_____ 12. America's president when the war began in 1914

_____ 13. Russia's czar who stepped down in 1917

_____ 14. Austrian archduke who was assassinated on June 28, 1914

_____ 15. Created a plan for Germany to make manageable war payments

*(continued on next page)*

## Short Answer

**Write the correct answer to each question in the provided blank.**

16. What term denotes a cease-fire? ____________________

17. What term denotes payment for war damages? ____________________

18. What German word means "the political unification of Germany and Austria"? ____________________

19. What is another name for German submarines? ____________________

20. What was the name of the anti-French coalition composed of Germany, Austria-Hungary, and Italy?

____________________

21. Who was the Italian prime minister who attended the Paris Peace Conference? ____________________

22. What was the name for the German strategy to fight a two-front war? ____________________

## Essay

**Write the correct answer to each question in the provided blank.**

23. How was Article 231 of the Treaty of Versailles partly responsible for the Second World War? ____________________

____________________

____________________

____________________

____________________

24. In what ways was the Washington Naval Conference a failure? ____________________

____________________

____________________

____________________

____________________

____________________

25. Was the Kellogg-Briand Pact destined to fail? Why? ____________________

____________________

____________________

____________________

____________________

Name ____________________

# Fireside Chat: September 6, 1936

**Answer the questions at the end after reading the following excerpt from a speech by Franklin D. Roosevelt.**

I have been on a journey of husbandry. I went primarily to see at first hand conditions in the drought States, to see how effectively Federal and local authorities are taking care of pressing problems of relief and also how they are to work together to defend the people of this country against the effects of future droughts.

I saw drought devastation in nine States.

I talked with families who had lost their wheat crop, lost their corn crop, lost their livestock, lost the water in their well, lost their garden and come through to the end of the summer without one dollar of cash resources, facing a winter without feed or food—facing a planting season without seed to put in the ground.

That was the extreme case, but there are thousands and thousands of families on Western farms who share the same difficulties.

I saw cattlemen who because of lack of grass or lack of winter feed have been compelled to sell all but their breeding stock and will need help to carry even these through the coming winter. I saw livestock kept alive only because water had been brought to them long distances in tank cars. I saw other farm families who have not lost everything but who because they have made only partial crops must have some form of help if they are to continue farming next spring.

I shall never forget the fields of wheat so blasted by heat that they cannot be harvested. I shall never forget field after field of corn stunted, earless and stripped of leaves, for what the sun left the grasshoppers took. I saw brown pastures which would not keep a cow on fifty acres.

Yet I would not have you think for a single minute that there is permanent disaster in these drought regions, or that the picture I saw meant depopulating these areas. No cracked earth, no blistering sun, no burning wind, no grasshoppers are a permanent match for the indomitable American farmers and stockmen and their wives and children who have carried on through desperate days, and inspire us with their self-reliance, their tenacity and their courage. It was their fathers' task to make homes; it is their task to keep those homes; it is our task to help them win their fight.

First, let me talk for a minute about this autumn and the coming winter. We have the option, in the case of families who need actual subsistence, of putting them on the dole or putting them to work. They do not want to go on the dole and they are one thousand percent right. We agree, therefore, that we must put them to work for a decent wage; and when we reach that decision we kill two birds with one stone, because these families will earn enough by working, not only to subsist themselves, but to buy food for their stock, and seed for next year's planting. Into this scheme of things there fit of course the Government lending agencies which next year, as in the past, will help with production loans. . . .

I want to make it clear that no simple panacea can be applied to the drought problem in the whole of the drought area. Plans must depend on local conditions, for these vary with annual rainfall, soil characteristics, altitude and topography. Water and soil conservation methods may differ in one county from those in an adjoining county. Work to be done in the cattle and sheep country differs in type from work in the wheat country or work in the corn belt. . . .

On my trip I have been deeply impressed with the general efficiency of those agencies of the Federal, State and local Governments which have moved in on the immediate task created by the drought. In 1934 none of us had preparation; we worked without blueprints and made

*(continued on next page)*

the mistakes of inexperience. Hindsight shows us this. But as time has gone on we have been making fewer and fewer mistakes. Remember that the Federal and State Governments have done only broad planning. Actual work on a given project originates in the local community. Local needs are listed from local information. Local projects are decided on only after obtaining the recommendations and help of those in the local community who are best able to give it. And it is worthy of note that on my entire trip, though I asked the question dozens of times, I heard no complaint against the character of a single work relief project.

The elected heads of the States concerned, together with their State officials and their experts from agricultural colleges and State planning boards, have shown cooperation with and approval of the work which the Federal Government has headed. I am grateful also to the men and women in all these States who have accepted leadership in the work in their locality.

In the drought area people are not afraid to use new methods to meet changes in Nature, and to correct mistakes of the past. If over-grazing has injured range lands they are willing to reduce the grazing. If certain wheat lands should be returned to pasture they are willing to co-operate. If trees should be planted as wind-breaks or to stop erosion they will work with us. If terracing or summer fallowing or crop rotation is called for they will carry it out. They stand ready to fit, and not to fight, the ways of Nature.

1. What national calamity had befallen America at the time of this fireside chat? How severe was the disaster?

______

______

2. What factors aggravated this disaster? ______

______

3. Which of the president's comments indicate his belief that a strong centralized government will solve the problems created by the drought? ______

______

______

______

______

______

4. Where do you think the government would get the money to pay for Roosevelt's plans? ______

______

______

______

Name ______________________

# Execution of the Czar and His Family

**Answer the questions at the end after reading the following account by Pavel Medvedeff, a member of the squad of soldiers guarding Nicholas II and his family.**

In the evening of July 16th the time of my duty had just begun, when between seven and eight p.m. the commandant, Iourovsky, ordered me to take all the Nagan revolvers from the guardsmen and to bring them up to him. I took twelve revolvers from the sentries as well as from some other guardsmen and brought them to the commandant's office. Iourovsky announced to me: "We will have to shoot them all tonight; notify the guardsmen not to be alarmed if they should hear the shots." I understood that Iourovsky had in mind to shoot the whole of the czar's family as well as the doctor and servants who lived with them, but I did not ask him where or by whom the decision was made. . . . At about ten o'clock in the evening, in accordance with Iourovsky's order, I informed the guardsmen not to be alarmed if they should hear firing. About midnight Iourovsky woke up the czar's family. I do not know if he told them the reason they were wakened and where they were to be taken, or not. I positively affirm that it was Iourovsky who entered the rooms where the czar's family was. . . . In about an hour the whole of the family, the doctor, maid and two waiters got up, washed and dressed themselves. Just before Iourovsky went to wake the family up, two members of the extraordinary commission arrived at Ipatieff's house. Shortly after one o'clock in the night the czar, czaritza, their four daughters, the maid, the doctor, the cook and the waiter left their rooms. The czar carried the heir in his arms. The emperor and heir were dressed in "Gimnasterkas" (soldiers' shirts) and wore caps. The empress and the daughters were dressed, but their heads were uncovered. The emperor with the heir proceeded first. The empress, her daughters and the others followed him. Iourovsky, his assistant, and the two above-mentioned members of the extraordinary commission were accompanying them. I was also present. During my presence nobody of the czar's family asked anybody any questions. They did not either weep or cry. Having descended the stairs to the first floor, we went out into the court, and from there by the second door (counting from the gate) we entered the lower floor of the house. When the corner room, adjoining the storeroom with a sealed door, was entered, Iourovsky ordered chairs to be brought. His assistant brought three chairs. One chair was given to the emperor, one to the empress, and the third to the heir. The empress sat by the wall with the window, near the back pillar of the arch. Behind her stood three of her daughters (I knew their faces very well, because I saw them every day when they were walking, but I didn't know them by name). The heir and the emperor sat side by side, almost in the middle of the room. Dr. Botkin stood behind the heir. The maid, a very tall woman, stood by the left post of the door leading to the storeroom; by her side stood one of the czar's daughters (the fourth). Two servants stood at the left from the entrance of the room, against the wall separating the storeroom.

The maid had a pillow. The czar's daughters also brought small pillows with them. One pillow was put on the empress's chair; another on the heir's chair. It looked as if all of them guessed their fate, but not a single sound was uttered. At the same time eleven men entered the room: Iourovsky, his assistant, two members of the extraordinary commission, and seven Letts.

*(continued on next page)*

Iourovsky ordered me to leave, saying: "Go to the street, see if there is anybody there and if the shots can be heard." I went out to the court which was enclosed by a fence, and before I could get out to the street I heard the firing. Immediately I returned to the house (only two or three minutes having elapsed), and on entering the room where the execution took place, I saw all the members of the czar's family lying on the floor, having many wounds in their bodies. The blood was running in streams, the doctor, the maid and the waiters were also shot. When I entered[,] the heir was still alive and moaned. Iourovsky went up and fired two or three more times at him. The heir grew still.

George Gustav Telberg and Robert Wilton. *The Last Days of the Romanovs.* (New York: George H. Doran, n.d.), 199–202.

1. How did the czar and his family respond when they faced execution? __________

2. How did Medvedeff know that all members of the family were assassinated? __________

3. Compare the events of this account with the assassination of Louis XVI. Examine the outcome of the deaths and the conditions following the deaths. (Refer to Chapters 16, 17, and 21 in the student text.)

Name ______________________________

## Union of Soviet Socialist Republics

**Locate each term on the map and place the corresponding number in the appropriate blank.**

_______ Arctic Ocean

_______ China

_______ Georgian S.S.R.

_______ Japan

_______ Kazakh S.S.R.

_______ Lithuanian S.S.R.

_______ Moldavian S.S.R.

_______ Mongolia

_______ Moscow

_______ North Pacific Ocean

_______ Russian Soviet Federated Socialist Republic

_______ Sweden

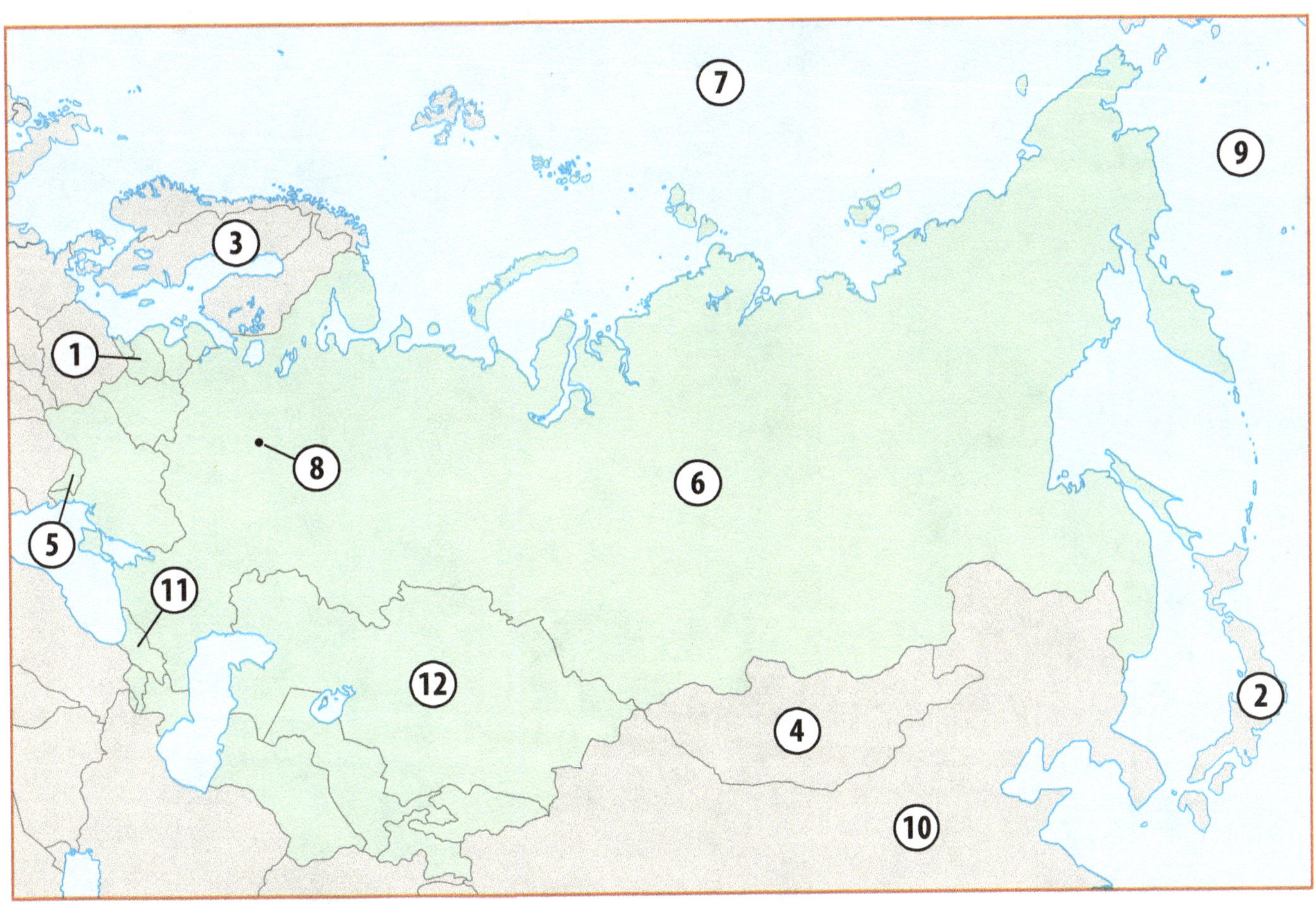

Name ______________________

# Hitler's Impact on the Youth of Germany

**Answer the questions below after reading the following excerpts from the writings of Susan Campbell Bartoletti.**

"... I swear to devote all my energies and my strength to the Savior of our country, Adolf Hitler. I am willing and ready to give up my life for him, so help me, God."

When all Jungvolk [boys] and Jungmädel [girls] had recited the oath, the trumpets blared a fanfare, and a military band burst out in National Socialist songs. The children were now trial members of the Hitler Youth....

"We had to get an *Abnenpass*, a stamped and signed official document that proved our racial heritage.... We had to write to check with the church registers. What the Nazi authorities were looking for, of course were Jewish names." ... The Hitler Youth were taught that the Aryan race was superior to all other races.

The boys and girls also had to prove that they were healthy and had no hereditary diseases. ... During the trial period, boys and girls demonstrated their physical fitness: They ran races, threw baseballs, swam, and performed gymnastics stunts. Girls completed a two-hour hike, whereas boys undertook a three-day cross-country hike....

The Hitler Youth philosophy maintained that youth must be led by youth. Meetings, called "Home Evenings," took place in cellars, barns, empty buildings, and other places far away from adults. The meetings were run by leaders not much older than the other members. "The leader of the group that I belonged to was a boy who was seventeen," said one Hitler Youth. "He was my mentor in every respect.... He exerted more influence over me than any person, parent, teacher, or anyone else of the older generation."

Each month, the Hitler Youth headquarters sent letters to the leaders, spelling out how to run the meetings. At the meetings, the children sang songs, played games, learned slogans, listened to readings, and read propaganda leaflets—all intended to teach them how to be good Nazis....

The Nazis knew what appealed to kids—uniforms, flags, bands, badges, weapons, and stories about heroes—and they offered plenty. They organized the Hitler Youth as an army, complete with regiments. A boy could rise from the simple rank of *Pimpf* (boy) to lead a squad, platoon, company, battalion, or even a regiment. A girl to rise from *Mädel* (maiden) to become a BDM [Bund Deutscher Mädel; League of German Girls] leader.

But the Hitler Youth did not tolerate originality or individuality. Through military drills and marches, the Hitler Youth learned to think and act as one. Most important, they learned to obey their leader, no matter what. The Nazis called this philosophy the "leadership principle," and it required absolute obedience to superiors....

Every athletic event became an exercise in patriotism.... The boys' groups divided into platoons for war games, and they hunted down the "enemy." When the games erupted into fist-fights, it became survival of the fittest: Stronger boys often pummeled weaker boys, throwing them to the ground. Ripped shirts, scrapes, bruises, and bloody noses abounded....

At fourteen, the boys advanced to the Hitlerjugend where they stayed until age eighteen. There, the military training continued. "We met together, marched, and played together," said Henry Metelmann. "We were instructed about military formations and how soldiers move in the countryside unseen. We learned how to shoot, throw hand grenades, and how to storm trenches." The boys earned prestigious Hitler Youth merit badges for outstanding performance.

At fourteen, girls advanced to the BDM, where they stayed until age twenty-one. They worked on efficiency badges in sports, Nazi ideology, nursing, household training, social work, and later, air-raid training.



1. According to the Hitler Youth oath, who was the "Savior" of Germany? ____________________

2–3. Describe two things that were required in order to join the Hitler Youth. ____________________

4. What age group led the Hitler Youth meetings? ____________________

5–7. What items did the Nazis use to appeal to German children? (Give three.) ____________________

8–10. What three military skills did the German boys acquire in the Hitlerjugend? ____________________

11–13. What three things did German girls learn in the BDM? ____________________

Name ______________________________

# Chapter Review

## Complete the Statement

**Underline the term that accurately completes each of the following statements.**

1. (Alexander III/Nicholas II) became Russia's czar in 1881 and persecuted many minority groups in Russia.
2. The (Bolsheviks/Mensheviks) wanted to change Russia's policies through peaceful, moderate means.
3. Nicholas II established a national government assembly called the (Reichstag/Duma).
4. The (dole/syndicate) provided government relief for the unemployed.
5. The weakness of the Weimar Republic prepared the way for the rise of (Lenin/Hitler).

## Matching

**Choose the best answer and place the letter in the blank beside the corresponding description.**

A. Alexander III
B. T. S. Eliot
C. Sigmund Freud
D. Paul von Hindenburg
E. Aleksandr Kerensky
F. Vladimir Lenin
G. Ramsay MacDonald
H. Benito Mussolini
I. Nicholas II
J. Rasputin
K. Joseph Stalin
L. Igor Stravinsky
M. Leon Trotsky

_____ 6. Led a temporary government in Russia after the czar's fall

_____ 7. Became the Soviet Union's dictator in 1927

_____ 8. Developed theories about human behavior

_____ 9. British leader of the Labour Party

_____ 10. Organized the Communist Red Army in Russia's civil war

_____ 11. Fascist leader in Italy

_____ 12. Russian czar who organized pogroms

_____ 13. Appointed Hitler as Germany's chancellor in 1933

_____ 14. Religious fraud who was a bad influence on Russia's empress

_____ 15. Took over Russia in 1917 with the help of his followers

*(continued on next page)*

## Short Answer

**Write the correct answer to each question in the provided blank.**

16. What is the name of the unbiblical philosophy that is subjective and teaches that individuals must find their own purpose? ______

17. What was the name for the agreements that Mussolini made with the Roman Catholic Church?
______

18. What system did the French build to defend against German attack? ______

19. What book did Adolf Hitler write while in prison? ______

20. What did Britain approve in 1926 that gave Canada, Australia, New Zealand, and South Africa more autonomy? ______

21. How did some German Protestants attempt to reconcile Nazism with Christianity? ______
______
______

22. Why did Hitler encourage the construction of the *Autobahnen*? ______
______

23. The mobs of the Russian Revolution intended to correct the wrongs of the government. How did the revolution fail in its optimistic aims? ______
______

## Essay

**Write the correct answer to each question in the provided blank.**

24. During the early days of Nazi rule, many German churches supported Hitler. Even after they realized what Nazism really was, they failed to oppose it. How should Christians, who must be subject to the government (Rom. 13:1–5), respond under similar circumstances? (See Acts 4:18–20 and 5:29.)
______
______
______
______
______

25. Explain the reason Lenin used the New Economic Policy and why it was ironic. ______
______
______
______
______

Name ___________________________

## A Prisoner of War

**Answer the questions at the end after reading the following excerpt from the writings of Claude J. Letulle.**

Finally the train came to a stop and the door of our car was opened. Our first sight was five Nazis in light-brown uniform, and behind them were soldiers with machine guns aimed at us. The Nazis were youth leaders, each accompanied by two German shepherds. The youth were even more feared than the Gestapo, for their methods were crueler.

As we left the cattle car, I looked around the station to see if I could locate the name of the place. On one badly painted signboard I could distinguish only a few Polish letters. I eventually learned that the name of the place was Rawa Ruska. Who would ever think of coming to Poland to help us? We knew that the Germans had invaded Poland and that the Nazis were strong, but surely some country would be able to fight back. Maybe Russia would be the one.

During all the time of our captivity we had continued in ignorance of how the war was progressing. We were confused, depressed, and afraid, and in November, 1941, we could not imagine that one month later the United States would become involved in the war. As we walked toward the special camp, my ruminations [thoughts] were broken off by an uproar behind me. One of the prisoners had just killed a soldier by cutting his throat with a knife. How the prisoner had managed to hide a knife from the Nazis after all the inspection we had been through, no one could guess. Of course, he was shot instantly with his hand still clutching the knife. We knew that he had reached a breaking point and was afraid of special tortures in the new camp. He had wanted to die before reaching the camp, but not without having had the satisfaction of killing one of his enemies. We understood his feelings, but his irrational act was not going to make life easier for us. . . .

About half an hour later the camp came into view. It was surrounded by two rows of electric barbed wire, separated by a distance of about fifteen feet in which there was more barbed wire. No easy escape here. Above the entrance a large sign proclaimed: Arbeit Macht Frei (Freedom comes from work). Inside the camp some prisoners were exercising, which I soon learned was to keep them "in shape" for work. There was one soldier for every prisoner, and the orders were simple: sit, roll over, run, sit, and so on. When a man didn't move fast enough, he was bludgeoned [beaten]. The sequence lasted forty-five minutes. When the soldiers were not satisfied, the prisoner was hung by his wrists for two hours.

The camp was quite large. We were pushed into barracks Number 35. The inside was absolutely empty—nothing but walls and windows with iron bars. I sat on the floor leaning against the wall and saw that it was covered with bedbugs. No one said a word. After a short while, the door was opened and an SS officer in a black uniform came in, accompanied by an interpreter, a Frenchman dressed like an officer, with shining boots. The Frenchman must have done a favor to be so well treated.

"Up, all you pigs," the interpreter ordered. "Don't you know that when an officer comes to address you, you must be on your feet at attention?" I later learned that the officer was Obersturmführer [literally, "Attack-leader-overseer"] SS Kurt Schumacher. He strutted in front of us.

"A Wehrmacht [Armed Forces] officer has recommended you to me and begged me to treat you well. I intend to do that. This is your block. You will have neither beds nor blankets as long as I judge it necessary. You will start working tomorrow morning, and I advise you to work joyfully for the glory of the Reich. You will be awakened at 4 A.M. There will be a five-minute break at eleven, a ten-minute break at noon, another five-minute break at four. Work will stop at eleven. Any attempt at escape will be punished with immediate death."

*(continued on next page)*

Then with a smile he added, "If any of you should feel sick, don't hesitate to let us know. Here the treatment is free." He was telling us that they would shoot us. . . .

I believe that I survived because I was young and had always been healthy—I was only twenty-three—but some of the older prisoners were less fortunate. One man in his forties had been told to work close to me. We had been given a glass of water at 10 A.M. and, at noon, one slice of bread smeared with a dab of fat. The older man was fatigued, but he managed to move his pick until the 4 P.M. break, all the while talking to himself as if in a state of delirium. A few minutes after we resumed our work, he fell down. A nearby soldier fired a shot to make him get up, but the man did not move. Three other soldiers ran up and began to kick him. One of them turned the prisoner onto his back, meaning to step on his face, but the man was dead. The soldiers were frustrated at having been deprived of such a pleasure, and they picked him up by the arms and legs and threw him into the pit. Later I learned that the Nazis sometimes fed dead prisoners to the dogs to make them more ferocious. We were sick over the death of that man and had all paused for a few moments, but the soldiers goaded [forced] us to continue working. . . .

[Later, Letulle and other prisoners were forced to enter the cellblocks and carry out dead prisoners.]

With our guards, we went into the cells to pick up the dead. In the first cell, the Russians regarded us with apparent hostility, but one of them explained that they knew what we were doing. Their situation was awful. They had to sleep on the cement floor, and they were indeed being starved to death. Many were emaciated, and the legs of some who were near death were covered with wounds full of pus. There were no dead in that first cell. In the next cell the silent hostility was the same, but again it was not us whom they blamed. We picked up two puffy bodies of men who had been dead for days. Carrying them by the arms and feet, we took them outside and put them into large bags. By four that afternoon we had cleared the cells of some twenty bodies.

A truck drove the bodies to the pit we had dug and unloaded its cargo as if it were dumping a load of stones. We were forced to go into the pit and line up the bodies, and it remains the most horrible experience I have had in my life. . . . I got out of the pit sick to my stomach and nearly out of my mind.

Claude J. Letulle. *Nightmare Memoir: Four Years as a Prisoner of the Nazis.* (Baton Rouge: Louisiana State Univ. Press, 1987), 44–46, 48, 110.

1. Whom did the prisoners fear even more than the Gestapo? ________________

2. What was Letulle's "most horrible experience" during his imprisonment? ________________

3. How did the prisoners of war suffer? ________________

4. How could the Nazis do such cruel things to others? (Use Romans 3:10–18 as a reference for your answer.)

Name ____________________

## War in the South Pacific

**Answer the questions at the end after reading the following excerpt from the writings of Chaplain Arthur F. Glasser.**

Early Christmas morning the assault waves landed on the beaches of Cape Gloucester. The Marine attack came with such suddenness and power that the Japanese troops defending the beach were speedily annihilated. We had landed at a point where the enemy least expected, and as a result encountered only a small opposing garrison. The Japanese defensive positions had been designed to prevent an Allied landing at a beach two miles from the one selected, and they were all rendered useless by this initial stroke. Hence, the first forty-eight hours found the forces of Nippon in great confusion as they tried to reorganize their whole strategy of defense. When they struck back it was with real force and the fighting became very bitter and bloody. But during those forty-eight hours our division poured such great numbers of men, guns, and equipment into the rapidly expanded beachhead that the Japanese were never able to build up their strength to match us blow for blow when the fighting did begin in earnest. By their costly miscalculation they were doomed from the very start—although they fought with fanatical fury. . . .

About this time word came along that a large body of Japanese troops was trying to break through the thin line of our defense perimeter in a night counterattack. Naturally this increased the tension among the men and some of the younger, less experienced, fainted and had to be dragged from the trail. Because we could not leave them alone, the column would then halt again. Medical corpsmen feverishly did all they could to revive them, and those nearest would distribute their gear among the others and encourage the faltering to keep up with us.

It was a fantastic night if ever I saw one! Even the jungle shadows played strange tricks on us. At times they were surprisingly familiar, and then again they appeared to menace [threaten] us with terrible revenge for having intruded upon their sacred domain.

Finally the word came through that we would "camp here for the night." "Camp here?"—I found myself standing in a mysterious pool of mud. With nary a grimace [without a frown] and with a surprising measure of simple resignation, I slithered to a hummock-like bit of higher ground and without further ceremony stretched out for the night. Exhausted, perspiring profusely—that jungle was such a hot steamy place—we spent the remaining hours of darkness awaiting we knew not what.

Fortunately the Japanese night assault was unsuccessful. Our lines held and the next day the advance continued.

With the advance, our engineers now came into their own. Bridges had to be erected over many streams, and roads had to be constructed through treacherous, swampy terrain in order that the constant flow of supplies to the assaulting infantry and tank teams might be continuously maintained at all costs. Hence there was no dearth of the heaviest of work. In no time at all, I had obtained a job helping one of our bridge gangs throw a combat bridge over a fast flowing stream. Soaked to the skin by the intermittent rains and much bedaubed with mud, we struggled with our bridge while a growing line of trucks and combat vehicles impatiently waited to cross the river and get to the front. When the job was finally completed, the traffic snarl quickly eased. But there was no rest, for our bridge-building gang was then quickly moved up to the next stream and began on the next bridge. . . . For us, each bridge was the site of a constant battle against every conceivable difficulty. Some of them built close to the sea were even battered by high waves and were only made secure after heavy log walls had been built around the exposed piers. But no one felt this work to be in vain, for every so often a truck would return from the lines containing the bodies of Marines who had given their lives for the rest of us but a

*(continued on next page)*

few hours before. The most agonizing labor could hardly repay the debt we all felt as we saw our own dead being hauled to the place of burial.

During the noon hour of that first day I visited the spot where our lines had been the previous night when the Japanese had made their unsuccessful night assault.

It is difficult to describe a battlefield, especially a jungle battlefield. Barbed wire tangles, hastily constructed machine gun shelters and shallow, muddy foxholes were scattered throughout the slashed, partially destroyed undergrowth. Here and there were small heaps of equipment, clothing, half-empty ammunition and food cases and "C" ration cans. Everything bespoke [indicated] the awful wastage of war.

Arthur F. Glasser. *And Some Believed: A Chaplain's Experiences with the Marines in the South Pacific.* (Chicago: Moody, 1946), 151–55.

1. **How did the marines gain an initial advantage over the Japanese defenders of Cape Gloucester?** ______________________________

______________________________

______________________________

2. **How did several of the soldiers who were "younger [and] less experienced" respond to the tension?**

______________________________

3. **What physical and psychological difficulties did Glasser and the marines encounter in this battle experience?** ______________________________

______________________________

______________________________

______________________________

4. **What did Glasser do to help the marines advance and overcome natural obstacles?** ______________________________

______________________________

5. **What did Glasser see that indicated the destruction produced by war?** ______________________________

______________________________

______________________________

Name ______________________

# A Little Girl's Memories of Bombings in Berlin

**Answer the questions at the end after reading the following excerpt from the writings of Inge E. Stanneck Gross.**

Papa was ordered back to active duty early in the year, and sent to the Russian front. We resumed the nightly ordeals without him, sleeping fully dressed now so that we could just dive into our coats and run.

School was no longer fun. Whenever a girl was absent, it was assumed that something had happened to her during the previous night's air raid. Unfortunately, most of the time that was the case. Then the teacher would try to gently break the bad news to us. I remember thinking that the next day—or the day after—my name would be mentioned as one of the dead. I was sure of that. It was so hard for me to take the news of the deaths of little friends, and I became quite depressed. When I stopped eating, Mom kept me home from school.

Berlin was being heavily bombed, and for a child which could not yet comprehend why this was happening, it was a very hostile world to live in. There were people out there who hated us so much that they were doing all those terrible things. I often wondered what they might look like. Being from other countries "far away" and being so nasty and hateful, they were sure to look like monsters with two heads, or worse. . . .

Two air raids devastated our neighborhood. The aim apparently was to destroy two targets—a military academy less than a mile away, and temporary barracks built on a vacant lot behind our house, next to which the army stored 110 gasoline barrels in the ground. During a raid at the end of February [1943], an extraordinary number of bombs were dropped on our neighborhood, but these two targets were not hit. Many buildings in our neighborhood were. We were worried.

In an effort to cheer me up, Grandma Stanneck took me to the circus on the afternoon of March first. I loved the circus, especially the animals. Mom was reluctant to let me go. Occasionally now there were air raids during the daytime.

I worried all day about the upcoming night and a repeat of another air raid like the big one we had a few days earlier. Even the fun of the circus could not block out my fear. The clowns' happy, smiling faces seemed ironic to me—as if they were saying "you laugh now, but wait until tonight!" I think I started to break right then. To me, the clowns' smiles suddenly turned into grimaces [scowls], and the audience's laughter into screeches of terror. I asked Grandma to take me home. I was feeling ill.

It was like the final straw—as if I had a premonition [forewarning]. That night, tons of incendiary bombs rained down on our neighborhood. Long before the end of the air raid, the men came into the cellar to report that they had extinguished a fire in the coal yard, but that the barracks behind us were burning, and the gasoline barrels in the ground could explode at any moment. There were 110 barrels. They told us we had better get out of our cellar and go somewhere else. If they exploded one at a time it would not be too serious, but if all of them exploded at once, it would take the apartment building down and bury us alive.

We started to run for our lives even though it was not yet the end of the air raid. We ran to put as much distance as possible between us and the fuel tanks. The whole world seemed to be on fire. The first barrel exploded. We ran faster. Nearly every other house on the street was burning, and there was no getting away from fire. Every so often we heard—and saw—the explosion of another fuel barrel. It is strange that we never gave a thought as to whether or not the house we lived in, and our belongings, would blow up. At the time we were completely detached from material possessions. They did not mean anything. Escaping with our lives was our main concern.

*(continued on next page)*

We ran endlessly through the inferno in the streets of our general neighborhood, wearing only our nightgowns, having shed our coats because of the intense heat from all the fires. We worried about where we would go if another air raid were to start. Most cellars were already overcrowded with people who were bombed-out earlier that night, and we might not be let in. Fortunately, there was no other air raid that night.

For a time, the explosions of the gasoline barrels became more numerous, often two or three together; and by dawn there was an eerie silence. There were burnt out houses everywhere. We returned to our street with much anticipation. The fire department had been there the whole time and had hosed down whatever they could, especially the coal yard and the house we lived in. The front building in which Tante [Aunt] Hilda lived had been saved as well. Wearily we went upstairs to our apartment and crawled into our beds. At least Peter and I did. Mom made plans. We were getting out of Berlin. . . .

The air raids were terrifying enough to experience in the cellar of the house, but to be out in the streets and totally unprotected was a devastating experience. The fires had been terrifying. I could not wait to return to "peaceful" Straupitz. Mom promised me that we would get out of Berlin immediately, and on the very next day—March 3—we left.

I was so traumatized that I have no recollection at all of the trip to Straupitz. We obviously had to go by train. There was no other way. I was truly at a breaking point. The cumulative impact of the bombs falling all around us—night after night—and going to school only to find—day after day—that another one of my classmates had been killed, impacted me beyond what words can describe. I was only eight.

Reprinted with permission from *Memories of World War II and Its Aftermath: By a Little Girl Growing Up in Berlin* by Inge E. Gross. Published by Island in the Sky Publishing Co., 2005.

1. Why was school "no longer fun" for Gross? ______________________________

______________________________

______________________________

______________________________

2. Why did her mother take her away from Berlin? ______________________________

3. What does this account reveal about Germany's military condition by 1943? ______________________________

______________________________

______________________________

______________________________

Name ______________________________

# Opposing Viewpoints on the Atomic Bomb

**Answer the questions at the end after reading the following sources:**

## Szilard Petition

The war has to be brought speedily to a successful conclusion and attacks by atomic bombs may very well be an effective method of warfare. We feel, however, that such attacks on Japan could not be justified, at least not unless the terms which will be imposed after the war on Japan were made public in detail and Japan were given an opportunity to surrender. . . .

The development of atomic power will provide the nations with new means of destruction. The atomic bombs at our disposal represent only the first step in this direction, and there is almost no limit to the destructive power which will become available in the course of their future development. Thus a nation which sets the precedent of using these newly liberated forces of nature for purposes of destruction may have to bear the responsibility of opening the door to an era of devastation on an unimaginable scale. . . . [I]f we were to violate this obligation our moral position would be weakened in the eyes of the world and in our own eyes. It would then be more difficult for us to live up to our responsibility of bringing the unloosened forces of destruction under control.

In view of the foregoing, we, the undersigned, respectfully petition: first, that you exercise your power as Commander-in-Chief, to rule that the United States shall not resort to the use of atomic bombs in this war unless the terms which will be imposed upon Japan have been made public in detail and Japan knowing these terms has refused to surrender; second, that in such an event the question whether or not to use atomic bombs be decided by you in light of the considerations presented in this petition as well as all the other moral responsibilities which are involved.

http://www.dannen.com/decision/45-07-04.html

. . . .

[The excerpts below are from oral history interviews with Hiroshima survivors 40 years after the attack.]

Ms. Toshiko Saeki was 26 at the time of the bombing. . . . Ms. Saeki lost thirteen members of her family in the A-bomb attack.

My hair started to fall out, I vomited blood. My teeth were coming out. And I had a fever of about 40 degrees. Nuclear war has nothing good. Whether you win or lose, it leaves your [sic] feeling futile with only your rage and with fear about the aftereffects of a radioactivity. The survivors have to live with this fear. At times I have thought I should have died then, it would have been better. But I must live for the sake of the people, all the people who lost their lives then. So I relate my experiences hoping that my talk would discourage people from making war. Our experience must not [be] forgotten. What we believed in during the war turned out to be worth nothing. We don't know to whom we should turn our rage. I went through hell on earth of Hiroshima should not be repeated again. That is why I keep telling the same old story over and over again. And I'll keep repeating it.

http://www.atomicarchive.com/Docs/Hibakusha/Toshiko.shtml

*(continued on next page)*

. . . .

Mr. Akira Onogi was 16 years old when the bomb was dropped.

INTERVIEWER: Wasn't it possible to help them?

ANSWER: No, there were too many people. We took care of the people around us by using the clothes of dead people as bandages, especially for those who were terribly wounded. By that time we somehow became insensible to all those awful things. After a while, the fire reached the river bank and we decided [to] leave the river. We crossed over this railway bridge and escaped in the direction along the railway. The houses on both sides of the railroad were burning and railway was the hollow in the fire. I thought I was going to die here. It was such an awful experience. You know for about 10 years after [the] bombing I always felt paralyzed we never saw the sparks made by trains or lightning. Also even at home, I could not sit beside the windows because I had seen so many people badly wounded by pieces of glass. So I always sat with the wall behind me for about 10 years. It was some sort of instinct to self-preservation.

http://www.atomicarchive.com/Docs/Hibakusha/Akira.shtml

1. Summarize some nuclear scientists' position on the use of the atomic bomb. ______________________________

2. To whom did the scientists send the petition? ______________________________

3. Why does Ms. Toshiko Saeki keep telling her story? ______________________________

4. Mr. Akira Onogi states that many were wounded by what objects? ______________________________

5. Argue whether the atomic bombs should have been used. ______________________________

Name ______________________________

# Chapter Review

## Complete the Statement

**Underline the term that accurately completes each of the following statements.**

1. (Bernard L. Montgomery/Dwight D. Eisenhower) was an American commander in North Africa.
2. (Hideki Tojo/Hirohito) was a general in Japan's military and appointed to serve as the virtual dictator of Japan.
3. Operation (Overlord/Barbarossa) was the code name for Germany's invasion of Russia.
4. The Atlantic Charter was an agreement of alliance drawn up by Franklin Roosevelt and (Joseph Stalin/Winston Churchill).
5. Japan invaded (Manchuria/Taiwan) in 1931 and seized the region from Chinese control.

## Matching

**Choose the best answer and place the letter in the blank beside the corresponding description.**

A. Neville Chamberlain
B. Winston Churchill
C. Édouard Daladier
D. Francisco Franco
E. Charles de Gaulle
F. Hirohito
G. Chiang Kai-shek
H. Bernard L. Montgomery
I. Henri Pétain
J. Vidkun Quisling
K. Erwin Rommel
L. Harry Truman
M. Mao Zedong

_____ 6. House of Commons member who predicted Nazi tyranny

_____ 7. German commander in North Africa who was called the "Desert Fox"

_____ 8. Kuomintang leader who tried to drive communism out of China

_____ 9. Norwegian traitor who delivered his country over to the Germans

_____ 10. Tried to halt Hitler's expansionist plans by appeasement

_____ 11. Chinese Communist leader

_____ 12. Fascist leader in Spain

_____ 13. French leader who organized an armistice with Germany

_____ 14. Leader of the Free French movement

_____ 15. Prime minister of France who met Hitler's demands at Munich

*(continued on next page)*

## Short Answer

**Write the correct answer to each question in the provided blank.**

16. What was the name of the German air force? ______________________

17. What was the goal of the Yalta Conference? ______________________

18. What legislation allowed the military supply of the Allies by the United States? ______________________

19. What was the code name for the invasion of France? ______________________

20. Give the name for France under German rule. ______________________

21. To what group of islands did General Douglas MacArthur promise to return? ______________________

22. How was Spain's civil war preparatory for the Second World War? ______________________

23. Which two countries did Germany annex without triggering a war as a result of appeasement?

______________________

## Essay

**Write the correct answer to each question in the provided blank.**

24. Note the similarities between Hitler's invasion of Russia and Napoleon's invasion of Russia in 1812. (See Chapters 16 and 22 of the student text.) ______________________

25. Compare the Holocaust with the events of Exodus 1:8–14; 5:5–14; and Esther 3:5–10. ______________________

Name ______________________

## Cold War Europe

**Locate each term on the map and place the corresponding number in the appropriate blank.**

_______ Albania

_______ Atlantic Ocean

_______ Black Sea

_______ Bulgaria

_______ Czechoslovakia

_______ East Germany

_______ France

_______ Great Britain

_______ Greece

_______ Hungary

_______ Italy

_______ Mediterranean Sea

_______ Poland

_______ Portugal

_______ Romania

_______ Spain

_______ Turkey

_______ USSR

_______ West Germany

_______ Yugoslavia

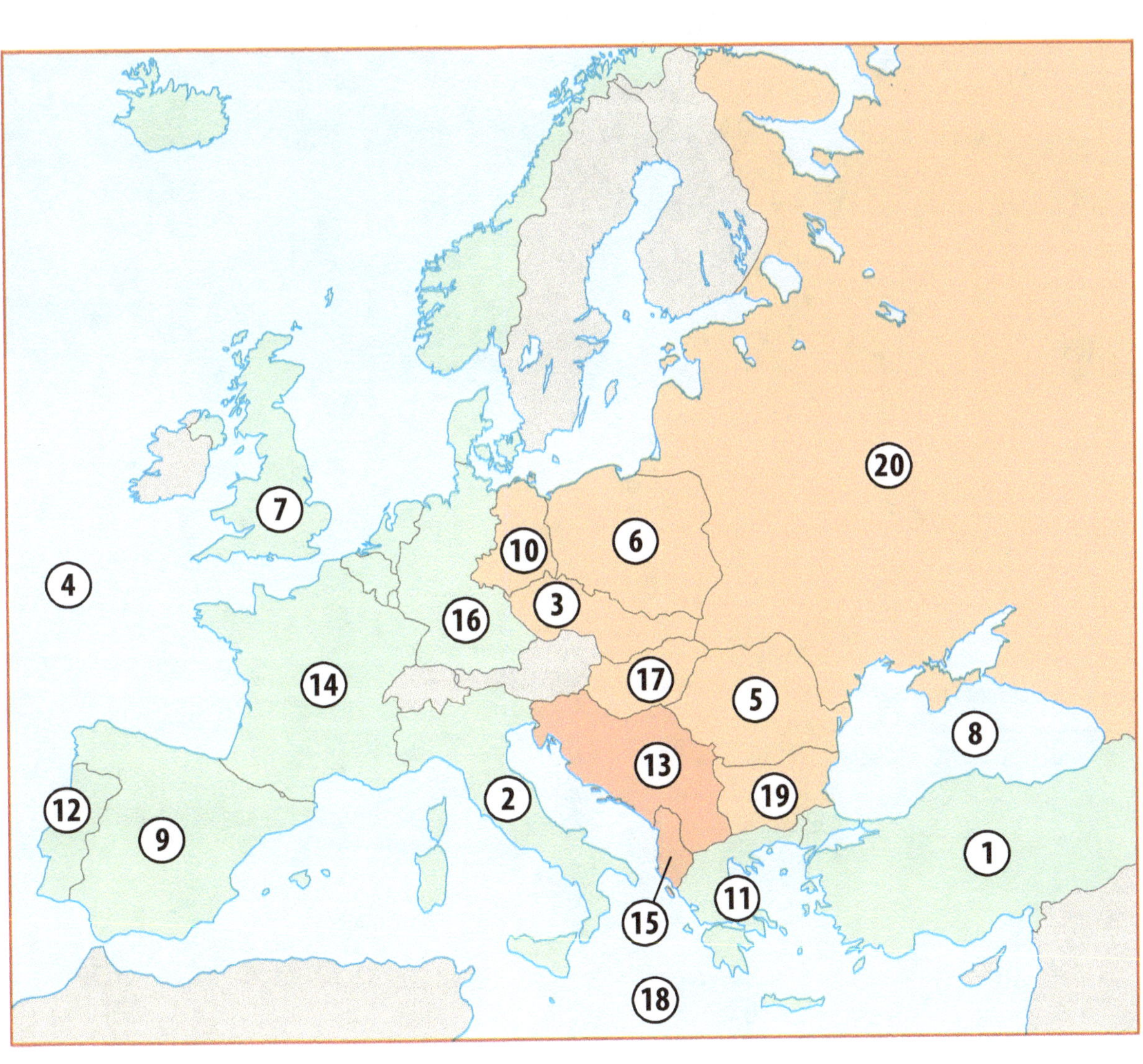

Name ____________________

# One Marine's Experience in Vietnam

**Answer the questions at the end after reading the following excerpt from Thomas J. Vogel's book *Growing Up in Vietnam*.**

The assignment of my first daytime patrol brought a sense of anticipation and excitement. Those were emotions that only a new guy would have. We were going to have a patrol in an area of the jungle that the Marines called "Dodge City." The veterans had no illusions about Dodge City.

We lined up with the engineers at the front of the column and two columns of Marines on the left and right sides of the road. We started walking slowly down the road and had been out about ten minutes when I saw a sniper round hit the road about 50 feet in front of me. I did not even bother to get down when others around me were jumping in the ditch. The hit seemed so far away from me, I did not see any call for alarm. (Another dumb thought that only a new guy would have.)

My squad leader appropriately yelled at me, and in less-than-kind words, roared, "Get down!" I have no doubt that my squad leader must have wondered what kind of rookie he had on his hands!

Nothing developed from that one sniper round, so the columns rose to their feet and started moving again. In a few minutes, we received another sniper round. This one hit the road just a few feet in front of me, and I needed no special invitation to hit the ditch! However, I kept lifting my head to see from where the round had come. Again, my squad leader yelled at me, "Keep your head down!"

The platoon sergeant yelled for the third squad, and we started off in a column across the field toward the position from which the sniper round had come. About halfway through the field, we received a third round. Again no one was hit, but we got down and stayed down for quite some time while the squad leader called in a fire mission. For some reason, the artillery never came; but at least the squad leader had registered the target with the artillery unit. Within just a few minutes, this would come in very handy. Word came again to move, and we approached the tree line without incident.

Upon entering the tree line, we came upon a hooch [a hut] about ten meters from a rice paddy. The squad sat down behind the hooch in a column, parallel to the tree line. I was at the far left end of the line, and I believe the squad leader was at the other end. Word was passed that we would take a break. I dropped down in the grass with my rifle pointed away from the hooch toward the jungle. A small water buffalo corral was located behind the hooch, immediately in front of me. To my front left and on the other side of the corral was jungle.

The heat was enough to make anyone sweat, but my fear of the unknown just added to my sweat and discomfort. I imagined a gook [derisive term for a member of the Viet Cong] hiding behind every tree. I recalled reading a Civil War book when I was in grade school. The author related how his father had shown him how to hunt for squirrels and how he had applied those same techniques to hunting snipers. After a while, my tenseness gave in to my weariness; I began to relax.

I guess we had been at the hooch for 20 minutes when, all of a sudden, the whole world seemed to erupt in a gigantic explosion and a crescendo of AK-47's. The enemy was shooting at us from behind the water buffalo corral, just a few feet away from me. However, I could not see anything, so I did not shoot. Suddenly, I heard some yelling, and as I looked to my right, I saw the NVA [North Vietnamese Army] in olive-green uniforms moving across the corral. They were assaulting our position. One guy in particular attracted my attention. He had his arm up in the air and was yelling. I aimed at him and squeezed off three rounds into his chest.

*(continued on next page)*

He jerked backward and disappeared from my sights. As I pivoted to shoot the man next to him, my rifle just went "click."

I panicked, dropped to one knee, cleared my rifle of the round in the chamber, and chambered in a new round. I stood up, fired again, and the rifle went "click" again. By now, the enemy was moving closer to our line with apparently nothing to stop them. They weren't more than 20 feet away from me at this point.

My mind was screaming. I pulled my magazine out of the M16, inserted in a new one, shouldered my rifle, aimed, and squeezed. This time, I got off one round when the rifle "clicked" ominously again. I don't know if I hit anything or anyone.

By this time, I was in a state of indescribable terror. I pulled out the magazine, threw it to the ground, jammed in another new one, and sent the charger forward which inserted a new round into the chamber. I aimed, and by this time, I was probably jerking my rounds all over Vietnam. I got off one round, and the rifle jammed again. I repeated the clearing process. . . . I looked to my right and saw no one. I was all alone. I really started to panic then. The enemy had moved past me; apparently, they did not see me on their far right flank.

As I ran to my right, looking for the rest of the squad, I came to the door of the hooch. I glanced in, and to my utter amazement, I saw the whole squad covered with blood. In the split second that I looked, they all seemed to turn and stare at me. All I can recall is seeing every man covered from head to foot with blood. They seemed to be in a state of shock.

As I stared, Seppi (Rene Sepulveda) came running from my right. He dropped to one knee, glanced in, and said, "We have to get them out of the hooch. They're right behind me—chasing me."

"Who?" (I asked one of the dumbest questions I have ever asked!)

No sooner had I asked the question than an explosion went off close by, showering us with black dust. I heard Seppi scream, but I did not see him again. All I could see was black dust and dirt. Just then my squad leader shouted, "Let's get out of here." His words were all the motivation I needed. I jumped up, broke through a hedge, ran across a rice paddy to a dike, and rolled down behind it. A black Marine by the name of Carver joined me. One Marine jumped into a ditch by the tree line and dropped flat on his back. He pointed his .45-caliber pistol straight up from his chest. A gook leaned over the ditch and stared directly into the barrel of that .45-caliber pistol! The gook immediately backed away from the ditch. He must have decided to leave well enough alone because he did not mess with that Marine again.

I crawled over to Carver who was crying. Blood was oozing out of his ears, and he was in terrible pain from a head concussion. I took out my canteen and poured water over his head in a vain effort to cool him and ease his pain. My efforts did not seem to do him any good.

Suddenly I saw some gooks crawling across the rice paddy toward us. I started firing my rifle, and this time, it fired to perfection. Though it wasn't but 20 meters to the tree line, I missed with every shot. However, the gooks did get up and run. Just then I saw why they ran—the rest of Second Platoon was right behind me! Was I ever glad to see them. I stood when they got to me, and we charged straight back into the tree line. As fast as we hit the tree line, the gooks melted away into the jungle—leaving us as quickly as they had arrived.

As suddenly as it started, the skirmish was over. It was my first firefight, and it seemed as if it had lasted for hours. In reality, it had probably lasted about five minutes. I have no idea because time seemed to stand still in a firefight. Everything was happening so fast, yet it was as if it happened in a slow motion dream. It was very loud, yet it was silent at the same time. It was terrifying.

My fire-team leader had been killed; his head was blown off in the opening barrage. Every other man in our squad had been wounded except for me. Whitey, our machine gunner, was the worst of the wounded. His machine gun had taken a direct hit by a gook rocket, and his body was covered with shrapnel. Still, his M60 machine gun had saved his life.

*(continued on next page)*

As we rode back to Hill 55, Seppi, who was sitting two guys away from me, suddenly stood up and started firing his rifle into the jungle. Someone grabbed him and pulled him down. "Seppi," he coaxed, "it's going to be okay."

Seppi sat down, but he had a faraway look in his eyes. To me, it appeared as if Seppi had just snapped. He had a minor wound, and he was considered "walking wounded." Seppi was medevaced, and when he returned after his wounds healed, the rest had done him a lot of good. He was back to his old, fun-loving self. Seppi would become one of the most-liked men in the company.

When we got back to Hill 55, I went back to my tent. No one was there; the whole squad had been medevaced. I don't believe that I had ever felt so alone in my life. I sat in my tent for a few minutes, but I was still so keyed up from the firefight that I could not sit still. I was still filled with adrenalin.

Just then, the company gunny called, "Mail call." I went, but nothing had come for me. I couldn't sit still. I walked down by the river where the road left the hill. I just stared at the jungle and turned to walk back.

As I started back up the hill toward . . . my tent, something came over me. I stepped into a nearby bunker, sat on a pile of sand bags, put my head in my hands, and sobbed uncontrollably. All of the tension of the last few days had finally erupted, and I unashamedly wept until I could cry no more.

That would be the last time I would cry for a long time. The next time I would cry was the day I left Vietnam. . . .

Before long, we were on a battalion-size operation. At the time, I did not know it was an operation. I just knew that we were heading somewhere to the east of Liberty Bridge. The next few days were a blur of humping through the bush, making evening patrols, and trying to make it through the terrifying nights.

One night, while I was on watch, it was very dark. I could hardly see my hand in front of my face. In the still and the silence of the night, I could hear gooks crawling up to my position. I strained to identify their location, but I could just barely hear their start-and-stop, stealthy movement. I positioned my grenades in front of me, and one-by-one loosened the pins a little. I did not want to fire my gun because the muzzle flash would give away my position. Besides, the bright light would have destroyed my night vision—not that I could see anything anyway.

I was sweating, and the adrenalin was rushing through my veins as I waited anxiously for the moment of truth. The gooks crawled forward ever so slowly. One minute, I would hear them to my right, and the next thing I knew, they would be off to my left. "What's going on here?" I thought. Their skulking movements were driving me crazy. The strain of continuing to listen to this activity for over an hour began to get to me. At some point, I realized I was listening to a small mouse just a few feet in front of me, moving to and from his hole as he looked for food. I was mentally, physically, and emotionally exhausted. I could hardly wait for my watch to be over. (Of course, I told no one about my watch the next morning. I didn't want anyone to know that I had been scared to death by a Communist mouse.)

Thomas J. Vogel. *Growing Up in Vietnam: Lessons in Life Learned from the Vietnam War.* (Schererville, IN: Bird Publications, 2000), 59–63, 85–86.



1. Why did Vogel fail to immediately seek cover during the sniper attack? ______________________

______________________________________________________________________

2. What various difficulties did Vogel experience around the time of the surprise attack? __________

______________________________________________________________________

______________________________________________________________________

*(continued on next page)*

3. When the Communists attacked, what recurring problem prevented Vogel from fighting back? ______

______

4. How long did the surprise attack last? ______

______

5. At what times during his service in Vietnam did Vogel cry? ______

______

6. What funny incident that occurred during Vogel's night watch indicated his alertness and fear of the enemy?

______

______

7. Why do you think the author entitled his book *Growing Up in Vietnam*? ______

______

______

Name ______________________

# The Berlin Wall

**Answer the questions at the end after reading the following excerpt from the writings of Inge E. Stanneck Gross.**

On Sunday morning, August 13, 1961, Berliners had awakened to construction in progress. Under the protection of heavy tanks and armed police and soldiers, concrete barriers and barbed wire fences were being put into place to seal off the borders of the Soviet-controlled sector of Berlin and the Soviet occupation zone, that is East Germany. The monstrous construction project, which was continuously reinforced over the following years, became known as the infamous Berlin Wall. This ugly wall was to stand for more than twenty-eight years and caused hundreds of deaths among those who tried to escape. It encircled, and therefore isolated, West Berlin, and cut it off from the eastern part of the city as well as from surrounding East Germany.

Berliners in both East and West Berlin went into shock. West Berliners who were visiting family or friends in East Berlin on that fateful weekend—including my cousin, Horst—were not allowed to return home. East Berlin residents who worked in West Berlin were cut off from their jobs. Any human contacts between families and friends that had still existed in the divided city were now totally cut. The *S-Bahn* (city train) and subway through-traffic was interrupted. Anyone who tried to escape in the years to come was ruthlessly shot.

Direct telephone service had been cut during the Blockade in 1948, but phone calls had been possible afterwards by routing a call through West Germany and East Germany, back to the other part of Berlin. Now even this circuitous way was no longer possible.

On this visit to Berlin a year after the construction of The Wall, I found that people had still not recovered from the shock. If anything, they were more disheartened than ever. The Wall affected their everyday lives. People could not attend weddings, births, and funerals on the "other side." There were sad scenes, where a bride and groom would stand on one side of The Wall on their wedding day and the parents or grandparents on the other, straining to get a glimpse of the happy couple.

Aunt Lotte and Uncle Martin had lost the sales personnel in their butcher shop. Help was extremely hard to find in West Berlin. At that particular time there were more jobs available than there were people to fill them. This led to the importation of guest workers from Turkey which, years later, turned into a migration, and some areas of West Berlin became wholly Turkish.

I also found a number of Berliners who were quite disappointed, and even angry, that the Americans had watched this happen and had done nothing to stop The Wall from being built.

In addition to the countless heart-wrenching experiences which befell the battle-weary Berliners, there were many tragedies. The Museum at Checkpoint Charlie tells some of the stories of the many people who tried to escape under, over, and through the fortified "wall system." It tells of the lucky ones who made it, and of the many who died trying to reach precious freedom. The museum has numerous ingenious inventions on display with which people tried to escape, such as inconceivably small and hidden spaces in cars, homemade flying machines, underground tunnels, and many more.

My term "wall system" means the following: The wall or barbed wire fence was not just a wall of concrete, or posts between which barbed wire had been strung. The fifteen foot high reinforced wall with rolled barbed wire on top which was visible from the West Berlin side, was not all there was to it. On the East Berlin side there was the "death strip" which consisted of alternating barbed wire fences with strips of loose, raked sand to see footprints. There were mine fields, deep trenches, tank traps, and another reinforced barricade on the east side. In addition, there were spotlights every three hundred feet as well as watchtowers, each manned by two

*(continued on next page)*

military men with binoculars. In some areas there were dog runs—each about half a mile long. Dog runs were fenced in strips of land in which trained vicious dogs were kept. . . .

A few words about the reason for building The Wall. At the end of World War II, Germany as well as Berlin, the capital city of the former Third Reich, were divided among the four Allies. While the three Western Allies jointly treated their sectors of Germany and Berlin as democracies, the Soviets forced their respective sectors into Communism. In the years following the war, quite a few people from both East Berlin and East Germany who were against Communism, fled to the West. As the years went by refugees arrived in West Berlin and West Germany by the thousands as the East German people became so dissatisfied with the Communist system that they preferred to leave all belongings behind in favor of freedom. Their numbers increased steadily and dramatically until by August 1961, refugees streamed into West Berlin by the thousands each day. The Wall was built by the communist government to stop this mass migration. . . .

The hardest part for the refugees was that they had to leave everything behind in order not to arouse suspicion with cumbersome baggage. It was also necessary for all family members to leave at the same time, as anyone left behind would encounter the punishment of the Communist system. Still, to gain precious freedom people left everything they owned and came to live in refugee camps in the West where they received help with starting a new life. This help initially consisted of shelter, food, and clothing, and then jobs and aid in finding housing. Shortage of housing was, and still is, one of the biggest problems in Germany.

With the building of The Wall, the "door to freedom" had been shut mercilessly.

Reprinted with permission from *Memories of World War II and Its Aftermath: By a Little Girl Growing Up in Berlin* by Inge E. Gross. Published by Island in the Sky Publishing Co., 2005.

1. How did the people of East and West Berlin respond to the building of the wall? ____________________
____________________________________________

2. According to Gross, what did the Americans do to stop the building of this wall? ____________________
____________________________________________

3. Why did the Soviets build the wall? ____________________
____________________________________________

Name ____________________

# Immediate Post-Communist Eastern Europe

**Locate each term on the map and place the corresponding number in the appropriate blank.**

_____ Albania
_____ Black Sea
_____ Bosnia and Herzegovina
_____ Bulgaria
_____ Croatia
_____ Czech Republic
_____ Germany
_____ Greece
_____ Hungary
_____ Italy
_____ Macedonia
_____ Moldova
_____ Poland
_____ Romania
_____ Slovakia
_____ Slovenia
_____ Switzerland
_____ Turkey
_____ Ukraine
_____ Yugoslavia

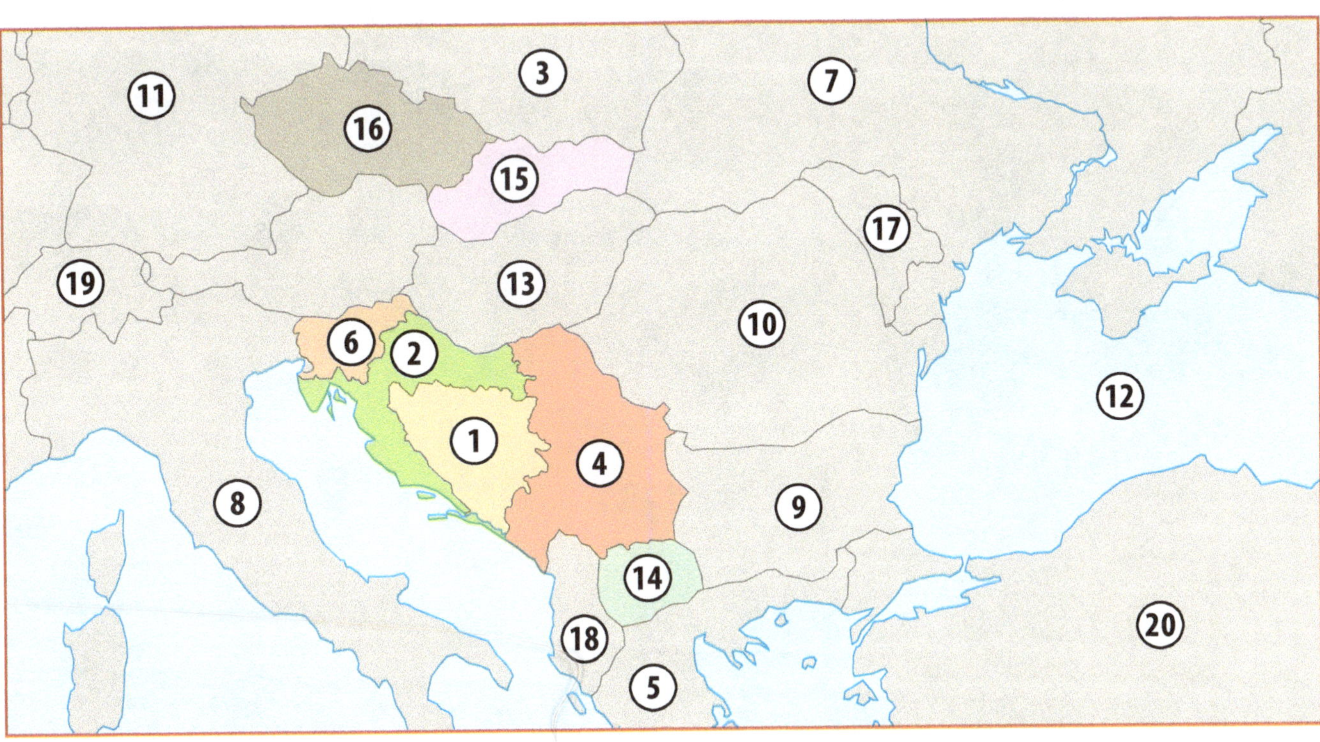

Name ______________________________

# Chapter Review

## Complete the Statement

**Underline the term that accurately completes each of the following statements.**

1. The policies of the Truman Doctrine are best summarized with the term (*appeasement*/ *containment*).
2. In the context of the Cold War, the term (*limited*/*total*) *war* denotes the practice of avoiding direct military confrontation and instead supporting like-minded nations.
3. The term (*perestroika*/*détente*) denotes a relaxation of tensions between opposing forces.
4. Tiananmen Square was the scene of a violent suppression of protestors in (China/Russia).

## Matching

**Choose the best answer and place the letter in the blank beside the corresponding description.**

| | | |
|---|---|---|
| A. Konrad Adenauer | E. Nikita Khrushchev | I. Lech Walesa |
| B. Fidel Castro | F. Douglas MacArthur | J. Boris Yeltsin |
| C. Bill Clinton | G. Ronald Reagan | |
| D. Mikhail Gorbachev | H. Marshal Tito | |

_____ 5. Soviet leader who pursued a "peaceful coexistence" with America

_____ 6. Led the Solidarity movement in Poland

_____ 7. Mayor of Cologne and first chancellor of West Germany

_____ 8. American president who was elected in 1980

_____ 9. Communist dictator in Cuba

_____ 10. Communist leader of Yugoslavia

_____ 11. General of UN forces in the Korean War before his dismissal

_____ 12. Brought reform that led to the end of the Soviet Union

## Short Answer

**Write the correct answer to each question in the provided blank.**

13. What does the acronym SEATO stand for? ______________________________

______________________________

14. Who was the civil rights movement's most visible spokesman? ______________________________

*(continued on next page)*

15. What was the name given to the Viet Cong attack that made Americans think victory was further away?

________________

16. What Communist alliance was formed by Eastern European countries in response to NATO?

________________

17. Who was the leader of the Free French during the war? ________________

18. What was the name of the economic plan intended to thwart the advance of communism in Western Europe? ________________

19. What was the name of the first man-made earth satellite? ________________

20. Who was the Communist leader of Vietnam? ________________

21. What event in November 1989 in Germany ended a symbol of Communist isolation from the Western world? ________________

22. What congressional resolution authorized President Johnson to defend Southeast Asia and drastically increased the number of American soldiers in Vietnam? ________________

## Essay

**Write the correct answer to each question in the provided blank.**

23. What actions did Margaret Thatcher take to oppose socialism in Great Britain? ________________

________________

________________

________________

24. How did events in Vietnam following World War II indicate France's waning power in the world?

________________

________________

________________

________________

________________

25. How did the collapse of the Soviet Union illustrate the truths of Daniel 2:36–44 and Psalm 75:6–7?

________________

________________

________________

Name ____________________

## The Middle East

Locate each term on the map and place the corresponding number in the appropriate blank.

_______ Afghanistan

_______ Egypt

_______ Iran

_______ Iraq

_______ Kuwait

_______ Pakistan

_______ Saudi Arabia

_______ Syria

_______ Turkey

_______ Yemen

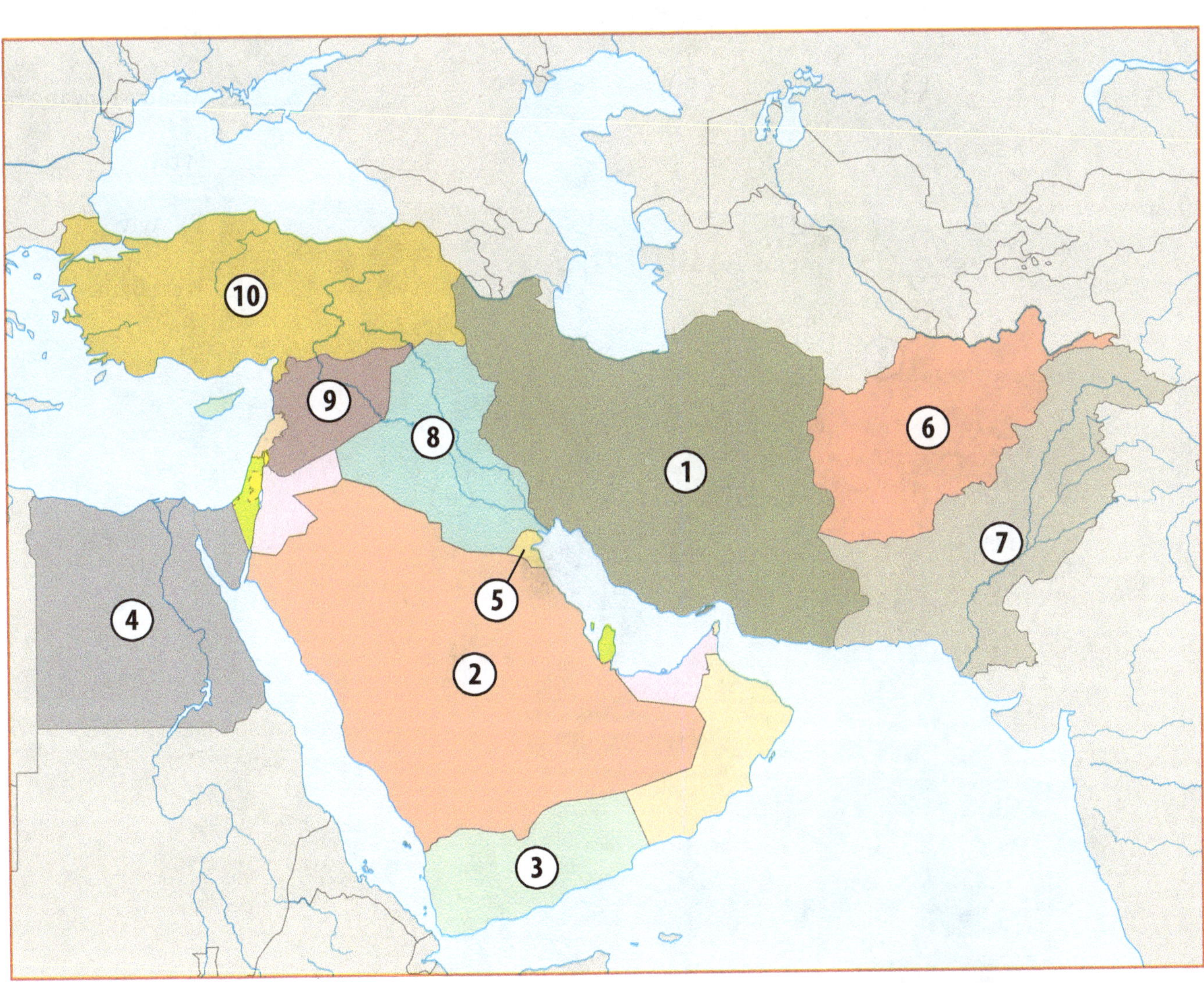

Name ______________________________

## Israel

Locate each term on the map and place the corresponding number in the appropriate blank.

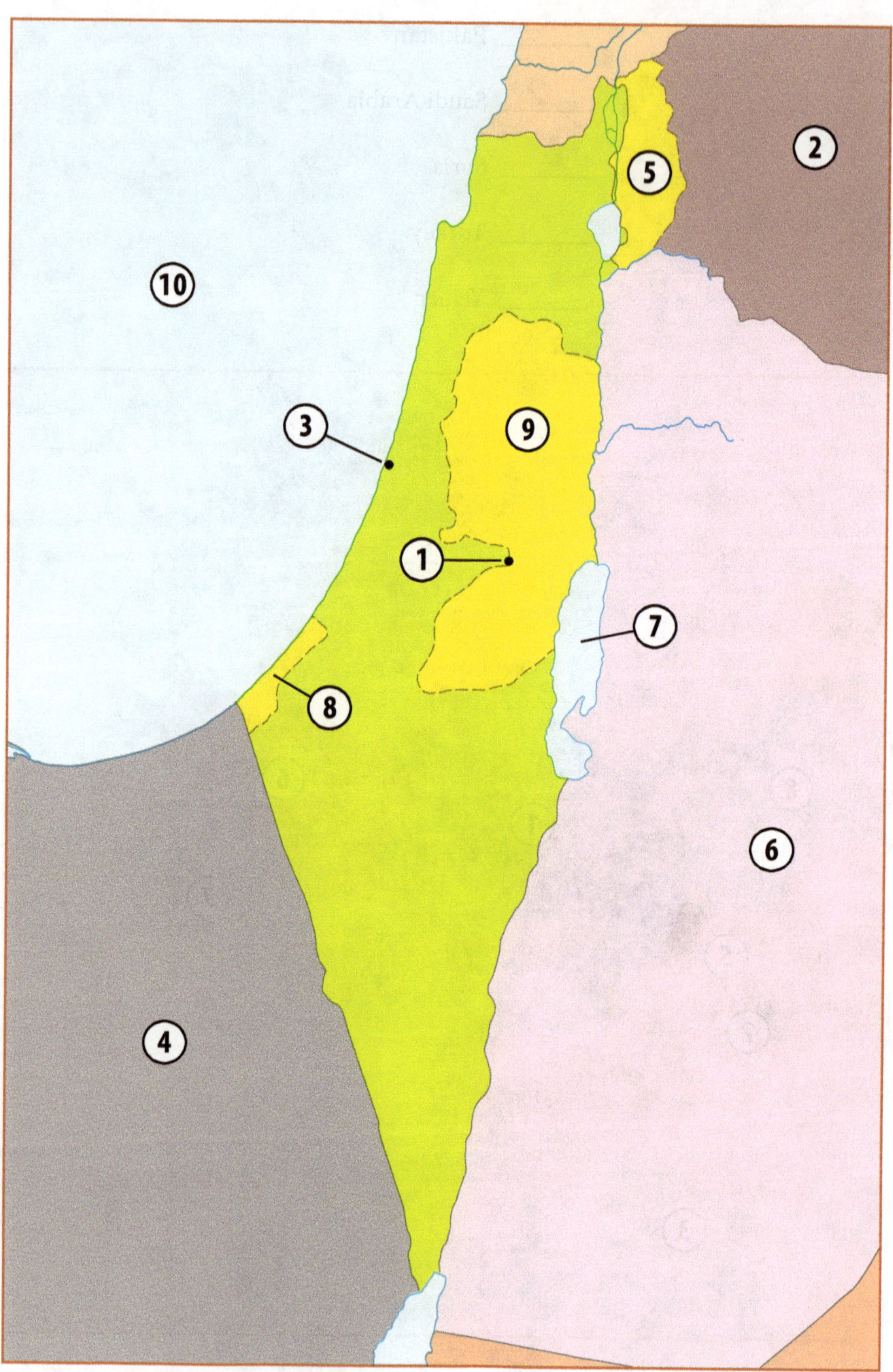


_______ Dead Sea

_______ Egypt

_______ Gaza Strip

_______ Golan Heights

_______ Jerusalem

_______ Jordan

_______ Mediterranean Sea

_______ Syria

_______ Tel Aviv

_______ West Bank

Name ______________________________

## Country Comparison Chart

**Use this chart to record updated information for countries mentioned in this chapter or other countries that you are interested in comparing/contrasting.**

| *Country/Region* | *Area (sq. mi.)* | *Population (M)* | *Pop. Density (per sq. mi.)* | *GDP (B) ($US)* | *Per Capita GDP ($US)* |
|---|---|---|---|---|---|
| | | | | | |
| | | | | | |
| | | | | | |
| | | | | | |
| | | | | | |
| | | | | | |
| | | | | | |
| | | | | | |
| | | | | | |
| | | | | | |
| | | | | | |
| | | | | | |
| | | | | | |
| | | | | | |
| | | | | | |
| | | | | | |
| | | | | | |
| | | | | | |

Name ______________________

# Chapter Review

## Complete the Statement

**Underline the term that accurately completes each of the following statements.**

1. (Ayatollah Khomeini/Mahmoud Ahmadinejad) became president of Iran in 2005 and led his country to develop nuclear technology.
2. Ukraine gained its independence from Russian dominance during the (Orange Revolution/ Rose Revolution).
3. (Chain migration/Brexit) refers to Britain's plans to leave the EU.
4. (EU/NAFTA) was intended to lower trade barriers and enhance trade between Canada, the United States, and Mexico.

## Matching

**Choose the best answer and place the letter in the blank beside the corresponding description.**

| | | |
|---|---|---|
| A. Osama bin Laden | E. Saddam Hussein | I. Vladimir Putin |
| B. George H. W. Bush | F. Xi Jinping | J. Kim Il Sung |
| C. George W. Bush | G. Kim Jong Un | K. Hassan Rouhani |
| D. Mahatma Gandhi | H. Ayatollah Khomeini | |

_____ 5. Belligerent third-generation dictator in North Korea

_____ 6. Saudi who masterminded the attack on the United States on September 11, 2001

_____ 7. President of China

_____ 8. Installed by Muslim forces in Iran after the shah was overthrown

_____ 9. Leader of the Indian nationalists who resisted the British Empire

_____ 10. President of Russia

_____ 11. Iraqi dictator who invaded Kuwait

_____ 12. US president when Saddam Hussein invaded Kuwait

_____ 13. Launched the United States and many others into a second war in the Persian Gulf region

## Short Answer

**Write the correct answer to each question in the provided blank.**

14. A nonviolent program used in India to defy British rule ______________________

*(continued on next page)*

15. Give the name for the monetary value of all goods and services produced within a geographic border.

______________________________

16. Name the Islamic terrorist network that was responsible for the terrorist attack on September 11, 2001.

______________________________

17. What does the acronym ISIS stand for? ______________________________

18. What terrorist group gained control of Afghanistan, enforcing radical Muslim rule? ______________________________

19. What is the primary religion of India? ______________________________

20. Why is September 11, 2001, a significant day in recent history? ______________________________

______________________________

______________________________

21. How has China made sinful choices in addressing its population growth? ______________________________

______________________________

______________________________

22. Name a current Communist nation. ______________________________

## Essay

**Write the correct answer to each question in the provided blank.**

23. What challenges has Japan encountered in recent years? ______________________________

______________________________

______________________________

______________________________

______________________________

24. What challenges and opportunities have many African states faced in recent years? ______________________________

______________________________

______________________________

______________________________

______________________________

______________________________

______________________________

______________________________

25. Explain globalization. ______________________________

______________________________

______________________________